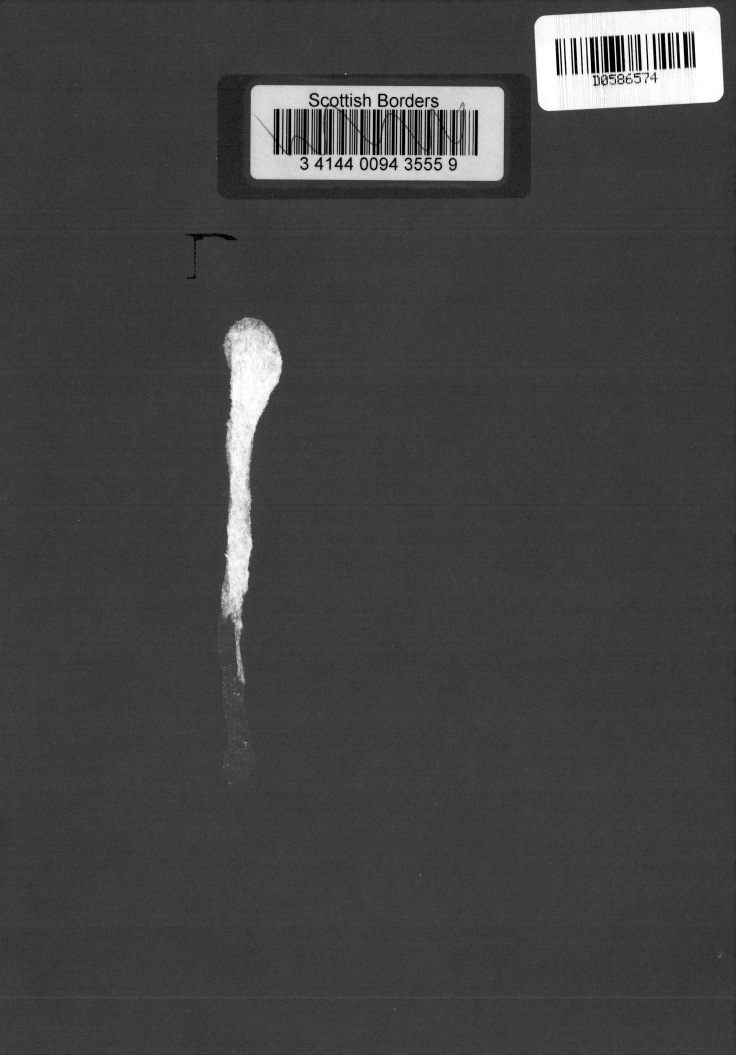

AGA WEEKEND
COOKBOOK

AGA WEEKEND
COOKBOOK

OVER 150 RECIPES INCLUDING SUNDAY ROASTS AND TEATIME BAKES

EBURY
PRESS

10 9 8 7 6 5 4 3 2 1

This edition published in 2011 by Ebury Press,
an imprint of Ebury Publishing

A Random House Group Company

First published by Ebury Press in 1998

Text and photography © Ebury Press or
the National Magazine Company Ltd 1998

The Random House Group Limited Reg. No. 954009

Addresses for companies within the Random House Group
can be found at www.randomhouse.co.uk

A CIP catalogue record for this book is available
from the British Library

The Random House Group Limited supports The Forest
Stewardship Council® (FSC®), the leading international
forest certification organisation. All our titles that are printed
on Greenpeace approved FSC® certified paper carry the
FSC® logo. Our paper procurement policy can be found
at www.randomhouse.co.uk/environment

To buy books by your favourite authors and register
for offers visit www.randomhouse.co.uk

Project editor Gillian Haslam
Designed by Christine Wood
Special photography by James Murphy
Illustrations by Madeleine David
Recipe testing by Miranda Hall
Other photographs: Jean Cazals, Harry Cory-Wright,
Laurie Evans, Gus Filgate, Graham Kirk, James Murphy
and Philip Webb

Printed and bound by Tien Wah Press, Singapore
ISBN 9780091945145

COOKERY NOTES

Both metric and imperial measures are given for the recipes. Follow one set of measures throughout, as they are not interchangeable.

All spoon measures are level unless otherwise stated. Sets of measuring spoons are available in metric and imperial for accurate measurement of small quantities.

These recipes are suitable for both 2-oven and 4-oven Aga cookers. When the cooking instructions differ for a recipe, both are given. The following symbols apply:
■ ■ for a 2-oven Aga
■ ■ ■ for a 4-oven Aga

Where a stage is specified for freezing, the dish should be frozen at the end of that stage.

Large eggs should be used except where otherwise specified. Free range eggs are recommended.

Use freshly ground black pepper and sea salt unless otherwise specified.

Use fresh rather than dried herbs unless dried herbs are suggested in the recipe.

Stocks should be freshly made if possible. Alternatively buy ready-made stocks or use good quality stock cubes.

CONTENTS

ABOVE: LEMON AND LIME PAVLOVA PIE
ILLUSTRATED ON HALF-TITLE PAGE: ARTICHOKE AND MUSHROOM LASAGNE

INTRODUCTION

The Aga is a cast-iron heat storage cooker which was invented in 1922 by the Swedish physicist, Dr Gustaf Dalen. It was introduced into England in 1929, and has become so popular that 'Aga' is now an established household name.

An Aga may be expensive to buy but it is an excellent investment, as it serves many purposes and will last a lifetime if properly used and maintained. Its timeless, classic design has changed little over the years, although you can now choose from a range of vitreous enamel colours to co-ordinate or contrast the cooker with the rest of your kitchen.

You will find that the Aga immediately becomes the focus of the kitchen, creating a special, all-year-round warm and welcoming atmosphere. Ensure that your cooker is positioned to take full advantage of this, especially if you eat in the kitchen – which you will almost certainly want to do once your Aga is installed! During hot weather simply open the windows to maintain a comfortable temperature.

HOW AN AGA WORKS
The fuel for your Aga may be natural gas, propane, solid fuel, oil or off-peak electricity but, whatever the heat source, all Agas basically function in the same way. The heat is generated in the burner unit and conducted around the walls of the cast-iron ovens and hot plates. The cast-iron surfaces store heat and release it as radiant heat at a steady rate when needed. As you cook, the heat lost is automatically restored because the Aga is thermostatically controlled. Different areas of the cooker are maintained at different temperatures in order to provide a range of cooking options. Food smells and vapours are conveniently ducted away from the ovens to the external flue.

TWO-OVEN AND FOUR-OVEN AGAS
Agas are available in two different sizes: two-oven and four-oven models. The two-oven Aga has a roasting oven and a simmering oven. In addition to these, the four-oven has a warming oven and a baking oven. These ovens are deceptively large, with a capacity of nearly 45 cu cm (2 cu ft) and every part of the ovens can be used. On top, both appliances have a fast boiling plate and a gentle simmering plate, protected by chrome insulated lids. The four-oven cooker also has a gentle warming plate. Again, the hot plates are large, each allowing room for up to four pans. The most popular model in this country is the two-oven cooker.

Some Aga models will also provide domestic hot water. Your choice of model will obviously depend on your individual requirements. Agas are assembled in your own home by the manufacturer's engineers.

Some of the earlier electric Agas have a hotter than average simmering oven so overnight cooking may not be suitable and long, slow cooking times should be reduced a little. With electric Agas, it is not recommended to cook poultry overnight in the simmering oven due to increased possibility of bacterial growth.

DIFFERENCES BETWEEN USING AN AGA AND A CONVENTIONAL COOKER
■ The Aga is a constant source of heat: there's no need to wait for the oven or hob to heat up.
■ The Aga operates on the principle of heat storage and is surprisingly efficient to run.
■ The Aga has no dials or knobs to adjust for a change in temperature. Once you are used to your Aga, you will find this simplification an advantage.
■ The Aga does not have a separate grill, but grilling takes place at the top of the roasting oven, or in a grill pan on the boiling plate.
■ Because most Aga cooking takes place in the large, versatile ovens rather than on the hot plates, condesation and cleaning are minimised.
■ The Aga is vented through a flue, so there are virtually no cooking smells from the ovens.
■ Because the cast-iron walls of the Aga ovens retain heat so well, you don't need to worry about losing heat as you open the door, to peep at a soufflé or cake for example. With a conventional oven, this can cause such a drop in temperature that a soufflé or cake may collapse.

CONSERVING HEAT IN THE AGA
The secret to success with an Aga is to cook inside, rather than on the top with the lids up, whenever possible – this way you conserve heat. Few foods need to be cooked entirely on the hot plates and those which do, such as stir-fries and green vegetables, cook quickly. Many dishes which would be cooked on the top of a conventional cooker, such as soups, stews and steamed puddings, are started off on the hot plates, then transferred to the appropriate oven. The following tips on conserving heat may help:
■ Always keep hot plate lids shut unless they are in use.
■ When using the hot plates, cover as much of the surface area as possible, with one large pan or several smaller ones.

■ Allow chilled items to stand at room temperature (for 1-2 hours) before placing in the ovens, especially turkeys, joints, casseroles, soups, etc.

■ Thaw frozen food before cooking. Ideally leave in the refrigerator overnight, then at cool room temperature for 1-2 hours.

■ Plan your menu carefully when you are entertaining or cooking for large family gatherings to avoid trying to cook several dishes at the same time which all need a very hot oven. This is particularly important if you have a 2-oven Aga. Of course, many dishes can be cooked in advance and reheated to serve.

■ If you are batch baking, bread for example, at a high temperature, allow up to 2 hours for your oven to return to temperature if you need maximum heat for your next batch of cooking. Alternatively, take advantage of the slightly cooler oven to bake cakes and biscuits after cooking family meals.

■ When there is going to be a heavy demand on your cooker, turn up the Aga heat dial slightly, about an hour in advance, remembering to return it to the normal setting before going to bed.

■ Some oil Agas lose heat in high winds so you may wish to turn up the heat dial as before.

■ Agas that heat water may cool a little if a lot of water is run off, e.g. for baths. You may wish to boost the water heat with an immersion heater if this affects your Aga when entertaining.

THE HEAT INDICATOR

The gauge on the front of your cooker indicates whether your Aga has the correct amount of heat stored.

■ When the heat indicator is on the thin black line, your Aga has the right amount of heat stored and is operating at its optimum.

■ If the indicator is towards the black shaded area, there is less heat stored and cooking will therefore take longer.

■ If the mercury reaches the red area, there is more than the required amount of heat stored and it is possible that there may be something wrong. Before calling your local approved Aga engineer, check that the control dial hasn't been altered.

■ During cooking, the temperature will fluctuate a little, but should soon return to its normal setting. If you've been using the hot plates extensively, the cooker may take 2-3 hours to recuperate.

GETTING TO KNOW YOUR OWN AGA

Each Aga is slightly different from the next: its position in the kitchen, whether situated between units or free-standing, on an inside or outside wall; the type of fuel used, and whether or not your Aga also supplies the hot

water; these factors will all add to its individuality. You may find it takes a little time to get to know and love your Aga with its own personality!

BASIC PRINCIPLES OF AGA COOKING

■ As different areas of the Aga are kept at different temperatures, you simply need to choose the right position for the dish you are cooking, depending upon whether it requires a low, moderate or high temperature, fast or slow cooking.

■ Each oven presents a range of options, because the temperature varies slightly within each oven, from top to bottom, front to back, and side to side. The top is the hottest part; the back will be a little hotter than the front; the side nearest the burner unit will be hotter than the opposite side.

THE ROASTING OVEN

Apart from roasting and baking, this versatile hot oven is used for shallow-frying, grilling, steaming and simmering. The oven has four shelf positions; the floor of the oven, and the grid shelf placed on the floor of the oven give two more cooking positions.

THE COLD PLAIN SHELF supplied with the Aga allows you to use the roasting oven for baking items which require a more moderate temperature. You simply slide in the cold shelf, usually two sets of runners above the food being cooked, to deflect the top heat and create a moderate heat below. With the 2-oven Aga, this is an important function. If your cold plain shelf is already in use, the large Aga roasting tin can fulfil the same function; to maintain the lower temperature throughout longer cooking, half-fill the tin with cold water after 20-30 minutes.

COOKING IN THE ROASTING OVEN

The recommended shelf positions for the recipes in this book are, of course, provided, but you may wish to adapt conventional recipes from elsewhere. You can, of course, purchase an oven thermometer to check the operational temperature of the different positions within your oven, if you wish. As a rough guide, the roasting oven shelf positions are used as follows:

TOP (OR FIRST) RUNNERS
Grilling (on oiled preheated rack over roasting tin)
SECOND RUNNERS
Browning dishes, gratins, roast potatoes, scones
THIRD RUNNERS
Fast-roasting, bread-baking, jacket potatoes
BOTTOM (FOURTH) RUNNERS
Medium-roasting, pastry

THE TWO-OVEN AGA

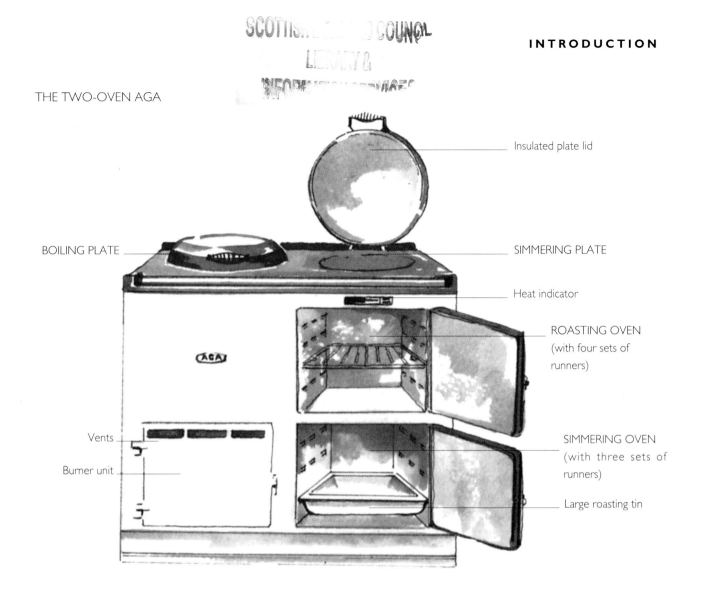

Insulated plate lid

BOILING PLATE

SIMMERING PLATE

Heat indicator

ROASTING OVEN
(with four sets of
runners)

AGA

SIMMERING OVEN
(with three sets of
runners)

Vents

Large roasting tin

Burner unit

GRID SHELF ON OVEN FLOOR
Slower-roasting (e.g. pork, poultry)
OVEN FLOOR
Crisp pastry bases (flans, etc); to crisp roast potatoes, frying, fast reduction of sauces, preheating griddles and frying pans
GRID SHELF ON OVEN FLOOR
WITH COLD PLAIN SHELF ABOVE
(in a 2-oven Aga)
Baking fish, biscuits and cakes

THE SIMMERING OVEN .
This oven has a minimum of three cooking positions: the floor, the grid shelf on the floor of the oven, and the middle runners which take the cold plain shelf and the Aga roasting tins, as well as the grid shelf. In addition, the 2-oven Aga has a further 2 sets of runners. The temperature of the oven can vary, but is generally around

100°C (212°F), within an ideal range for slow, gentle cooking. Almost all dishes need to be started off at a higher temperature (on one of the hot plates or other ovens), then transferred to the simmering oven to complete cooking.

The main uses of this oven are as follows:
■ ROOT VEGETABLES Place in a saucepan, cover with cold water, put the lid on the pan and bring to the boil on the boiling plate. Cook for 3-5 minutes, then drain off all but about 1 cm (½ inch) water. Salt lightly, recover and transfer to the simmering oven to steam until tender, about 20-30 minutes. Potatoes, in particular, benefit from being cooked in this way: they will be soft through to the centre without falling apart.
■ STOCKS Bring stocks to the boil in a covered pan on the boiling plate, then transfer to the floor of the simmering oven. In this way, you will be able to make

9

flavoursome, jellied stocks, without the unpleasant cooking smells usually associated with boiling stocks.

■ CASSEROLES These cook superbly in the gentle heat of this oven. First bring to a simmer on one of the hot plates, then place in the simmering oven to cook slowly. To speed up cooking, you can place the casserole on the grid shelf on the floor of the roasting oven for 15-20 minutes of each hour.

■ MERINGUES Perfect light, crisp meringues can be cooked entirely in the simmering oven; the floor is the ideal position.

■ PORRIDGE can be cooked overnight in this oven.

■ CAKES With a 2-oven Aga, the simmering oven is often used to complete the cooking of cakes which have been part-baked in the roasting oven. Large rich fruit cakes can be cooked overnight on the grid shelf on the floor of the simmering oven without being started off elsewhere – to delicious effect.

■ KEEPING FOODS HOT/REHEATING The temperature of the simmering oven is perfect for keeping foods warm, without spoiling.

■ RESTING MEAT If you have a 2-oven Aga, the simmering oven is most useful for resting roasted poultry and joints of meat.

THE FOUR-OVEN AGA BAKING OVEN

This is situated below the roasting oven and has the same number of runners and corresponding versatile cooking positions. The temperature in the middle of this oven averages 180°C (350°F) – ideal for many baking purposes.

■ The top of the oven is used for baking biscuits, small cakes, roulades, etc.

■ The middle is used for sandwich cakes, crumbles, poaching and baking fish.

■ The bottom of the oven with the grid shelf in position is used for casseroles, deep cakes, and poaching ham.

THE FOUR-OVEN AGA WARMING OVEN

This is maintained at approximately 70°C (160°F) and is very temperate.

■ It is the ideal place to warm plates and serving dishes, and to keep foods warm without spoiling, including delicate sauces.

■ Allow roasts to rest in this oven for 20 minutes before carving.

■ Meringues and porridge can be cooked overnight in this oven.

THE BOILING PLATE

The main function of this hot plate is to bring foods up to a fast boil, before continuing to cook elsewhere in, or on

the Aga. It is also used for quick frying, stir-frying, cooking green vegetables and making toast (with the special Aga toaster).

THE SIMMERING PLATE

This is used for bringing foods up to a gentle simmer; slow-frying, including sweating vegetables; foods which require gentle cooking with constant attention, such as delicate sauces.

■ The hot plate also doubles up as an excellent griddle: simply lightly oil or butter the clean surface and cook drop scones, crumpets, tortillas, nan bread and poppadoms etc, directly on it.

THE FOUR-OVEN AGA WARMING PLATE

This is a useful additional warm surface – ideal for holding dishes taken out of one of the ovens, and warming the teapot.

■ It is also suitable for melting chocolate, butter, etc.

■ Bread dough can be risen on this hot plate: place the bowl on a folded towel to avoid direct contact.

■ Note that the area at the back of an Aga is also a good source of warmth.

AGA EQUIPMENT

The following items are supplied with your Aga:-

GRID SHELF This has non-tilt runners, so it can be drawn out to the full extent without danger of tipping.

COLD PLAIN SHELF This is used as a shelf, a full-size baking sheet, and to lower the temperature in the roasting oven (see page 8). When not in use, the cold plain shelf should be stored outside the cooker. A second one of these is most useful.

AGA ROASTING TINS These have many uses and two are supplied: the full-size tin and a half-size roasting tin, both of which can be hung from the runners in the ovens. Apart from the obvious functions, the roasting tins can be used for grilling, with the rack in position; traybakes, such as flapjacks; bain-maries, for custards etc. The large roasting tin can also be used as an alternative cold shelf (see page 8).

THE AGA TOASTER This is used to toast bread, crumpets, etc of any thickness on the boiling plate.

Other items of equipment which you will find useful:-

SPLATTER GUARD This is most useful for covering pans during frying, to protect the Aga surface.

THE AGA GRILL PAN This ridged cast-iron non-stick pan is excellent for cooking steaks, chops, etc. It is first preheated on the floor of the roasting oven for 5-10 minutes, then used on the boiling plate. (A similar ovenproof ridged cast-iron skillet can be used.)

THE AGA CAKE BAKER A non-essential item, but one that you will find most useful if you are a 2-oven Aga owner and often bake large cakes that take longer than 45 minutes to cook, such as Madeira, rich fruit cakes, etc. It can also be used as a large pan for stocks, or large scale entertaining.

PANS AND COOKWARE

Although it isn't essential to buy a whole new range of pots and pans when you become an Aga owner, it is important to make sure that the bases of your existing pans are perfectly flat, to ensure good contact with the hot plate. Good quality pans with thick ground bases which conduct heat well should really be used. (Ask the Aga shop or cooker centre in your area for advice on the suitability of your pans.)

■ All of your saucepans should be suitable for use in the simmering oven (with handles and lids heat resistant to the temperature range of this oven), as well as on the hot plates. For the recipes in this book, it is assumed that this is the case.

■ Ovenproof is used in these recipes to denote that the pan (or casserole) must be suitable for use in the roasting oven.

■ Hard anodised aluminium, stainless steel and cast-iron pans are the most suitable choices. Aga manufacture their own ranges of cookware in these materials, so you may prefer to choose from these if you are buying new cookware. The pans are designed with flat lids, so that they can be stacked on top of each other to save space in the oven if required.

■ Cast-iron cookware is particularly efficient to use with an Aga, and is most attractive. You may, however, find that the very large pans are heavy to lift in and out of the ovens.

If you are buying new pans, consider the following basic selection:-

■ 4 saucepans, ranging from 2-4 litre (3½-7 pint) capacity (you may prefer to have some of these with short, ovenproof handles so they are more versatile)

■ 1 large 25-30 cm (10-12 inch) ovenproof frying pan (some come with detachable handles)

■ 1 omelette pan (which can also be used as a crêpe pan)

■ 2-3 casseroles, ranging from 2-4 litre (3½-7 pint) capacity – suitable for use on the hot plates)

■ The Aga grill pan (or other ridged skillet)

Note: The largest pan which will fit into the oven has a 13 litre (22 pint) capacity. This is useful for preserves and cooking for crowds!

CLEANING THE AGA

This is an easy task because most of the cooking takes place in the ovens and you therefore have very little grease to contend with.

■ The hot plates, roasting oven and 4-oven Aga baking oven are largely self-cleaning. Any thing which is spilt will carbonise and can be brushed away easily with the wire brush provided.

■ The other areas of the cooker do not become as dirty, due to the type of cooking they are used for. Simply wipe down with warm soapy water, then polish with a soft, dry cloth.

■ Clean the enamel and chrome areas regularly with a cream cleaner, such as Astonish, then spray with silicone polish so they wipe clean easily.

■ Wipe away any spills as soon as they occur. This is particularly important for spilled milk, fruit juice, preserves and other acidic foods which might otherwise damage the enamel with prolonged contact.

SPRING CLEANING YOUR AGA

Aim to give your Aga a thorough clean to coincide with its recommended regular service:

■ Carefully lift off the oven doors and lay, enamel-side down, on a cloth. Clean the inside of the doors with a cream cleanser, or soap-filled wire pad if necessary. Wipe over the seal but do not allow it to become wet.

■ Clean the chrome shelves and the inside of the hot plate covers with a cream cleanser. Brush out the ovens.

■ Clean the rest of the enamel and chrome areas with a cream cleaner, such as Astonish. For best results, polish this off with a soft, dry cloth.

THE AGA ISN'T JUST A COOKER...

Your Aga will make your kitchen an efficient drying and airing room.

■ An old-fashioned clothes airer can be suspended from a high kitchen ceiling to provide plenty of additional drying space. Traditional cast-iron and pine ones are available, and these are an attractive feature in any kitchen, without any running costs. You may even find that your tumble dryer becomes obsolete!

■ Herbs, flowers and petals for pot pourri can be hung near the cooker to dry in the gentle warmth.

■ On a bitterly cold night, you may wish to leave the kitchen door ajar. You will find that the warmth from the Aga will take the chill off the house.

POACHED EGGS WITH
SMOKED HADDOCK AND MUFFINS

PREPARATION TIME:
10 MINUTES

COOKING TIME:
10 MINUTES

430 CALS PER
SERVING

SERVES 6

FREEZING:
UNSUITABLE

Smoked haddock is always a traditional breakfast time choice. Combined with muffins, spinach and Béarnaise sauce, this makes a delicious brunch.

225 g (8 oz) smoked haddock fillets
25 g (1 oz) butter
225 g (8 oz) washed spinach
salt and freshly ground black pepper
15 ml (1 tbsp) vinegar

6 fresh eggs
3 English muffins
60 ml (4 level tbsp) bought Béarnaise sauce

1 Thinly slice the haddock.
2 Melt the butter in a saucepan then, when hot, add the spinach and cook on the BOILING PLATE until just wilted; season, drain (reserving the juices) and set aside.
3 Bring the juices to the boil. When hot add the haddock; cook for 1 minute on each side. Set aside.
4 Bring a large, shallow non-stick pan or small roasting tin of water to a gentle simmer and add the vinegar (see Aga Tip). Carefully break the eggs into the water and cook for 2-3 minutes or until the whites are just set; remove and drain on kitchen paper.
5 To assemble, split the muffins and lightly toast directly on the SIMMERING PLATE until golden. Divide the spinach between each half muffin and top with the smoked haddock. Place one egg on top of each muffin and coat with 10 ml (2 level tsp) Béarnaise sauce.
6 Place on the plain shelf on the second runners at the back of the ROASTING OVEN and cook for 4-5 minutes or until the Béarnaise is bubbling.

AGA TIP
If using the roasting tin in step 4, break one egg into each corner of the tin and the remaining eggs in the centre.

THE ULTIMATE SCRAMBLED EGGS

PREPARATION TIME:
5 MINUTES

COOKING TIME:
10 MINUTES

270 CALS PER
SERVING

SERVES 4

FREEZING:
UNSUITABLE

Everyone has their own favourite method of cooking scrambled eggs, but for the best results use the freshest eggs possible and plenty of butter. The eggs should be evenly creamy when cooked, not half liquid and half set.

8 eggs
salt and freshly ground black pepper
50 g (2 oz) butter

POACHED EGGS WITH SMOKED HADDOCK AND MUFFINS

1 Beat the eggs well, adding plenty of salt and black pepper. Melt half the butter in a heavy, non-stick pan and add the beaten eggs. Stir with a wooden spoon over a very gently heat on the side of the SIMMERING PLATE until they just begin to thicken. Add the remaining butter and continue stirring over the heat until the first scrambled pieces appear.

2 Remove the pan from the heat immediately and continue stirring – the scrambled eggs will finish cooking in the heat from the saucepan without becoming rubbery in texture. Serve immediately.

13

KEDGEREE WITH HERB BUTTER

PREPARATION TIME:
10 MINUTES

COOKING TIME:
ABOUT 20 MINUTES

540 CALS PER
SERVING

SERVES 4

FREEZING:
UNSUITABLE

This simple combination of basmati rice, lightly poached smoked haddock, boiled eggs and subtle spice makes the perfect traditional breakfast dish to set you up for the day.

450 g (1 lb) smoked haddock or fresh salmon (see Cook's Tip)
150 ml (¼ pint) milk
75 g (3 oz) cooked cockles
5 ml (1 level tsp) coriander seeds
3 hard-boiled eggs
225 g (8 oz) basmati rice
30 ml (2 tbsp) double cream

45-60 ml (3-4 level tbsp) chopped chives
salt and freshly ground black pepper
50 g (2 oz) butter
5-10 ml (1-2 tsp) lemon juice
30 ml (2 level tbsp) chopped fresh tarragon
lemon or lime wedges and herbs, to garnish

1 Place haddock in a shallow pan with the milk. Cover and cook on SIMMERING PLATE for 8 minutes or until cooked. Drain; reserve 30-45 ml (2-3 tbsp) cooking liquor. Flake the fish, discarding skin and bones.
2 Thoroughly drain the cockles. Finely crush coriander seeds. Quarter the eggs.
3 Cook the rice by bringing to the boil in salted water, then transferring to SIMMERING OVEN for 10-12 minutes or until just tender. Drain, rinse with boiling water and drain again.
4 Return rice to the pan; add haddock, reserved liquor, cockles, crushed coriander seeds, eggs, cream and chives. Season lightly; heat gently on the SIMMERING PLATE for 2 minutes.
5 Place the butter, lemon juice, tarragon and seasoning in a jug. Warm in the SIMMERING OVEN for 10 minutes until the butter melts. Garnish the kedgeree and serve with herb butter.

COOK'S TIP
Undyed smoked haddock generally has a superior flavour to the familiar yellow smoked haddock.

STICKY GLAZED HAM WITH SPICED ORANGES

PREPARATION TIME:
15 MINUTES +
SOAKING

COOKING TIME:
1½ HOURS

170 CALS PER
SERVING

SERVES 6

FREEZING: SLICE THE
HAM THINLY AND
OVERLAP THE SLICES
ON A SHEET OF
FOIL. WRAP TIGHTLY
AND FREEZE. THAW
OVERNIGHT AT
COOL ROOM
TEMPERATURE.

The strong flavours of marmalade and Dijon mustard combine to give a delicious glaze on this classic ham. Spiced oranges (see next recipe) make the ideal accompaniment.

1.1 kg (2½ lb) gammon joint
125 g (4 oz) carrot, roughly chopped
125 g (4 oz) onion, roughly chopped
125 g (4 oz) celery, roughly chopped
15 ml (1 level tbsp) Dijon mustard

15 ml (1 level tbsp) light soft brown (muscovado) sugar
45 ml (3 level tbsp) marmalade
300 ml (10 fl oz) cider

1 Soak the gammon overnight in cold water.
2 Drain the gammon and place in a large saucepan with the vegetables. Add enough water to cover. Bring to the boil on the SIMMERING PLATE, then cover and simmer very gently for 20 minutes. Leave to cool in the water for about 1 hour, then drain and remove the rind.
3 Place the gammon in a small roasting tin. Combine the mustard with the sugar and marmalade and spread over the ham fat. Pour in the cider.
4 ▪▪ Bake in the front of the ROASTING OVEN with the roasting tin on the bottom runners for 20-25 minutes until the fat is crisp and golden, basting occasionally during the final 7 minutes.
▪▪▪▪ Bake at the back of the BAKING OVEN with the roasting tin on the bottom runners for 30 minutes.
4 Remove the joint from the tin and allow to cool. Reduce the juices to a syrupy consistency by cooking on the floor of the ROASTING OVEN or on the BOILING PLATE. Pour the juices over the ham. Serve thinly sliced with the Spiced Oranges (see right).

SPICED ORANGES

PREPARATION TIME:
15 MINUTES

COOKING TIME:
1½ HOURS

100 CALS PER
SERVING

SERVES 6

FREEZING:
UNSUITABLE

These delicious oranges are also excellent served with cold turkey and with duck or pork pâté, so make more than you need for just one meal.

1.1 kg (2½ lb) oranges
750 ml (1¼ pint) white wine vinegar
1.1 kg (2½ lb) granulated sugar

half cinnamon stick
30 cloves

1 Slice the whole oranges thinly, place in a large pan with just enough water to cover. Bring to the boil and simmer for 5 minutes, then drain in a colander and set aside.
2 Add remaining ingredients to the pan and bring to the boil, stirring occasionally. Return oranges; return to the boil, cover and transfer to the SIMMERING OVEN for 50 minutes.
3 Lift the oranges out of the syrup and place in sterilized vinegar-proof jars. Boil remaining syrup uncovered on the floor of the ROASTING OVEN for 25-30 minutes until reduced to 1.1 litres (2 pints). Pour over the oranges, cover and leave in a cool, dark place for at least two weeks.

COOK'S TIPS
Choose smaller, thin skinned oranges (ruby or blood oranges are very good).
Recycled coffee jars with plastic lids are ideal (some metal lids rust easily).
Spiced oranges make a lovely present for dinner party hosts or as Christmas gifts.

AGA TIP
Reducing the syrup in the Aga ensures that the smell of the vinegar does not permeate the house.

SAUSAGE AND BACON OATCAKES

PREPARATION TIME:

COOKING TIME:
20-25 MINUTES

395 CALS PER
SERVING

SERVES 8

FREEZING: PROVIDED
THE SAUSAGEMEAT
HAS NOT ALREADY
BEEN FROZEN,
OATCAKES FREEZE
WELL, WITHOUT THE
EGG AND OATMEAL
COATING.
INTERLEAVE WITH
GREASEPROOF PAPER
AND PACK IN A
RIGID CONTAINER.
FREEZE FOR UP TO
1 MONTH. THAW
OVERNIGHT IN THE
REFRIGERATOR
BEFORE COATING.
COMPLETE FROM
STEP 3 ONWARDS.

These savoury oatcakes are also extremely good sandwiched burger-style in warm baps with a selection of relishes.

175 g (6 oz) lean back bacon, minced or very finely chopped
1 small onion, skinned and minced or very finely chopped
225 g (8 oz) pork sausagemeat
10 ml (2 tsp) wholegrain mustard
15 ml (1 tbsp) chopped fresh parsley or 10 ml (2 tsp) dried parsley
125 g (4 oz) medium oatmeal

salt and freshly ground black pepper
1 egg, beaten
oil for shallow frying
8 rashers streaky bacon, rinded and thinly stretched
stuffed olives threaded onto wooden cocktail sticks, to garnish

1 Mix the minced or chopped bacon and onion with the sausagemeat, mustard, parsley, thyme, 15 ml (1 tbsp) of the oatmeal and plenty of salt and pepper. Alternatively, combine briefly in a food processor.
2 Divide the mixture into 8 equal portions. On a lightly floured surface, form each portion into a 7.5-8.5 cm (3-3½ in) round cake. Dip into the beaten egg, then coat in the remaining oatmeal, pressing on firmly with fingertips. Cover and chill in the refrigerator for at least 30 minutes (or overnight, if wished).
3 Heat the oil in a large frying pan on the BOILING PLATE and cook the sausage cakes, in two batches if necessary, for about 30 seconds-1 minute on each side until golden brown.
4 Wrap a streaky bacon rasher around each cake and place in the small roasting tin, join-side down. Cook for 20-25 minutes on the floor of the ROASTING OVEN, turning once. Drain on absorbent kitchen paper.
5 Serve the oatcakes hot, garnished with stuffed olives threaded onto wooden cocktail sticks.

MUSHROOM AND SPINACH PANCAKES

**PREPARATION TIME:
1 HOUR +
STANDING AND
SOAKING**

**COOKING TIME:
1½ HOURS**

**375 CALS PER
SERVING**

SERVES 4

**FREEZING:
SUITABLE – SEE
COOK'S TIPS**

Pancakes layered with savoury fillings to form a large 'cake' are ideal to whip out of the fridge and straight into the Aga for a trouble-free brunch when you have weekend guests.

**50 g (2 oz) plain white flour
50 g (2 oz) plain wholemeal flour
1 egg
350 ml (12 fl oz) skimmed milk
salt and freshly ground black pepper
300 ml (½ pint) vegetable stock
25 g (1 oz) dried mushrooms
15 ml (1 tbsp) vegetable oil, plus extra for greasing**

**450 g (1 lb) fresh spinach, washed and prepared, or 350 g (12 oz) frozen-leaf spinach, thawed
225 g (8 oz) reduced-fat soft cheese
450 g (1 lb) brown-cap mushrooms
1 bunch spring onions
flat-leafed parsley, to garnish**

1 Blend together the flours, egg, milk and a pinch of salt in a food processor. Cover and set aside for 30 minutes. Pour stock over the dried mushrooms and leave to soak for 30 minutes.

2 Wipe the SIMMERING PLATE with kitchen paper dipped in oil. Lightly oil a small non-stick crepe pan and place on the BOILING PLATE. When hot, add enough batter to coat base of pan thinly. Cook the pancake for 1-2 minutes until golden brown, then turn onto the SIMMERING PLATE, shut the lid and cook for a further 30 seconds to brown the underside. Transfer to a plate. Continue with remaining batter to make 10-12 pancakes (see Cook's Tips).

3 Cook the spinach in a pan for 2-3 minutes until just wilted. Cool, squeeze and chop. Mix with the soft cheese and season to taste.

4 Roughly chop the brown-cap mushrooms and spring onions. Heat 15 ml (1 level tbsp) oil in a pan, add the chopped mushrooms and spring onions and cook very briskly on the BOILING PLATE until lightly browned. Add the soaked dried mushrooms and stock, bring to the boil, then reduce heat and cook uncovered in the ROASTING OVEN for 15-20 minutes or until syrupy. Season with salt and pepper. Blend half the mushroom mixture in a food processor until smooth. Return to pan and combine with remaining mushrooms.

5 Place half the spinach mixture in a lightly oiled, 1.1-litre (2-pint) round, shallow, ovenproof dish. Using about six pancakes (see Cook's Tips), layer them with the mushroom mixture and remaining spinach mixture, finishing with a mushroom layer.

6 Cook in the ROASTING OVEN with the shelf on the bottom runners for 30 minutes or until well browned and hot. Serve garnished with flat-leafed parsley.

COOK'S TIPS
Ready-made pancakes are available from supermarkets.
Interleave leftover pancakes with greaseproof paper, wrap and freeze.
To prepare ahead, complete to the end of step 5, then chill overnight. To use, complete step 6, allowing 35-40 minutes to cook.

POTATO PANCAKES WITH MUSTARD CHICKEN LIVERS

PREPARATION TIME: 20 MINUTES

COOKING TIME: 25-30 MINUTES

335 CALS PER SERVING

SERVES 4

FREEZING: SUITABLE: PANCAKES ONLY. THAW AT ROOM TEMPERATURE. REHEAT PANCAKES BRIEFLY ON THE SIMMERING PLATE OR WRAP IN FOIL AND REHEAT ON THE FLOOR OF THE SIMMERING OVEN FOR 15-20 MINUTES.

As you eat this tasty dish, the light fluffy potato pancakes melt in the mouth along with the just cooked chicken livers. The whole dish is perfectly rounded off by a mustard crème fraîche sauce. Always check that your guests are happy to eat offal before choosing this recipe.

PANCAKES
225 g (8 oz) floury potatoes
1 small egg (size 5), or ½ size 2 egg
30 ml (2 tbsp) milk
20 ml (1½ tbsp) self-raising flour
5 ml (1 tsp) chopped fresh thyme
1.25 ml (¼ tsp) salt
1 egg white
a little vegetable oil, for frying

SAUCE
50 g (2 oz) crème fraîche
15 ml (1 tbsp) wholegrain mustard
7.5 ml (½ tsp) lemon juice
15 ml (1 tbsp) chopped fresh chives

CHICKEN LIVERS
2 shallots
25 g (1 oz) butter
225 g (8 oz) chicken livers, thawed if frozen
salt and freshly ground black pepper

TO SERVE
50 g (2 oz) lamb's lettuce
extra-virgin olive oil
lemon juice, to taste
chives and lemon wedges, to garnish

1 Peel the potatoes and cut into even-sized pieces. Cook in lightly salted boiling water for 12-15 minutes or until tender. Drain well and mash until very smooth. Allow to cool slightly, then whisk in the egg, milk, flour, thyme and salt to form a thick smooth batter.

2 Meanwhile, make the sauce. In a bowl, mix together the crème fraîche, mustard, lemon juice and chives. Set aside to allow the flavours to develop.

3 Whisk the egg white and carefully fold into the pancake batter.

4 Heat a very thin layer of oil in a frying pan on the BOILING PLATE. Wipe the SIMMERING PLATE with slightly oiled kitchen paper. Pour in 2 large spoonfuls of the batter to form small pancakes and cook for 1-2 minutes until golden. Flip the pancakes over onto the SIMMERING PLATE, shut the lid and cook the other side until golden. Drain on kitchen paper and keep warm in the SIMMERING OVEN. Repeat with the remaining mixture to make 8 pancakes in total.

5 Peel and slice the shallots. Melt the butter in a small frying pan, add the shallots and fry gently for 5 minutes until just golden. Increase the heat, add the chicken livers and stir-fry for 3-4 minutes until the livers are well browned on the outside, but still a little pink in the centre. Season with salt and pepper to taste.

6 Toss the lamb's lettuce with a little oil and lemon juice. Arrange the potato pancakes on warmed serving plates. Sit the livers on top, scraping over any pan juices, and add a spoonful of the mustard sauce. Garnish with the salad, chives and lemon wedges.

BASIC MUFFIN MIXTURE

PREPARATION TIME:
10 MINUTES

COOKING TIME:
15-20 MINUTES

250 CALS PER
SERVING

MAKES 7-8 MUFFINS

FREEZING: BAG AND
FREEZE. THAW
OVERNIGHT IN THE
FRIDGE. PLACE ON
THE GRID SHELF ON
THE FLOOR OF THE
ROASTING OVEN
FOR 5 MINUTES.

Freshly baked muffins are marvellous for breakfast. Have the dry ingredients weighed up and ready the night before, and you will have them in the oven before the kettle has boiled for tea or coffee.

12 brown sugar cubes
150 g (5 oz) plain flour
7.5 ml (1½ level tsp) baking powder
1.25 ml (¼ level tsp) salt
1 egg, beaten

40 g (1½ oz) sugar
50 g (2 oz) melted butter
2.5 ml (¼ tsp) vanilla essence
100 ml (4 fl oz) milk

1 Roughly crush the sugar cubes and set aside. Sift together the plain flour, baking powder and salt. In a large bowl, combine the beaten egg, sugar, melted butter, vanilla essence and milk. Fold in the sifted flour and spoon the mixture into 7-8 muffin tins lined with paper cases. Sprinkle with the brown sugar.
2 Bake at the front of the ROASTING OVEN on the grid shelf on the floor for 15-20 minutes. Cool on a wire rack.

Variations
APPLE AND CINNAMON
255 cals per serving
Fold 75 ml (5 level tbsp) ready-made chunky apple sauce and 5 ml (1 level tsp) ground cinnamon into the basic mixture with the flour and complete as above.

MAPLE SYRUP AND PECAN
335 cals per serving
Lightly toast 50 g (2 oz) pecan nuts and roughly chop. Fold half of the nuts and 75 ml (3 tbsp) maple syrup into the basic mixture. Mix the remaining nuts with the crushed sugar and sprinkle over the muffins before baking. Drizzle with maple syrup to serve.

CREAMY OVERNIGHT PORRIDGE WITH CRUNCHY OAT TOPPING

PREPARATION TIME:
2 MINUTES

COOKING TIME:
OVERNIGHT
+12–16 MINUTES

SERVES 2 (TOPPING:
6–8 PORTIONS)

160 CALS PER
SERVING,
+ 115 CALS FOR
THE TOPPING IF
SERVING 6,
85 CALS IF
SERVING 8

FREEZING:
UNSUITABLE

A wonderful everyday treat. For speed and ease this recipe is given using a teacup as a measure (180 ml/6 fl oz). If you like larger portions of porridge, then use a mug, allowing up to half a cup or half a mug of oats per person. The topping can be made in bulk in advance and kept in an airtight tin or jar.

1 cup whole oatflakes, conservation grade,
or whole rolled oats
60 ml (4 tbsp) organic natural yoghurt
cream or extra yoghurt, to serve

FOR THE TOPPING
100 g (3½ oz) jumbo oats
75 g (3 oz) pale muscovado sugar
1.25 ml (¼ tsp) salt

1 For the topping, place the oats, sugar and salt in the small roasting tin. Set on front of bottom runners of ROASTING OVEN. Bake for 6–8 minutes, turn the tin round or stir well and cook for a further 5–8 minutes or the sugar just begins to melt and the oats are palest golden colour – take care not to burn. Leave to cool and store in an airtight jar or tin.
2 For the porridge, put 1 cup of oats in an ovenproof earthenware or glass casserole and add 2 cups of water.
3 Place at the front of the grid shelf on the floor of the SIMMERING OVEN. Leave overnight.
4 Stir in yoghurt and return to the oven for 2–3 minutes, then serve topped with crunchy toasted oats and milk, extra yoghurt or cream.

COOK'S TIP
The flavour of the whole rolled or flaked oats is retained much better than finely milled oats. If you cannot easily obtain jumbo oats, use the same rolled oats for the topping.

AGA TIP
If making a double quantity of the topping in the large roasting tin, stir every 5 minutes or so to ensure the mixture does not burn at the back of the oven.

SMOOTHIE DRINKS
Banana and Mango

PREPARATION TIME:
5 MINUTES

220 CALS PER
SERVING

SERVES 2

FREEZING: SEE
COOK'S TIPS

Mangoes are rich in betacarotene, as well as providing vitamin C and fibre. Bananas provide potassium, vitamin B6 and a slow-release carbohydrate to stave off hunger pangs.

1 ripe mango
1 banana (see Cook's Tips)
200 ml (7 fl oz) semi-skimmed milk
150-200 ml (5-7 fl oz) unsweetened orange juice

45 ml (3 level tbsp) Greek yogurt (see Cook's Tips)
15 ml (1 level tbsp) icing sugar (optional)

1 Peel and roughly chop the mango. Place in a blender or food processor with the remaining ingredients, then blend for 1 minute or until smooth. Serve well chilled.

COOK'S TIPS
Bananas freeze well: chop them into smaller pieces and use straight from the freezer.
For 200 cals per serving, use any low-fat fruit yogurt instead.

Dried Fruit

PREPARATION TIME:
5 MINUTES +
SOAKING

175 CALS PER
SERVING

SERVES 2

You can use any combination of dried fruits for this drink.

75 g (3 oz) dried fruit, e.g. apples, pears, apricots, prunes

300 ml (½ pint) unsweetened orange juice
200-250 ml (7-9 fl oz) semi-skimmed milk

1 Chop the dried fruit into small pieces, then place in a bowl and pour the orange juice over the top. Cover the bowl and leave to stand overnight.
2 Place the fruit in a blender or food processor, along with any remaining soaking liquor, then add the milk and blend for 1 minute or until smooth. Serve well chilled.

Apricot and Orange

PREPARATION TIME:
5 MINUTES

170 CALS PER
SERVING

SERVES 2

This smoothie recipe uses canned apricots rather than fresh, so it is particularly useful during winter when the variety of fresh fruits available can be limited. Some of the vitamin C is lost during the canning process, but you gain in other ways – canned apricots actually provide more betacarotene than fresh.

400 g (14 oz) canned apricots in natural juice
150 ml (5 fl oz) apricot yogurt

200-250 ml (7-9 fl oz) unsweetened orange juice

1 Place all the ingredients in a blender or food processor and blend for 1 minute or until smooth. Serve well chilled.

19

CHEESE PARKERHOUSE ROLLS

PREPARATION TIME:
25 MINUTES +
RISING

COOKING TIME:
17-22 MINUTES

125 CALS PER
SERVING

MAKES 24

FREEZING: COOL,
WRAP AND FREEZE.
RE-HEAT FROM
FROZEN FOR 10-15
MINUTES ON THE
BOTTOM RUNNERS
OF THE ROASTING
OVEN, OR THAW
AND PLACE IN THE
SIMMERING OVEN
FOR 20 MINUTES.

Use a good quality Farmhouse Cheddar for the best flavour.

700 g (1½ lb) strong white flour
7.5 ml (1½ tsp) salt
1 sachet fast action dried yeast
25 g (1 oz) butter

450 ml (¾ pint) tepid water
melted butter
125 g (4 oz) mature Cheddar cheese, grated

1 Put the flour, salt and yeast into a bowl. Rub in the butter until the mixture resembles fine breadcrumbs. Make a well in the centre of the bowl, then pour in the water. Beat thoroughly until the dough leaves the sides of the bowl clean. Alternatively, mix in a food processor using the plastic dough blade.

2 Turn onto a lightly floured surface and knead for about 10 minutes until smooth and elastic, or for 1-2 minutes in the food processor. Roll out the dough until it is about 1 cm (1½ in) thick. Cut out rounds using a plain 6.5 cm (2½ in) cutter. Knead and re-roll the trimmings as necessary.

3 Brush with a little melted butter. Mark a crease across each round, then fold carefully in half along the crease.

4 Place on a baking sheet, cover with a clean tea towel and leave in a warm place (such as on a folded thick towel on top of the lid of the SIMMERING PLATE) for about 40 minutes or until doubled in size.

5 Brush the risen rolls with melted butter then bake in the ROASTING OVEN on the top runners for 10 minutes. Sprinkle with cheese, turn the tray round, place on the bottom runners and bake for a further 7-12 minutes, until well risen and golden brown. Remove from the baking tray and cool on a wire rack.

CINNAMON BREAD WITH STRAWBERRY COMPOTE

PREPARATION TIME:
20 MINUTES +
SOAKING

COOKING TIME:
20-25 MINUTES

430 CALS PER
SERVING

SERVES 6

FREEZING:
UNSUITABLE

Steeping chunks of bread in sweetened milk, then frying it to a crisp case has long been a thrifty way of revitalizing stale bread. This recipe enhances the idea, tossing the bread in spiced sugar and serving it with lightly poached strawberries. Served with whipped cream, the flavour combination is really delicious.

STRAWBERRY COMPOTE
450 g (1 lb) strawberries
25 g (1 oz) caster sugar
1 cinnamon stick, halved
45 ml (3 tbsp) redcurrant jelly
squeeze of lemon juice, to taste

CINNAMON BREAD
6 thick slices white bread, about 2 cm (¾ in) thick (see Cook's Tip)
3 egg yolks

2.5 ml (½ tsp) vanilla essence
65 g (2½ oz) caster sugar
150 ml (¼ pint) double cream
50 ml (2 fl oz) milk
50 g (2 oz) unsalted butter
15 ml (1 tbsp) oil
1.25 ml (¼ tsp) ground cinnamon
lemon balm or mint sprigs, to garnish

1 To make the compote, hull the strawberries and halve any large ones. Place in a saucepan with the sugar and cinnamon stick. Cover and cook in the SIMMERING OVEN for 15-20 minutes until the strawberries begin to soften.

2 Melt the redcurrant jelly in a separate saucepan with 15 ml (1 tbsp) water. Pour over the strawberries. Stir lightly and remove from the heat. Add a little lemon juice to taste.

CINNAMON BREAD WITH STRAWBERRY COMPOTE

3 Cut a 7.5 cm (3 in) square from each bread slice. Cut each square in half diagonally to make triangles. Lightly beat the egg yolks with the vanilla essence, 15 ml (1 tbsp) sugar, cream and milk.
4 Place the bread slices in a single layer on two large plates. Pour the egg mixture over them and leave to stand for 10 minutes until absorbed.
5 Melt the butter with the oil in a large frying pan on the BOILING PLATE. Add half the bread triangles and fry for 2 minutes or until golden on the undersides. Turn the bread and fry for another minute. Drain and keep warm in the SIMMERING OVEN while frying the remainder, adding a little more butter to the pan if necessary.
6 Mix the remaining sugar and the cinnamon together and use to coat the fried bread. Arrange on serving plates with the strawberries and juice. Decorate with lemon balm or mint sprigs and serve with cream or crème fraîche.

COOK'S TIP
Use bread that is one or two days old if available, as it will be easier to cut and soak.

VARIATIONS
Use raspberries instead of strawberries, heating them briefly in the melted redcurrant jelly, rather than softening them first. Lightly poached sweet plums or apricots would also work well.

21

SOUPS AND STARTERS

BAKED RED ONION SOUP

PREPARATION TIME:
20-25 MINUTES

COOKING TIME:
1¼-1½ HOURS

575 CALS PER
SERVING

SERVES 4

FREEZING:
UNSUITABLE

A delicious variation on the classic French onion soup.

4 large red onions, about 1.1 kg (2½ lb) total weight
60 ml (4 tbsp) olive oil
1 garlic clove
10 ml (2 level tsp) chopped fresh sage or small pinch dried
salt and freshly ground black pepper

8 slices ciabatta bread (see Cook's Tip)
900 ml (1½ pints) hot, home-made vegetable stock
175 g (6 oz) grated Gruyère or Cheddar cheese
50 g (2 oz) freshly grated Parmesan cheese

1 Peel the onions and cut each one into eight wedges; places in a large roasting tin lined with foil. Combine the olive oil, peeled and crushed garlic and the sage; add to the onions and toss well. Cook on the top rungs of the ROASTING OVEN for 20 minutes. Stir well, then place on the floor of the ROASTING OVEN for a further 15-20 minutes, ensuring the onions brown evenly. Season generously with salt and pepper.

2 Divide half the onions among four individual ovenproof soup bowls. Using the toasting rack on the BOILING PLATE, toast the ciabatta bread on both sides, then place one slice in each soup bowl. Add sufficient vegetable stock to cover, then scatter half the Gruyère or Cheddar cheese over the top, followed by half the Parmesan cheese.

3 Sprinkle with the remaining onions, then repeat the layers of toasted ciabatta, vegetable stock and grated cheeses.

4 Place the bowls in a large roasting tin and bake on the bottom rungs of the ROASTING OVEN for about 20 minutes or until the cheese is melted and browned. Stand for 5-10 minutes in the SIMMERING OVEN before serving.

COOK'S TIP
The ciabatta bread should be cut on the diagonal into 1 cm (½ in) thick slices

CAULIFLOWER SOUP

PREPARATION TIME:
25 MINUTES

COOKING TIME:
40 MINUTES

540 CALS PER
SERVING

SERVES 6

FREEZING: FREEZE
AT STEP 3 BEFORE
ADDING SPRING
ONIONS AND
CORIANDER.

Thai spices and flavourings combine well with cauliflower to make a fragrant soup.

4 stalks lemon grass
4 kaffir lime leaves (optional)
2 x 400 g (14 oz) cans coconut milk
750 ml (1¼ pints) vegetable stock
4 garlic cloves
5 cm (2 in) piece fresh root ginger
4 red chillies
30 ml (2 tbsp) groundnut oil
10 ml (2 tsp) sesame oil
1 large onion

10 ml (2 level tsp) ground turmeric
10 ml (2 level tsp) sugar
900 g (2 lb) cauliflower florets
30 ml (2 tbsp) lime juice
30 ml (2 tbsp) light soy sauce
salt and freshly ground black pepper
4 spring onions
60 ml (4 level tbsp) chopped fresh coriander

22

1 Roughly chop the lemon grass; shred the kaffir lime leaves. Put coconut milk and stock into a pan. Peel and finely chop garlic and ginger. Add to the pan with the lemon grass, lime leaves and chillies. Bring to the boil, cover and transfer to the SIMMERING OVEN for 15 minutes. Strain and reserve the liquid.

2 Heat the oils together in the cleaned saucepan. Thinly slice the onion; add with the turmeric and sugar and fry gently for 5 minutes. Cut the cauliflower florets into pieces. Add to the pan and stir-fry for 5 minutes or until lightly golden.

3 Add the reserved liquid, lime juice and soy sauce. Bring to the boil, then cover and cook in the SIMMERING OVEN for 15-20 minutes until the cauliflower is tender. Season. Trim and shred the spring onions; add to the soup with coriander and serve.

CARROT, PARSNIP AND LENTIL SOUP

PREPARATION TIME:
20 MINUTES +
SOAKING

COOKING TIME:
55 MINUTES

280 CALS PER
SERVING

SERVES 6

FREEZING: COOL,
PACK AND FREEZE
THE SOUP AND
CHORIZO
SEPARATELY AT THE
END OF STEP 3.
THAW OVERNIGHT
AT COOL ROOM
TEMPERATURE AND
COMPLETE TO THE
END OF THE
RECIPE.

The lentils and spicy chorizo make this a robust and hearty soup, most welcome after winter country walks. This is very much a meal in itself or just followed by bread and cheese.

75 g (3 oz) green lentils
200 g (7 oz) chorizo sausage or peppered salami
350 g (12 oz) onions
225 g (8 oz) carrots
225 g (8 oz) parsnips
30 ml (2 tbsp) oil
5 ml (1 level tsp) ground cumin

1.7 litres (3 pints) vegetable stock or boiling water with 3 vegetable stock cubes
2 bay leaves
a few thyme sprigs
salt and freshly ground black pepper
croûtons, to garnish

1 Soak the lentils in double their volume of cold water for 6 hours or overnight. Cut the chorizo into cubes. Roughly chop the onions, carrots and parsnips.

2 Heat the oil in a large pan on the BOILING PLATE, then add the chorizo sausage and cook, stirring, for 5 minutes or until golden. Remove with a slotted spoon and set aside. Add the onions to the pan and cook until soft and golden. Add the carrots, cumin, parsnips and drained lentils and cook, stirring, for 5 minutes. Stir in the stock (see Cook's Tip), bay leaves and thyme. Bring to the boil and transfer to the SIMMERING OVEN for 30 minutes or until the vegetables are tender.

3 Cool slightly, remove the herbs and purée the soup in batches in a food processor or liquidiser.

4 Return to the wiped-out pan, bring back to the boil and correct the seasoning. Serve with the fried chorizo, garnished with croûtons.

COOK'S TIP
If using stock cubes, do not add the cubes or salt to the soup until the lentils are tender.

ROAST PEPPER SOUP

PREPARATION TIME:
25 MINUTES

COOKING TIME:
1½ HOURS

390 CALS PER
SERVING

SERVES 4

FREEZING: SUITABLE
FOR THE SOUP, NOT
FOR THE SAFFRON
CREAM. COMPLETE
TO END OF STEP 5
(OMITTING STEP 4).
COOL, PACK AND
FREEZE THE SOUP.
THAW OVERNIGHT
AT COOL ROOM
TEMPERATURE.

There is something very special about the flavour of roasted peppers – they cook to perfection in the Aga and combine well with the traditional Mediterranean herbs of oregano and basil.

2 large red peppers
90 ml (3½ fl oz) olive oil
1 large aubergine
1 large onion
2 garlic cloves
5 ml (1 level tsp) grated lemon rind
15 ml (1 level tbsp) chopped fresh thyme, or 5 ml (1 level tsp) dried
5 ml (1 level tsp) dried oregano
400 g (14 oz) can chopped tomatoes
900 ml (1½ pints) vegetable stock

30 ml (2 level tbsp) chopped fresh basil
salt and freshly ground black pepper
fresh basil leaves, to garnish

FOR THE SAFFRON CREAM
small pinch saffron threads
1 egg yolk
1 garlic clove, crushed
2.5 ml (½ level tsp) cayenne pepper
10 ml (2 tsp) lemon juice
150-175 ml (5-6 fl oz) olive oil

1 Place the peppers in a roasting tin on the top runners of the ROASTING OVEN for 40-50 minutes until charred and tender. Cool in a covered bowl, then cut in half, de-seed, peel and chop the flesh, retaining any juices.

2 Meanwhile, halve the aubergine lengthways. Score the flesh with the point of a knife, sprinkle with salt and leave for 20 minutes. Squeeze out the bitter juices. Brush with oil and place cut side down in a roasting tin on the floor of the ROASTING OVEN. Bake for 20-30 minutes until dark brown underneath. Cool and chop.

3 Peel and chop the onion and garlic. Heat remaining oil in a pan and fry onion, garlic, rind, and herbs on the BOILING PLATE, stirring, for 3-5 minutes until browned. Add peppers, aubergine, tomatoes and stock. Bring to boil; cover and simmer in the SIMMERING OVEN for 30 minutes.

4 To make the saffron cream, soak the saffron in 15 ml (1 tbsp) boiling water for 5 minutes. Whisk the yolk with the garlic, cayenne pepper, lemon juice and seasoning until pale and slightly thickened. Slowly whisk in the olive oil until thick. Stir in the saffron liquid and adjust seasoning.

5 Transfer the soup to a blender. Add the basil; process until smooth. Return soup to pan and heat through. Adjust seasoning. Serve topped with the saffron cream. Garnish with basil.

COOK'S TIP
The raw egg in the saffron cream makes this an unsuitable topping for the very young and elderly.

SPINACH AND RICE SOUP

PREPARATION TIME:
10 MINUTES

COOKING TIME:
25-30 MINUTES

305 CALS PER
SERVING

SERVES 4

FREEZING:
UNSUITABLE

Choose small leaved spinach for the best flavour, stripping the leaves from the coarse stem. If you use frozen spinach, select frozen leaf in preference to frozen chopped spinach.

1 onion	**1.25 ml (¼ level tsp) cayenne pepper**
60 ml (4 tbsp) extra-virgin olive oil	**125 g (4 oz) arborio rice**
2 garlic cloves	**1.1 litres (2 pints) vegetable stock**
10 ml (2 level tsp) chopped fresh thyme or large pinch dried	**225 g (8 oz) fresh or frozen spinach (see Cook's Tip)**
10 ml (2 level tsp) chopped fresh rosemary or large pinch dried	**60 ml (4 level tbsp) pesto sauce**
grated rind of ½ lemon	**salt and freshly ground black pepper**
10 ml (2 level tsp) ground coriander	**extra-virgin olive oil and freshly grated Parmesan cheese, to serve**

1 Finely chop the onion. Heat half the oil in a saucepan. Add the onion, peeled and crushed garlic, herbs, lemon rind and spices, then cook gently on the SIMMERING PLATE in a covered pan for 5 minutes.

2 Add the remaining oil along with the rice and cook, stirring, for 1 minute. Add the stock, transfer to the BOILING PLATE and bring to the boil. Place in the back of the SIMMERING OVEN for 20 minutes or until the rice is tender.

3 Meanwhile, shred the spinach and stir into the soup with the pesto sauce. Boil on the BOILING PLATE for 2 minutes and season to taste.

4 Serve drizzled with a little oil, topped with Parmesan cheese.

COOK'S TIP
If using frozen spinach, thaw and drain thoroughly before stirring into the soup.

SPINACH AND RICE SOUP

TOMATO, CELERY AND APPLE SOUP

PREPARATION TIME: 15 MINUTES

COOKING TIME: 50 MINUTES

160 CALS PER SERVING

SERVES 6

FREEZING: COOL, PACK AND FREEZE SOUP AT THE END OF STEP 3. TO USE, THAW OVERNIGHT AT COOL ROOM TEMPERATURE. BRING THE SOUP BACK TO THE BOIL AND SIMMER FOR 5 MINUTES. IF THE SOUP SEEMS TOO THICK, DILUTE IT TO THE DESIRED CONSISTENCY WITH VEGETABLE STOCK OR WATER.

If using a food processor, you may wish to reserve part of the liquid (either juice or stock) to add after the soup has been puréed. Food processors are better puréeing thicker rather than thinner mixtures.

275 g (10 oz) onions
1 head green celery, about 400 g (14 oz)
400 g (14 oz) cooking apples
50 g (2 oz) butter
2 garlic cloves
2 x 400 g cans plum tomatoes

300 ml (½ pint) apple juice
450 ml (¾ pint) vegetable stock
pinch of sugar
salt and freshly ground black pepper
basil leaves, to garnish

1 Roughly chop the onions and celery. Peel, core and roughly chop the cooking apples.
2 Melt the butter in a large, heavy-base saucepan. Add the onions and celery and cook for 5 minutes on the BOILING PLATE stirring occasionally, until the onion is soft and golden. Add the crushed garlic and apples and cook for a further 3 minutes, then stir in the tomatoes, apple juice and vegetable stock. Bring the soup to the boil and simmer, uncovered, for 30-40 minutes in the SIMMERING OVEN until the vegetables are tender.
3 Cool the soup slightly, then purée in batches in a food processor or liquidiser until smooth. Push purée through a fine sieve.
4 Return the soup to the wiped-out pan. Bring back to the boil, add a pinch of sugar and adjust the seasoning. Garnish and serve.

COOK'S TIP
For a richer-tasting soup, replace the apple juice with the same quantity of medium cider.

ICED ASPARAGUS AND SHALLOT SOUP

PREPARATION TIME: 15 MINUTES + CHILLING

COOKING TIME: 30 MINUTES

95 CALS PER SERVING

SERVES 6

FREEZING: COMPLETE TO THE END OF STEP 4. COOL, PACK AND FREEZE. THAW OVERNIGHT AND CONTINUE STEPS 5 AND 6.

Make sure the soup is served very well chilled in chilled bowls; if not, it will lose its refreshing taste.

1.1 kg (2½ lb) asparagus
4 large shallots
200 g (7 oz) leeks

45 ml (3 tbsp) oil
salt and freshly ground black pepper
chervil sprigs, to garnish

1 Using a sharp knife, trim the asparagus (see Cook's Tips) – this will yield around 700 g (1½ lb). Cut the tips off the asparagus and set aside. Thinly pare the stalks with a vegetable parer and chop into 2.5 cm (1 in) pieces. Finely chop the shallots and leeks.
2 Heat the oil in a large saucepan, add the shallots and cook gently on the SIMMERING PLATE for 2-3 minutes. Add the leeks and continue to cook for about 5 minutes or until soft. Add the chopped asparagus and 900 ml (1½ pints) water; season and bring to the boil.
3 Cook, uncovered, in the SIMMERING OVEN for 10-20 minutes or until the asparagus is very soft. Allow to cool a little.
4 Pour the soup into a food processor or blender and process until very smooth. If using a food processor, push through a fine sieve (see Cook's Tips).

5 Halve the reserved asparagus tips lengthways if they are large and cook in boiling, salted water for 2-3 minutes or until just tender, then drain and refresh with cold water. Add the asparagus tips to the soup, cover and chill for at least 4 hours, preferably overnight.

6 Mix approximately 450-600 ml (¾-1pint) iced water into the soup; season well. Serve in chilled soup bowls, garnished with chervil.

COOK'S TIPS
To trim asparagus, break off the tough stalk ends and use a potato peeler or small knife to remove the bitter outer bracts.
The easiest way to push the asparagus purée through a sieve is with the bowl of a ladle.

SQUASH, PUY LENTIL AND PRAWN SOUP

PREPARATION TIME: 20 MINUTES

COOKING TIME: 55 MINUTES

470 CALS PER SERVING FOR 6; 350 CALS PER SERVING FOR 8

SERVES 6-8

FREEZING: COMPLETE SOUP TO THE END OF STEP 3, THEN COOL QUICKLY, PACK AND FREEZE. THAW THE SOUP OVERNIGHT AT COOL ROOM TEMPERATURE, THEN COMPLETE THE RECIPE.

If you have vegetarian guests, this recipe can easily be adapted by using vegetable stock and omitting the prawns.

75 g (3 oz) each carrots, onions, celery and leeks
175 g (6 oz) Puy lentils
75 g (3 oz) butter
2 garlic cloves
900 ml (1½ pints) fish stock
200 ml (7 fl oz) vermouth
142 ml (5 fl oz) carton double cream

2 thyme sprigs
2 bay leaves
salt and freshly ground black pepper
6-8 small squashes, each weighing about 700 g (1½ lb)
18-24 large raw prawns
chives, to garnish

1 Roughly chop the carrots, onions, celery and leeks. Rinse the lentils in cold water.

2 Heat 50 g (2 oz) butter in a large ovenproof pan on the SIMMERING PLATE and cook vegetables, stirring occasionally, for 5 minutes. Add crushed garlic; cook for 1 minute. Stir in lentils, stock, 150 ml (¼ pint) vermouth, cream, herbs, seasoning and 300 ml (½ pint) water. Transfer to the BOILING PLATE and bring to boil; cover and cook on the floor at the back of the SIMMERING OVEN for 40-45 minutes until vegetables are tender; discard herbs.

3 Meanwhile, trim the bases of the squashes so they are flat and cut the tops off at the stalk end; scoop out the seeds. Place squashes in a roasting tin, hang on the bottom runners of the ROASTING OVEN and cook for 35-40 minutes or until tender. Scoop out some of the flesh and add to the soup. Cool slightly; liquidize in batches in a food processor until smooth. Pass through a fine sieve, if wished, and adjust the seasoning.

4 If soup is too thick, dilute with stock or water, return to the wiped-out pan and keep warm. Peel and de-vein the prawns; rinse in cold water. Place in a pan with remaining butter and vermouth. Simmer on the SIMMERING PLATE for 2-3 minutes until prawns turn pink. Strain prawn liquid into the soup. Ladle into the hollowed-out squashes; garnish with the prawns and chives.

WILD MUSHROOM AND PARMESAN WAFERS WITH CHAMPAGNE SAUCE

PREPARATION TIME:
35 MINUTES +
CHILLING

COOKING TIME:
45 MINUTES

480 CALS PER
SERVING

SERVES 8

FREEZING:
UNSUITABLE

When wild mushrooms are out of season, try this recipe with chestnut (brown) mushrooms which have a better flavour than button mushrooms.

75 g (3 oz) butter
75 g (3 oz) Parmesan cheese
450 g (1 lb) mixed wild mushrooms (see Cook's Tips)
225 g (8 oz) shallots
350 g (12 oz) puff pastry

salt and freshly ground black pepper
300 ml (½ pint) champagne
300 ml (½ pint) vegetable stock
284 ml (10 fl oz) carton double cream
sprigs of fresh thyme, to garnish

1 Melt 25 g (1 oz) butter and grate the Parmesan cheese. Rinse and quarter the mushrooms (see Cook's Tips). Finely chop the shallots.

2 Roll pastry out on a lightly floured worksurface to a rectangle 23 × 33 cm (9 × 13 in) and cut widthways into three, even-sized pieces. Brush with the melted butter, sprinkle with half the grated Parmesan cheese and season with pepper. Stack the pieces of pastry on top of one another, then re-roll the pastry out to the same dimensions and refrigerate for 15 minutes. Cut out eight 10 cm (4 in) diameter rounds and place on a greased baking sheet. Sprinkle with the remaining grated Parmesan cheese, season with pepper and refrigerate for 30 minutes (see Cook's Tips). Cook on the third runners of the ROASTING OVEN for 5-7 minutes. Then slit the sides to let out the steam and turn the tray around before returning to the oven for a further 3-5 minutes. Set aside to cool, then split each round in two.

3 Heat the remaining butter in a large, shallow ovenproof pan, add the shallots and cook, stirring, for 2-3 minutes or until soft. Add the mushrooms. Cook for 5 minutes, stirring, then add the champagne and stock. Bring to the boil and cook in the SIMMERING OVEN for 5 minutes. Lift the mushrooms out of the pan with a slotted spoon and set aside. Add the cream to the liquor in the pan. Bring to the boil, then reduce for 15-20 minutes or until syrupy on the floor of the ROASTING OVEN. Add seasoning to taste and stir in reserved mushrooms.

4 To serve, warm the pastry in the SIMMERING OVEN for 10 minutes. Place a pastry base on each plate, then spoon the mushrooms and sauce over. Cover with a pastry lid and garnish with sprigs of fresh thyme.

COOK'S TIPS
Most major supermarkets now sell wild mushroom selections. Look out for morels, chanterelles, ceps and pieds de mouton. Rinse the mushrooms well under cold, running water; fine soil is often trapped in the gills.
Chill pastry after rolling or it will shrink and lose its shape during baking. If you wish, you can use ready rolled pastry to save time on the first rolling.

PARMA HAM WITH MANGO AND ORANGE

PREPARATION TIME:
20 MINUTES +
MARINATING

COOKING TIME:
5 MINUTES

250 CALS PER
SERVING

SERVES 4

FREEZING:
UNSUITABLE

When choosing mangos, they should be slightly soft under thumb pressure. Also, when under-ripe there is little or no smell; when ripe, they are fruity and fragrant; when over-ripe they smell earthy or musty.

I orange
30 ml (2 tbsp) virgin olive oil
45 ml (3 tbsp) sweet sherry
5 ml (I tsp) balsamic vinegar

salt and freshly ground black pepper
2 large mangoes
75 g (3 oz) Parma ham
tarragon sprigs, to garnish

I Pare the rind from the orange and place in a small bowl with the oil; cover and set aside for 30 minutes. Divide the orange into segments.
2 Meanwhile, pour the sherry into a small saucepan, bring to the boil on the SIMMERING PLATE and bubble to reduce by half. Remove from the heat and whisk in the balsamic vinegar; season to taste. Set aside to cool.
3 Peel the mangoes and halve to remove the stone; slice the flesh.
4 Arrange the mango and orange segments on individual plates with the ham. Add the orange-flavour oil to the sherry mixture; drizzle over the mango and Parma ham (see Cook's Tip).

COOK'S TIP
Keep orange oil in a cool place for up to I week. Add to other salad dressings.

SCAMPI PROVENÇAL

PREPARATION TIME:
25 MINUTES

COOKING TIME:
20-25 MINUTES

205 CALS PER
SERVING

SERVES 6

FREEZING: SUITABLE
FOR SAUCE ONLY

Serve this classic dish with crusty bread as a starter or with rice and salad as a main course.

700 g (I½ lb) tomatoes, preferably plum tomatoes
4 shallots or I small onion
45 ml (3 tbsp) olive oil
3 garlic cloves, crushed or chopped
15 ml (I level tbsp) tomato paste
150 ml (¼ pint) white wine

bouquet garni
salt and freshly ground black pepper
700 g (I½ lb) raw scampi, peeled tiger prawns or langoustines
spring onions, chives and prawns, to garnish

I Peel, de-seed and roughly chop the tomatoes. Finely chop the shallots. Heat the olive oil in a large frying pan, add the shallots and cook for 1-2 minutes on the BOILING PLATE. Add the garlic and cook for 30 seconds before adding the tomato paste; cook for I minute. Pour in the white wine, bring to the boil and bubble for about 5-10 minutes until very well reduced and syrupy.
2 Add the chopped tomatoes and bouquet garni, then season to taste. Bring to the boil and cook in the SIMMERING OVEN for 10 minutes or until pulpy.
3 Add the raw scampi to the hot sauce, then return to the boil and simmer gently, stirring, for 1-2 minutes or until the scampi are pink and just cooked through to the centre. Garnish with finely sliced spring onions, chopped chives and prawns; serve immediately.

COOK'S TIP
To prepare ahead, complete the recipe to the end of step 2, cool quickly, then cover and refrigerate for up to two days. To use, bring the sauce to the boil, then complete the recipe as in step 3.

SAVOURY HERB CUSTARDS WITH SMOKED SALMON

PREPARATION TIME:
15 MINUTES +
INFUSING +
COOLING

COOKING TIME:
25-30 MINUTES

555 CALS PER
SERVING

SERVES 4

FREEZING:
UNSUITABLE

Individual savoury herb custards provide delicate bases for slices of smoked salmon and salmon caviar. The herbs are gently heated in the cream, then left to infuse before being strained off; this is sufficient to flavour the custards without overpowering them, while ensuring a smooth creamy texture.

25 g (1 oz) fresh herbs, such as chives, parsley, tarragon, thyme, basil
350 ml (12 fl oz) double cream
3 eggs, lightly beaten
40 g (1½ oz) Gruyère cheese, finely grated
2.5 ml (½ tsp) celery salt

salt and freshly ground black pepper
125 g (4 oz) smoked salmon
25 g (1 oz) salmon caviar
15 ml (1 tbsp) chopped fresh chives
chives and salad leaves, to garnish

1 Lightly oil and base-line four 150 ml (¼ pint) timbale moulds or ramekin dishes. Wash and dry the herbs and bruise lightly with a rolling pin. Place in a small pan and add 300 ml (½ pint) of the cream. Bring slowly to the boil, remove from the heat, cover and place in the SIMMERING OVEN for 30 minutes to infuse.

2 Strain the cream through a fine sieve into a bowl and blend in the eggs, Gruyère, celery salt and seasoning to taste. Pour into the moulds or ramekins and place in a small roasting tin. Pour sufficient boiling water into the tin to come two-thirds of the way up the sides of the dishes.

3 ▨ ▨ Place at the front of the bottom runners of ROASTING OVEN and bake for 15-20 minutes. Cover with cold plain shelf on third runners. Then move to the SIMMERING OVEN for a further 10 minutes.

▨ ▨ ▨ ▨ Set on bottom runners of BAKING OVEN and bake for 25 minutes.

4 Set at the back of the Aga top for 30 minutes-1 hour in the roasting tin or on a folded tea towel on the lid of the Aga to keep just warm for 30 minutes. The custards will set completely as they cool. Run a sharp knife around the edge of each custard to loosen it, then invert onto a serving plate.

5 Whip the remaining cream and top each herb custard with a slice of smoked salmon, a little whipped cream, some salmon caviar and chives. Serve at once, garnished with a sprig of chives and some salad leaves. Crisp French bread is an ideal accompaniment.

COOK'S TIP
These savoury custards are at their best served slightly warm, so don't bake them too far in advance.

VARIATION
Finely chop 25 g (1 oz) watercress or rocket leaves and mix with the cream, eggs, Gruyère, celery salt and pepper. Pour into the moulds and cook as above. Serve with a fresh tomato sauce.

CRAB CAKES WITH MUSTARD SAUCE

PREPARATION TIME:
20 MINUTES +
CHILLING

COOKING TIME:
15-20 MINUTES

470 CALS PER
SERVING

SERVES 6

FREEZING: ONLY IF
USING FRESH CRAB
MEAT. FREEZE
AFTER STEP 2.
THAW OVERNIGHT
AT COOL ROOM
TEMPERATURE,
THEN COMPLETE
RECIPE.

This delicious mustard sauce can also be used with salmon, grilled white fish and chicken. Add more mustard if you like a more piquant sauce with these dishes.

4 spring onions
275 g (10 oz) white crab meat
60 ml (4 tbsp) mayonnaise
salt and freshly ground black pepper
50 g (2 oz) fresh white breadcrumbs
10 ml (2 tsp) Worcestershire sauce
3-4 drops Tabasco sauce
grated rind of 1 lemon
1 egg yolk

FOR THE SAUCE
25 g (1 oz) shallots
25 g (1 oz) button mushrooms
6 cooked, shell-on prawns
125 ml (4 fl oz) white wine
125 ml (4 fl oz) chicken stock
284 ml (10 fl oz) carton double cream
10 ml (2 level tsp) wholegrain mustard
olive oil for shallow-frying
diced tomatoes and black olives
cooked lobster tail or prawns, fresh dill sprigs and celery tops, to garnish
spinach salad, to serve

1 Finely chop the spring onions. In a bowl, flake the crab meat and mix with the spring onions, mayonnaise and seasoning. Stir in 25 g (1 oz) breadcrumbs with the Worcestershire and Tabasco sauces, lemon rind and egg yolk. Bind together well.

2 Divide the mixture into six and shape into round cakes. Coat each cake in the remaining breadcrumbs and chill for at least 2 hours or overnight.

3 Meanwhile, make the mustard sauce. Chop the shallots and slice with mushrooms. Put the prawns in a saucepan with the shallots, mushrooms, white wine and chicken stock. Bring to the boil on the BOILING PLATE and bubble until the liquid has reduced by two-thirds.

4 Add the cream and bring slowly to the boil. Continue to boil until the sauce thickens slightly. Strain the sauce and return to the rinsed-out saucepan. Stir in the mustard and set aside.

5 In a large frying pan on the BOILING PLATE, shallow-fry the crab cakes for 2-3 minutes on each side or until golden and crisp; reheat the mustard sauce. Serve crab cakes on a bed of diced tomatoes and olives; garnish and accompany with a spinach salad.

LOBSTER AND SUMMER VEGETABLE TARTLETS

LOBSTER AND SUMMER VEGETABLE TARTLETS

PREPARATION TIME:
45 MINUTES

COOKING TIME:
ABOUT 10 MINUTES

445 CALS PER
SERVING

SERVES 6

FREEZING:
UNSUITABLE

These individual poppy seed tartlets of filo pastry would make an elegant base for a wide variety of hot or cold starters.

about 200 g (7 oz) filo pastry
25 g (1 oz) butter, melted
15 ml (1 level tbsp) poppy seeds
large pinch saffron
200 ml tub crème fraîche
salt and freshly ground black pepper
125 g (4 oz) French beans

225 g (8 oz) slim asparagus tips
125 g (4 oz) broad beans
60 ml (4 tbsp) orange vinaigrette
two 700 g (1½ lb) cooked lobsters, split
fresh chervil, to garnish
lime slices, to serve

1 Cut 16 squares of filo pastry (see Cook's Tips), each 18 cm (7 in). Brush the squares with melted butter (see Cook's Tips) and layer four on top of each other to form a star shape. Place six ovenproof saucers or large tart tins upside down on a baking sheet. Brush with melted butter. Sprinkle filo shapes with poppy seeds and press each star shape on to a saucer or tin.

■ ■ Cook on the bottom runners of the ROASTING OVEN for 5 minutes, turn over and remove the tins or saucers, and cook for a further minute in the ROASTING OVEN, or transfer to the SIMMERING OVEN for a further 10 minutes or until golden and crisp.

■ ■ ■ ■ Cook on the third runners of the BAKING OVEN for 7-8 minutes, turn over and remove the tins or saucers, and cook for a further 1-3 minutes or until golden, crisp and dry. Cool, then ease off the saucers and set aside.

2 Place saffron in a small bowl, then pour on 15 ml (1 tbsp) boiling water and leave to stand for 15 minutes. Mix the soaking liquid and the saffron strands into the crème fraîche and season. Cover and chill.

3 Trim the French beans, then cook in boiling, salted water for about 5 minutes until they're just tender. Drain, then plunge immediately into ice-cold water. Cook the asparagus and broad beans in the same way for 3 minutes. Drain all the vegetables and dry on absorbent kitchen paper. Place in a large bowl and toss in sufficient orange vinaigrette to moisten. Season to taste. Remove the lobster meat from the claws and from the tail.

4 To serve, divide the vegetables between the pastry cases. Add the lobster meat and a spoonful of the crème fraîche. Garnish with chopped chervil and serve with lime slices.

COOK'S TIPS
When using filo pastry, make sure you keep it covered with a clean tea-towel or clingfilm as you work to prevent it from drying out.
Be sparing when brushing the pastry with melted butter as it needs only a light coating.
To prepare up to 24 hours in advance, complete to the end of step 2. Store the pastry cases in an airtight container and the crème fraîche mixture in a covered bowl in the fridge. Make the orange vinaigrette, cover and refrigerate. To use, complete the recipe

LEEK, POTATO AND GOAT'S CHEESE CAKES

PREPARATION TIME:
25 MINUTES

COOKING TIME:
45 MINUTES
+ CHILLING

195 CALS PER
SERVING

SERVES 8

FREEZING: COOL,
PACK AND FREEZE
THE CAKES AT THE
END OF STEP 3.
THAW THE CAKES
OVERNIGHT AT
COOL ROOM
TEMPERATURE AND
THEN COMPLETE
THE RECIPE.

When buying leeks, choose those that are slim, rather than the thicker ones. These will be melting in texture when cooked with a subtle flavour.

250 g (9 oz) leeks
550 g (1¼ lb) potatoes
salt and freshly ground black pepper
150 g (5 oz) soft goat's cheese
25 g (1 oz) butter

125 g (4 oz) feta cheese
50 g (2 oz) fresh breadcrumbs
flour, for dusting
oil, for brushing
fresh herbs, to garnish

1 Rinse and finely chop the leeks. Peel the potatoes and bring to the boil in salted water in an ovenproof pan. When boiling, transfer the pan to the SIMMERING OVEN and cook until tender. Drain and dry well. Mash the potato with the soft goat's cheese.

2 Melt butter in a saucepan, add the leeks and cook first on the SIMMERING PLATE for 2 minutes, then transfer to the SIMMERING OVEN for 10 minutes or until very soft. Transfer the pan to the BOILING PLATE and cook, stirring, until all the liquid has evaporated. Cool, then mix with potatoes, crumbled feta cheese and breadcrumbs. Season well. Cover and refrigerate for 3-4 hours.

3 Shape the chilled cheese and potato mixture into 16 cakes, each 6.5 cm (2½ in) across and 1 cm (½ in) deep.

4 Dust the cakes with flour and brush with oil. Cook for 1-2 minutes each side directly on the SIMMERING PLATE until golden and crisp, then place on a baking tray in the ROASTING OVEN on the fourth runners for 10 minutes until piping hot right through. Garnish with fresh herbs to serve.

WARM VEGETABLE SALAD WITH BALSAMIC DRESSING

PREPARATION TIME: 40 MINUTES

COOKING TIME: 20 MINUTES

270 CALS PER SERVING

SERVES 6

FREEZING: UNSUITABLE

Enhancing the flavour of even the humblest vegetable, such as carrots, can make quite a simple combination of fresh, young vegetables taste delectable when served with a good dressing.

450 g (1 lb) thin leeks
salt and freshly ground black pepper
700 g (1½ lb) carrots
75 ml (5 tbsp) vegetable oil
45 ml (3 level tbsp) caster sugar
60 ml (4 level tbsp) chopped fresh tarragon

150 ml (5 fl oz) white wine
75 ml (5 tbsp) olive oil
45 ml (3 tbsp) balsamic vinegar
2 Little Gem lettuces
1 bunch or 75 g (3 oz) watercress

1 Slice the leeks diagonally into 5 cm (2 in) lengths. Bring a large pan of salted water to the boil, add the leeks and boil for 30 seconds. Drain the leeks and plunge into ice-cold water. Drain again thoroughly and set aside.

2 Slice the carrots very thinly lengthways. Bring a pan of water to the boil, add the carrots and boil for 30 seconds. Drain and plunge into ice-cold water. Drain again thoroughly and set aside.

3 In a large frying pan, heat 30 ml (2 tbsp) vegetable oil. Add the leeks and fry on the BOILING PLATE until golden. Remove and set aside.

4 Fry the carrots in 2-3 batches on the BOILING PLATE in the remaining vegetable oil, adding caster sugar and 45 ml (3 level tbsp) tarragon. Cook, turning regularly, over a high heat for 2-3 minutes or until the carrots are brown around the edges. Remove and set aside.

5 Add the white wine to the pan, bring to the boil and bubble until reduced by half. Stir in the olive oil, balsamic vinegar and the remaining chopped tarragon. Season and set aside.

6 Tear the lettuce and mix it with the watercress and warm leeks and carrots. Pour the dressing over and serve immediately.

SOURED CREAM AND ONION TARTS

PREPARATION TIME: 20 MINUTES + CHILLING

COOKING TIME: ABOUT 1 HOUR

535 CALS PER SERVING

SERVES 6

FREEZING: UNSUITABLE

If you find pastry difficult to make, this is the recipe for you! Soured cream pastry melts in the mouth, and is simple to prepare – it takes only a few seconds in the food processor.

9 medium tomatoes, halved
salt and freshly ground black pepper
15 ml (1 level tbsp) chopped fresh thyme or 2.5 ml (½ level tsp) dried
30 ml (2 tbsp) olive oil
200 g (7 oz) chilled butter

175 g (6 oz) plain flour
90-105 ml (6-7 level tbsp) soured cream
800 g (1¾ lb) onions
125 g (4 oz) Roquefort, feta, or a good Red Leicester or Lanark Blue cheese
fresh thyme sprigs, to garnish

1 Place the tomatoes in a roasting tin, season, sprinkle with thyme, drizzle with oil and cook, uncovered, on bottom runners of the ROASTING OVEN for 40 minutes until slightly shrivelled.

2 Meanwhile, cut 150 g (5 oz) of the butter into small dice and place in a food processor with the flour. Pulse until butter is roughly cut up through the flour (you should still be able to see pieces of butter), then add the soured cream and pulse again for 2-3 seconds until just mixed.

3 On a floured surface, divide the pastry into six balls and thinly roll each into a 12.5 cm (5 in) round. Place on two sheets of foil placed on trays; cover and chill for 30 minutes.

4 Finely slice the onions. Melt the remaining butter in an ovenproof pan on the BOILING PLATE, add the onions, fry for 30 seconds, then transfer to the SIMMERING OVEN and cook slowly for about 15 minutes until very soft. Return to the BOILING PLATE and fry until well browned and caramelized. Cool.

5 Place the pastry on the foil in a roasting tin and position on the plain shelf. Spoon the onions into the centre of the pastries, leaving a 1 cm (½ in) edge. Crumble the cheese on top and add the tomatoes. Season, then roughly fold up the pastry edge, pinching it together tightly to hold the edge in place.

6 Cook the tarts on the floor of the ROASTING OVEN on the second runners for 25-30 minutes until golden, turning the tin round after 15-20 minutes to ensure even cooking. Garnish with fresh thyme sprigs. Serve immediately.

CRISPY DUCK SALAD

PREPARATION TIME:
30 MINUTES +
COOLING AND
CHILLING
OVERNIGHT

COOKING TIME:
1 HOUR 15 MINUTES

550 CALS PER
SERVING

SERVES 8

FREEZING:
UNSUITABLE

This delicious starter tastes just as good if made with cooked guinea fowl or chicken.

6 duck legs, each about 200 g (7 oz)
5 ml (1 level tsp) peppercorns
2 fresh thyme sprigs
2 bay leaves
salt and freshly ground black pepper
125 g (4 oz) kumquats
125 g (4 oz) pecan nuts

2 oranges
225 g (8 oz) cranberries
125 g (4 oz) caster sugar
60 ml (4 tbsp) white wine vinegar
135 ml (9 tbsp) sunflower oil
45 ml (3 tbsp) walnut oil
salad leaves, such as frisée

1 Place the duck legs in a large, flameproof casserole, cover with cold water and bring to the boil. Place in the SIMMERING OVEN for 10 minutes, skim the surface of the liquid and add the peppercorns, thyme, bay leaves and 10 ml (2 level tsp) salt. Cover and cook in the ROASTING OVEN with the grid shelf on the floor for 45 minutes or until tender. Cool quickly and refrigerate overnight (see Cook's Tips).

2 Cut the kumquats into quarters. Place the pecan nuts on a baking sheet and bake in the ROASTING OVEN for 3-5 minutes until pale golden.

3 Finely grate the rind and squeeze the juice from the oranges. Place the orange rind in a frying pan with 200 ml (7 fl oz) of the orange juice, plus the cranberries and sugar. Bring to the boil on the SIMMERING PLATE and cook gently for 5 minutes or until the cranberries are tender. Drain the cranberries, reserving the juice, and set aside. Bring the juice to a fast boil on the BOILING PLATE and bubble until syrupy, then add the reserved cranberries.

4 Place a good pinch of salt and black pepper in a small bowl, then whisk in the vinegar followed by the oils. Add the kumquats to the cranberry mixture with the dressing and pecans. Set aside. Skim the fat from the surface of the jellied duck liquor and set aside. Cut the duck into thick shreds, leaving the skin on.

5 Just before serving, heat 30 ml (2 tbsp) reserved duck fat (see Cook's Tips) in a large roasting tin placed on the floor of the ROASTING OVEN for 10 minutes until very hot. Add the duck, spread out well, return to the oven for 12-15 minutes until golden and crispy, turning the tin round after 10 minutes. To serve, carefully toss the duck with the cranberry mixture and serve with salad leaves.

COOK'S TIPS
The duck is chilled overnight so the fat solidifies and can be used in step 5. You'll be left with a wonderful jellied stock that can be frozen for use in other dishes. The duck fat can also be used for pate and roast potatoes. Take care - the duck fat may splutter, so cover your hands.
To prepare ahead, complete the recipe to the end of step 3 up to two days in advance, then cover and refrigerate the ingredients separately.

AUBERGINE TIMBALES

PREPARATION TIME:
30 MINUTES

COOKING TIME:
1½ HOURS +
COOLING

145 CALS PER
SERVING

SERVES 6

FREEZING:
UNSUITABLE

ILLUSTRATED OPPOSITE

Aubergines absorb oil like blotting paper, so use with restraint. Brush lightly with oil and sear on the boiling plate for a wonderful flavour and texture. Protect the plate with foil first.

4 garlic cloves
60 ml (4 tbsp) olive oil, plus oil for brushing
2 x 400 g cans chopped plum tomatoes
150 ml (5 fl oz) white wine
2 sprigs thyme
15 ml (1 level tbsp) sun-dried tomato paste

5 ml (1 level tsp) caster sugar
salt and freshly ground black pepper
4 long, thin aubergines
90 ml (6 level tbsp) Greek yogurt
Roasted Red Pepper Salsa (see recipe below)
rocket leaves, to serve

1 Finely chop the garlic. Heat the olive oil in a very large, shallow ovenproof casserole or pan with the garlic and fry for 30 seconds. Add the chopped plum tomatoes, white wine, thyme sprigs, tomato paste, caster sugar, salt and pepper. Bring to the boil and reduce briskly on the BOILING PLATE, uncovered, cooking steadily, stirring, for 7-10 minutes or until thick, then transfer to the SIMMERING OVEN for 20 minutes. Discard thyme sprigs and set mixture aside to cool.

2 Meanwhile, trim the aubergine tops and slice off six thin rounds. Cut remaining aubergines lengthways into 5 mm (¼ in) thick slices. Brush aubergine slices on both sides with olive oil. Cover the BOILING PLATE with foil, then cover with a layer of sliced aubergines. Put the lid down and allow to brown for about 1 minute. Turn the aubergine slices over with a palette knife and brown the other side. If necessary, cook the aubergines in batches.

3 Lightly oil six 175 ml (6 fl oz) ovenproof moulds such as ramekins. Place an aubergine round in the bottom of each mould and use the long strips of aubergine to line the sides, making sure there are no gaps. Leave the excess aubergine hanging over the edge of the moulds.

4 Divide the Greek yogurt between the moulds, then add the tomato mixture. Fold over the excess aubergine and cover the tops with foil. Place the moulds in a roasting tin half-filled with hot water.

5 ■ ■ Place the roasting tin on the grid shelf on the floor of the ROASTING OVEN with the cold plain shelf on the bottom runners and cook for 25-30 minutes.
■ ■ ■ ■ Place on the middle runners of the BAKING OVEN for 30-35 minutes.

6 Allow the timbales to cool, then turn out on to serving plates. Serve with Roasted Red Pepper Salsa (below) and a salad of rocket leaves.

ROASTED RED PEPPER SALSA

PREPARATION TIME:
10 MINUTES +
COOLING

COOKING TIME:
30 MINUTES

60 CALS PER
SERVING

SERVES 6

FREEZING:
UNSUITABLE

1 large red pepper
45 ml (3 tbsp) olive oil

10 ml (2 tsp) balsamic vinegar
salt and freshly ground black pepper

1 Roast the red pepper in a roasting tin on the top runners of the ROASTING OVEN for 25-30 minutes or until the skin is charred. Leave to cool in a plastic bag, then remove the skin, core and seeds, retaining the juice. Cut into strips or dice, then mix with the oil and balsamic vinegar and season. Keep the salsa covered in the fridge for up to 3 days.

COUNTRY TOMATO AND PARMESAN TART

PREPARATION TIME: 40 MINUTES + CHILLING

COOKING TIME: 40 MINUTES

285 CALS PER SERVING FOR 6; 210 CALS PER SERVING FOR 8

SERVES 6-8

FREEZING: UNSUITABLE

This tart would also be delicious served warm for a light lunch, accompanied by a good, strong Cheddar cheese and a delicious chutney.

75 g (3 oz) plain flour
140 g (4½ oz) finely grated fresh Parmesan cheese
75 g (3oz) butter
salt and freshly ground black pepper
1.25ml (¼ level tsp) cayenne pepper

900 g (2 lb) tomatoes, preferably plum
60 ml (4 level tbsp) sun-dried tomato paste
15 g (½ oz) fresh breadcrumbs
15 ml (1 level tbsp) chopped fresh thyme
fresh thyme sprigs, to garnish

1 In a food processor, blend the plain flour, 75 g (3 oz) grated Parmesan cheese, butter, 2.5 ml (½ level tsp) salt and the cayenne pepper until the mixture looks like rough breadcrumbs. Set aside one-third of the crumb mixture, cover and refrigerate. Press the remaining crumb mixture into the base of a 21cm (8¼ in) square, loose-based flan tin, using the back of a metal spoon to spread it out to the edges (see Cook's Tip). Chill for 10 minutes.

2 ■ ■ Bake on the grid shelf on the floor of the ROASTING OVEN with the cold plain shelf above on the third runners for 12-16 minutes until light golden brown. Cool.
■ ■ ■ ■ Bake in the middle of the BAKING OVEN for 15-20 minutes. Cool.

3 Cut the plum tomatoes into thick slices. Spread the sun-dried tomato paste all over the baked and cooled crumb base, then sprinkle with half the fresh breadcrumbs. Layer the tomato slices and chopped fresh thyme on top and sprinkle with the remaining fresh breadcrumbs, the remaining Parmesan cheese and the reserved pastry crumb mixture; season with salt and black pepper.

4 ■ ■ Cook the tart on the grid shelf on the floor of the ROASTING OVEN for a further 15-20 minutes or until golden brown.
■ ■ ■ ■ Cook on the top runners of the BAKING OVEN for a further 15-20 minutes or until golden brown.

5 Allow it to cool slightly, then cut into portions and garnish with fresh thyme. The tart can be served either warm or at room temperature.

COOK'S TIP
A square flan tin makes serving far easier, but if you don't have one, the same mixture can be cooked in a 23 cm (9 in) round flan tin.

ITALIAN BREAD WITH MELTED CHEESE FILLING

PREPARATION TIME:
25 MINUTES +
CHILLING

COOKING TIME:
35 MINUTES

390 CALS PER
SERVING

SERVES 6

FREEZING: WRAP
AND FREEZE AFTER
STEP 4. THAW AT
COOL ROOM
TEMPERATURE,
THEN COMPLETE
THE RECIPE.

Perfect at lunchtime, serve this dish cut into thick, satisfying wedges – the filling will ooze appetizingly from the centre.

50 g (2 oz) pecorino cheese (see Cook's Tips)
two 150 g packets mozzarella cheese
freshly ground black pepper
2 round focaccia breads, each about 350 g (12 oz)
75 g (3 oz) shallots or spring onions

1 red pepper
225 g (8 oz) courgettes
30 ml (2 tbsp) olive oil
fresh rosemary sprigs and sea salt, to garnish

1 Grate the pecorino cheese. Drain the mozzarella and cut into small dice, then combine with the pecorino and season generously with black pepper.

2 Carefully slice the focaccia bread in half horizontally, then set aside. Make a cut in the bottom piece about 1 cm (½ in) in from the edge of the bread and about 2.5 cm (1 in) deep all the way round the edge, then hollow out centre (see Cook's Tips). Repeat with the second focaccia loaf.

3 Peel and finely dice shallots. De-seed and finely dice the red pepper; finely dice the courgettes. Heat the oil in a large frying pan, then add shallots, red pepper and courgettes. Fry gently on the SIMMERING PLATE for about 10 minutes or until soft and golden. Leave to cool.

4 Stir the cooled vegetables into the cheese mixture; divide between the two hollowed-out bases. Place 'lids' on top and wrap in foil. Refrigerate for at least 4 hours or overnight.

5 Cook on the plain shelf on the bottom runners of the ROASTING OVEN. After 20 minutes, turn the tray round to ensure even cooking, then cook for a further 10-20 minutes or until the filling is heated through. Remove the foil; cut each loaf into six wedges. Garnish and serve.

COOK'S TIPS
Pecorino is a hard Italian cheese available from some supermarkets. If you cannot find it, use Parmesan cheese instead.
If your loaves are not very deep, make your cuts more shallow. The hollowed-out bread can be made into breadcrumbs, then frozen for stuffings and toppings.

PISSALADIERE PARCEL

PREPARATION TIME:
I HOUR 40 MINUTES
+ RISING

COOKING TIME:
I HOUR 45 MINUTES

470 CALS PER
SERVING FOR 6; 353
CALS PER SERVING
FOR 8

SERVES 6-8

FREEZING: SUITABLE.
THAW ON PLAIN
SHELF ON FLOOR
OF SIMMERING
OVEN FOR I HOUR.
TRANSFER TO
ROASTING OVEN
FOR 5-10 MINUTES.

ILLUSTRATED OPPOSITE

Serve this crisp, hot flan with a large bowl of mixed green salad leaves. Wedges are delicious served with summer barbecues. Re-heat the parcel in the Aga just before serving.

900 g (2 lb) onions
3 garlic cloves
200 g (7 oz) goat's cheese
8 anchovy fillets (see Cook's Tips)
90 ml (6 tbsp) olive oil
sprig of rosemary or 5 ml (1 level tsp) dried

375 g (12 oz) strong, plain white flour
2.5 ml (½ level tsp) easy-blend dried yeast
5ml (1 level tsp) salt
flour, for sprinkling
1 beaten egg
rosemary sprigs and sea salt, to sprinkle

1 Peel and finely slice the onions and garlic. Crumble the cheese; chop the anchovies. Heat 60 ml (4 tbsp) oil in an ovenproof pan; add the onions, garlic and rosemary. Lay a sheet of greaseproof paper over the onions; cover the pan with a tight-fitting lid. Simmer for 3-4 minutes on the SIMMERING PLATE, then transfer to the floor of the SIMMERING OVEN for 45 minutes-1 hour until the onions are soft. Drain the onions, reserving the liquid for use in the next step.

2 For the dough, stir together flour and yeast (see Cook's Tips); make a well. Add reserved onion liquid made up to 300 ml (½ pint) with warm water, remaining oil and salt, stirring until a soft dough is formed. Knead for 10 minutes (4-5 minutes in a mixer). Shape into a ball; place in a oiled bowl. Cover with clingfilm and leave for 45 minutes until doubled in size.

3 Mix the crumbled cheese and chopped anchovies into the cooked onion mixture.

4 Roll dough out to a 30 cm (12 in) round. Lift on to the floured plain shelf. Spread onion mixture over, leaving a 6.5 cm (2½ in) border. Lightly brush border with water. Bring up sides to cover the filling; seal well. Place the greased roasting tin on top of parcel and invert it, so the seal is underneath. Press down lightly.

5 Make deep, diagonal slashes across the top, 1 cm (½ in) apart; prove for 30 minutes or until spongy. Brush lightly with beaten egg. Sprinkle with rosemary and sea salt.

6 Cook on the top runners of the ROASTING OVEN for 20-30 minutes. Turn the tin round and cook on the bottom runners for a further 15-20 minutes until an even golden brown. Cool for 5 minutes.

COOK'S TIPS
If you omit the anchovies, this dish will be suitable for vegetarians.
You can use bought bread mix. Use 350 g (12 oz) mix and add 300 ml (½ pint) liquid, made up of warm water and onion liquid. Knead and shape the dough as in step 2.
To prepare ahead, complete to end of step 5. Refrigerate for up to 4 hours. To use, complete recipe.

CRUNCHY CHICKPEA EGGS

PREPARATION TIME:
30 MINUTES +
CHILLING

COOKING TIME:
15 MINUTES

415 CALS PER
SERVING

SERVES 6

FREEZING:
UNSUITABLE

If you do not like deep frying, bake the eggs in the small roasting tin in a little hot oil. Set the tin on the top runners of the roasting oven, pushing well to the back, for 15-20 minutes.

1-2 red chillies
2 tomatoes, preferably plum
4 spring onions
125 g (4 oz) pitted black olives
2 x 420 g cans chickpeas
2 garlic cloves
60 ml (4 level tbsp) chopped, fresh flat-leafed parsley

salt and freshly ground black pepper
6 hard-boiled eggs, shelled
1 egg, beaten
75 g (3 oz) fine fresh white breadcrumbs
oil for deep frying
aïoli mayonnaise, to serve

1 De-seed and finely chop the chillies and the tomatoes.
2 Roughly chop the spring onions and black olives. Place the drained chickpeas in a food processor with the crushed garlic, chillies, tomatoes, parsley and seasoning and process for 1 minute or until roughly chopped.
3 Divide the mixture into six equal portions. Form each into a flat cake and shape it round the shelled, hard-boiled eggs, making it as even as possible (see Cookery Editor's Tips). Brush with beaten egg and roll in breadcrumbs. Chill, uncovered, for up to 4hours or overnight.
4 To deep-fry, heat the oil in a deep-fat frying or large saucepan to 160°C (325°F) or until a cube of bread begins to sizzle, then gently lower each egg into the oil and fry for 7-8 minutes until golden brown. Remove and drain thoroughly on absorbent paper. To oven-bake, heat 120 ml (8 tbsp) oil in a small roasting tin for 5-10 minutes in the ROASTING OVEN eggs in the hot fat, then set on the top runners of the ROASTING OVEN and bake for 15-20 minutes until golden and crisp. Serve hot with aïoli mayonnaise.

COOK'S TIPS
Make sure the shelled eggs are dry as this will allow the chickpea mixture to stick more easily.
The chickpea mixture may seem too crumbly, but keep squeezing and pressing the mixture well around the egg and it will stick..
To prepare ahead, complete the recipe to the end of step 3 up to one day ahead.To use ,complete recipe.

WINTER SQUASH SALAD

PREPARATION TIME:
15 MINUTES

COOKING TIME:
55 MINUTES

275 CALS PER
SERVING (FOR 4);
185 CALS PER
SERVING (FOR 6)

SERVES 4-6

FREEZING:
UNSUITABLE

During late autumn and winter an ever-increasing variety of squash and pumpkins is available. Many have labels to help you choose a suitable variety and most can be roasted, sauteed, boiled and fried.

125 g (4 oz) onions
225 g (8 oz) yellow butternut squash
225 g (8 oz) courgettes
225 g (8 oz) plum tomatoes
50 g (2 oz) cheese, such as feta
75ml (5 tbsp) olive oil

2 garlic cloves
30 ml (2 tbsp) chopped fresh herbs, such as chives, mint or flat-leaf parsley
salt and freshly ground black pepper
50 g (2 oz) chopped black and green olives
warm crusty bread, to accompany

1 Finely slice the onions, squash, courgettes and tomatoes. Crumble the cheese. Heat 30 ml (2 tbsp) oil in an ovenproof pan and fry the squash for 3-4 minutes or until softened and golden. Remove and set aside. Add the crushed garlic and onions to the pan and cook slowly for 5 minutes on the SIMMERING PLATE, then transfer to the SIMMERING OVEN for a further 10 minutes.

2 Spoon the sliced squash, courgettes and tomatoes into an ovenproof dish or tin and top with the onions and garlic, herbs, seasoning and remaining oil. Cover with foil and cook on the grid shelf on the floor of the ROASTING OVEN. After 15 minutes, uncover and cook for a further 30-40 minutes, until tender.

3 Serve on individual plates, sprinkled with the olives and crumbled cheese. Accompany with warm, crusty bread.

CHEESE AND APPLE PARCELS

PREPARATION TIME:
35 MINUTES +
CHILLING

COOKING TIME:
ABOUT 15 MINUTES

260 CALS PER
PARCEL

MAKES 10

FREEZING:
COMPLETE RECIPE
TO THE END OF
STEP 5, THEN OPEN
FREEZE AND PACK.
THAW THE PARCELS
OVERNIGHT IN THE
FRIDGE AND
CONTINUE AS IN
STEP 6.

Tangy Cheshire cheese and sweet, juicy apples are wrapped in buttery, melt-in-the-mouth puff pastry (to save time, buy 500 g ready-made). Serve the pastries on a bed of lightly dressed salad leaves, as a light lunch or supper.

FOR THE PASTRY
175 g (6 oz) firm unsalted butter
225 g (8 oz) plain white flour
pinch of salt
5ml (1 tsp) lemon juice

FOR THE FILLING
125 g (4 oz) Cheshire cheese
1 large dessert apple
45 ml (3 level tbsp) chopped fresh parsley
salt and freshly ground black pepper
beaten egg, to glaze
salad leaves, to serve

1 To make the rough puff pastry, cut the butter into small dice, then sift the flour and salt into a bowl. Add butter, lemon juice and 100 ml (3½ fl oz) very cold water. Using a round-bladed knife, mix to a soft dough, adding extra water if too dry. Do not make this pastry in a food processor.

2 Knead lightly, then roll out on a lightly floured surface to an oblong, about 30 cm (12 in) long and 10 cm (4 in) wide. Fold the bottom third up and the lower third down, keeping edges straight, then give the pastry a quarter turn. Repeat the rolling, folding and turning four more times (see Cook's Tip). Wrap the pastry in greaseproof paper and refrigerate for at least 30 minutes.

3 For the filling, crumble the cheese into a bowl. Peel, core, quarter and dice the apple. Add to bowl with the parsley; season.

4 Roll out half the pastry thinly on a lightly floured surface; cut out five 12 cm (5 in) rounds, using a saucer as a guide.

5 Brush the edges of the circles with beaten egg; spoon a little filling onto one side of each of the rounds. Fold the other half over the filling and press the edges together to seal. Lightly flute the edges.

6 Transfer the parcels to a lightly greased plain shelf. Brush with beaten egg. Score each parcel several times across the top. Use the remaining pastry rounds and filling to make five more parcels. Bake on the second runners of the ROASTING OVEN for 12 minutes, then turn the shelf round and cook for a further 3-5 minutes until risen and golden. Serve warm with lightly dressed leaves.

COOK'S TIP
Chill the pastry if it becomes too sticky to handle when rolling and folding in step 2.

RISOTTO GALETTE WITH MELTED TALEGGIO

PREPARATION TIME: 15 MINUTES, + COOLING

COOKING TIME: 1 HOUR

540 CALS PER SERVING FOR 4; 405 CALS PER SERVING FOR 6

SERVES 4-6

FREEZING: UNSUITABLE

This recipe starts off as a classic risotto and is then converted into a crisp, golden, crusted 'cake' sandwiched with melted cheese..

large pinch of saffron threads
900 ml (2 pints) hot vegetable stock
1 onion
50 g (2 oz) butter
3 garlic cloves
350 g (12 oz) arborio rice
120 ml (4 fl oz) dry white wine
60 ml (4 level tbsp) chopped mixed fresh herbs, such as basil, chives, parsley and tarragon

25 g (1 oz) Parmesan or Cheddar cheese
2 large eggs
225 g (8 oz) taleggio cheese (see Cook's Tip)
salt and freshly ground black pepper
oil, for shallow frying

1 Infuse the saffron threads in the hot vegetable stock for 10 minutes; transfer to a saucepan. Peel and finely chop the onion.

2 Melt the butter in a large, heavy-based pan, add the onion and crushed garlic; fry on the BOILING PLATE for 10 minutes until soft and golden.

3 Add the rice to the onion; stir over the heat for 1 minute until grains are glossy. Add the wine; boil rapidly until almost all the liquid has evaporated.

4 Add a quarter of the saffron stock to the rice. Bring to a fast boil, stirring briskly, then place in the SIMMERING OVEN for 5 minutes until the liquid is absorbed. Repeat until the liquid is used up and the rice just cooked – about 20-25 minutes cooking overall.

5 Off the heat, stir in the herbs and grated Parmesan cheese. Cover with greaseproof paper, press down firmly and set aside to cool.

6 Stir the beaten eggs into the risotto; divide the mixture in half. Pour a little oil into a 23 cm (9 in) non-stick, ovenproof frying pan; heat gently.

7 Spoon half the risotto into the pan and spread evenly to the edges with a palette knife. Sprinkle the diced taleggio over and carefully spread the remaining risotto on top. Cook on the floor of the ROASTING OVEN for 10-15 minutes until golden underneath.

8 Place the grid shelf on the second runners of the ROASTING OVEN and bake for a further 10 minutes until the top is golden. Turn out on to a large plate and allow to cool slightly for 10-15 minutes in the SIMMERING OVEN. Serve warm, cut into wedges.

COOK'S TIP
Taleggio is a rich, soft cheese from Italy with a wonderful melting texture. As an alternative, use mozzarella or fontina.

PASTA WITH BROCCOLI PESTO

PREPARATION TIME: 10 MINUTES

COOKING TIME: 30 MINUTES

325 CALS PER SERVING

SERVES 6

FREEZING: UNSUITABLE

This quick and easy broccoli pesto is a great accompaniment to just about everything from grilled chicken to baked fish. Alternatively, if served with pasta, it makes a very good vegetarian supper dish.

700 g (1½ lb) broccoli
2 garlic cloves
1 lemon
salt and freshly ground black pepper
60 ml (4 tbsp) olive oil
175 g (6 oz) dried pasta, eg penne

142 ml (5 fl oz) carton double cream
15 g (½ oz) freshly grated Parmesan cheese
basil pesto sauce, to accompany
fresh basil leaves and pickled red chillies, to garnish

PASTA WITH BROCCOLI PESTO

1 Cut the large stalks from the broccoli and set aside to use in soups. Divide the tops into small florets. Peel and chop the garlic. Squeeze the juice from the lemon.

2 Cook the florets in a pan with 1 cm (½ in) boiling, salted water for 5-6 minutes or until very tender. Drain in a colander, reserving about 50 ml (2 fl oz) cooking liquor and refresh the broccoli in cold water to retain a good colour.

3 Heat the olive oil in the same pan, add the chopped garlic and cook for 1-2 minutes. Stir in the broccoli and cook on the SIMMERING PLATE for 10-15 minutes, stirring all the time, until the broccoli is a thick pulp.

4 Meanwhile, cook the pasta in plenty of boiling, salted water according to the packet instructions. When the pasta has come to the boil, transfer to the SIMMERING OVEN if the pasta variety takes more than 5 minutes to cook. Drain well.

5 Stir 45 ml (3 tbsp) lemon juice and the double cream into the broccoli mixture and simmer gently for a further 3-4 minutes. Thin the sauce to the consistency of single cream with a little of the reserved cooking liquor. Stir in the Parmesan cheese. Season with plenty of salt and black pepper.

6 Toss the pasta into the Broccoli Pesto and serve immediately with a little basil pesto spooned over. Garnish with basil leaves and pickled red chillies.

AGA TIP
Cooking pasta in the SIMMERING OVEN after it has come to the boil ensures it does not boil over.

SAUSAGE AND RED ONION PASTA

PREPARATION TIME:
15 MINUTES

COOKING TIME:
30 MINUTES

825 CALS PER
SERVING

SERVES 4

FREEZING:
COMPLETE STEP 3,
COOL QUICKLY
AND FREEZE. THAW
OVERNIGHT AT
COOL ROOM
TEMPERATURE.
RE-HEAT SAUCE ON
SIMMERING PLATE,
TRANSFER TO
SIMMERING OVEN
WHILE COOKING
PASTA.

A most useful 'store cupboard' recipe. Chillies and sausages of the Toulouse variety keep well in the fridge and can also be frozen.

350 g (12 oz) small red onions
3 garlic cloves
I large red chilli
450 g (I lb) Toulouse or any other strongly flavoured coarse sausages
45 ml (3 tbsp) olive oil
15 ml (I tbsp) balsamic vinegar
400 g (14 oz) can chopped tomatoes
45 ml (3 level tbsp) tomato paste

300 ml (½ pint) white wine
bay leaf
15 ml (I level tbsp) chopped fresh oregano or 5 ml (I level tsp) dried
salt and freshly ground black pepper
225 g (8 oz) dried pasta noodles, e.g. pappardelle
purple or green basil leaves, to garnish

I Peel and quarter the onions. Peel and slice the garlic. Halve, de-seed and finely chop the chilli (see Cook's Tip). Skin the sausages and crumble the meat.

2 In a large pan, fry the sausagemeat in half the oil. Stir continuously on the BOILING PLATE for 4-5 minutes until deep golden brown. Remove with a slotted spoon and set aside. Add the onions to the pan with the remaining oil and fry for 5-10 minutes or until soft and golden.

3 Stir in the balsamic vinegar with the chilli and garlic. Fry for about 5 minutes. Return the sausagemeat to the pan with the chopped tomatoes, tomato paste, wine, bay leaf and oregano. Season well and bring to the boil, simmer for 2-3 minutes and then transfer to the SIMMERING OVEN for 20 minutes.

4 Meanwhile, cook the pasta in an ovenproof pan in plenty of boiling, salted water according to packet instructions. When the pasta has come to the boil, transfer to the SIMMERING OVEN. Drain well and stir in the sauce. Serve immediately, garnished with basil.

COOK'S TIP
When handling chillies, wear rubber gloves to avoid skin irritation.

AGA TIP
Cooking pasta in the simmering oven ensures it does not boil over.

ARTICHOKE AND MUSHROOM LASAGNE

PREPARATION TIME:
20 MINUTES

COOKING TIME:
I HOUR 40 MINUTES

785 CALS PER
SERVING FOR 4; 525
CALS PER SERVING
FOR 6

SERVES 4-6

FREEZING:
UNSUITABLE

This variation on a classic lasagne is perfect for vegetarian guests and is also very quick to prepare. Served with a mixed green salad, this makes a good supper dish.

225 g (8 oz) onions
1.1 kg (2½ lb) mixed mushrooms, e.g. brown-cap and button
397 g can artichoke hearts in water
45 ml (3 tbsp) olive oil
3 garlic cloves
25 g (I oz) walnuts
125 g (4 oz) cherry tomatoes
50 g (2 oz) butter, plus extra for greasing

50 g (2 oz) plain flour
1.1 litres (2 pints) full-fat milk
2 bay leaves
30 ml (2 tbsp) lemon juice
salt and freshly ground black pepper
200 g (7 oz) fresh chilled lasagne
75 g (3 oz) freshly grated Parmesan cheese
fresh oregano, to garnish

I Peel and roughly chop the onions and mushrooms. Drain and halve the artichokes.

2 In a large ovenproof pan, fry the onions gently in the oil for I minute, then transfer to the SIMMERING OVEN until soft. Add the crushed garlic and walnuts and fry for 3-4 minutes. Stir in

the mushrooms and fry briskly on the BOILING PLATE for 5-10 minutes until no liquid is left. Add the tomatoes and set aside.

3 Melt the butter in a saucepan on the SIMMERING PLATE, add flour and stir for 1 minute. Slowly whisk in the milk until you have a smooth mixture. Bring to the boil, add bay leaves, cover and place in the SIMMERING OVEN for 10 minutes. Add lemon juice and season. Discard the bay leaves.

4 Grease a shallow ovenproof dish and layer one-third of the lasagne over the base. Spoon half the mushroom mixture over, then half the artichokes. Cover with a layer of lasagne and half the sauce. Spoon remaining mushroom mixture over, then remaining artichokes. Top with remaining lasagne. Stir the Parmesan into the remaining sauce and spoon evenly over the top.

5 Place the dish in a roasting tin and set on the bottom runners of the ROASTING OVEN for 40-55 minutes until the pasta is tender and the top is golden and bubbling. Garnish with oregano.

COOK'S TIP

To prepare ahead, complete to the end of step 4, up to 3 hours ahead. Cover and keep in the fridge. To use, remove from the fridge about 30 minutes before cooking as in step 5.

AGA TIP

If the lasagne browns too quickly, place the cold plain shelf above on the second runners for the final 10-15 minutes and turn the dish around if the back is darker than the front.

BEST EVER BOLOGNAISE

PREPARATION TIME: 15 MINUTES + SOAKING

COOKING TIME: 1½-3 HOURS

680 CALS PER SERVING

SERVES 6

FREEZING: COMPLETE TO END OF STEP 3; COOL QUICKLY AND FREEZE. THAW OVERNIGHT AT COOL ROOM TEMPERATURE. BRING TO THE BOIL SLOWLY, ADDING EXTRA STOCK IF NEEDED. SIMMER UNTIL HOT THROUGH. COMPLETE THE RECIPE.

Minced lamb, pork or turkey can also be used to make this delicious bolognaise which is always popular. For a special occasion, use venison.

275 g (10 oz) onions
75 g (3 oz) carrot
75 g (3 oz) celery
125 g (4 oz) brown-cap mushrooms
225 g (8 oz) rindless streaky bacon
10 g packet dried porcini mushrooms (optional)
15 ml (1 tbsp) olive oil
2 garlic cloves
450 g (1 lb) minced beef
300 ml (½ pint) white wine

300 ml (½ pint) chicken stock
15 ml (1 level tbsp) tomato paste
10 ml (2 level tsp) dried oregano
90 ml (6 tbsp) double cream
30 ml (2 level tbsp) chopped, fresh flat leaf parsley
salt and freshly ground black pepper
350 g (12 oz) dried spaghetti
crème fraîche or mascarpone cheese, to serve (optional)
fresh thyme sprigs, to garnish

1 Finely chop the onions, carrot and celery. Roughly chop the mushrooms and bacon. Soak dried mushrooms, if using, in 100 ml (4 fl oz) water for 30 minutes.

2 Fry the onion, carrot and celery in the oil on the BOILING PLATE until soft. Add the fresh mushrooms and crushed garlic and fry for 1 minute. Add the beef and bacon; stir until browned. Stir in the wine, stock, tomato paste and oregano. Bring to the boil, cover.

■ ■ Cook slowly in the SIMMERING OVEN for 2-3 hours.

■ ■ ■ ■ Cook in the BAKING OVEN with the grid shelf on the floor for 20-30 minutes, then transfer to the SIMMERING OVEN for 1 hour.

3 Uncover the meat mixture, stir in the dried mushrooms and their soaking liquid and simmer for 7-10 minutes (if not using dried mushrooms, add an extra 100 ml (4 fl oz) stock at this stage). Add the cream and parsley and bubble for 1 minute. Adjust the seasoning.

4 Meanwhile, cook the spaghetti in an ovenproof pan in boiling, salted water according to packet instructions. When the pasta has come to the boil, transfer to the SIMMERING OVEN. Drain and serve with the Bolognaise. Top with a spoonful of crème fraîche or mascarpone; garnish with thyme.

INDIAN KOFTAS

PREPARATION TIME: 15 MINUTES

COOKING TIME: 20 MINUTES + 1½ HOURS

SERVES 4–6

625-420 CALS PER SERVING

FREEZING: PREPARE TO END OF STEP 4 AND FREEZE. THAW FOR 8 HOURS OR OVERNIGHT IN THE REFRIGERATOR. ALLOW TO STAND AT ROOM TEMPERATURE FOR 2 HOURS BEFORE COOKING.

These are cooked entirely in the oven for ease and to avoid cooking smells in the house. They are ideal to prepare in advance.

60 ml (4 tbsp) oil
600 g (1 lb 5 oz) onions
5 garlic cloves
2 slices bread
500 g (1 lb 2 oz) minced beef
10 ml (2 tsp) ground coriander
20 ml (4 tsp) ground cumin

5 ml (1 tsp) salt
5 ml (1 tsp) chilli powder
5 ml (1 tsp) turmeric
5 ml (1 tsp) garam masala or mixed spice
15 ml (1 tbsp) fresh ginger, grated
500 g (1 lb 2 oz) large pot plain yoghurt
50 g (2 oz) coconut cream, chopped

1 Place half the oil in the large roasting tin and half in the small roasting tin. Peel the onions and reserve one large or two small. Slice the remainder and put in the small roasting tin. Set on the top runners of the ROASTING OVEN to cook for 15–20 minutes until golden. Place the large roasting tin on the floor of the ROASTING OVEN to heat the oil.

2 Chop the reserved onions. Peel and slice the garlic. Put half the garlic in the food processor with the bread and work to fine crumbs. Add the onions, beef and half the coriander, cumin, salt and chilli powder, reserving the remainder for the sauce. Work to combine lightly, then using oily or wet fingers, roll the meat into 40–45 balls the size of an egg yolk.

3 Toss the meatballs in the oil in the large roasting tin and return to the floor of the ROASTING OVEN for 10 minutes until just firm. Add the reserved spices and garlic, plus turmeric and garam masala or mixed spice to the onions, toss well and roast for a further 3–4 minutes.

4 Layer the meatballs, onion mixture, ginger, yoghurt and coconut cream in an ovenproof dish. Cover, cool and chill if you are preparing in advance.

5 Cook for 1-1½ hours in the SIMMERING OVEN, then place on the grid shelf on the floor of the ROASTING OVEN for 5-15 minutes or until just bubbling. Serve with basmati rice, chutneys and popadoms.

COOK'S TIP

To cook popadoms, choose varieties that do not need deep-frying. Place directly on the SIMMERING PLATE, put the lid down for 20–25 seconds, turn over to cook on the other side and stack at the side or the back of the Aga to keep crisp. Follow instructions for basmati rice on the packet: bring to the boil uncovered on the BOILING PLATE, then cover and place in the SIMMERING OVEN until cooked and the liquid is absorbed for perfect, light, dry rice.

TAGLIATELLE WITH MASCARPONE AND BACON

PREPARATION TIME: 15 MINUTES

COOKING TIME: 30 MINUTES

745 CALS PER SERVING

SERVES 4

FREEZING: UNSUITABLE

This is a very quick and delicious pasta dish. If entertaining vegetarian guests, serve the crispy bacon in a separate bowl.

150 g (5 oz) thinly cut streaky bacon or pancetta (see Cook's Tips)
2 bunches watercress or rocket, about 50 g (2 oz)
125 g (4 oz) shallots
15 ml (1 tbsp) olive oil
250 g (9 oz) mascarpone cheese
60 ml (4 tbsp) single cream

15 ml (1 level tbsp) chopped fresh sage
salt and freshly ground black pepper
125 g (4 oz) Gorgonzola cheese
225 g (8 oz) dried pasta, e.g. tagliatelle or pappardelle
deep-fried sage leaves (see Cook's Tips) and fresh rocket, to garnish

1 Cut the bacon into rough pieces. Trim and roughly tear the watercress. Peel and finely slice the shallots.

2 In a large ovenproof frying pan, fry the bacon in its own fat on the floor of the ROASTING OVEN for about 10 minutes until crisp. Remove and set aside. Add the oil and shallots to the pan and fry on the BOILING PLATE for 5-10 minutes until soft and golden. Stir in the watercress and cook for 2 minutes until just wilted.

3 Add the mascarpone and cream and simmer for 2-3 minutes until hot through. Add the sage and season with pepper. Roughly crumble half the Gorgonzola over. Heat through gently for 1-2 minutes.

4 Meanwhile, cook pasta in boiling, salted water in an ovenproof pan according to packet instructions. When the pan of pasta comes to the boil, transfer to the SIMMERING OVEN. Drain and stir in the sauce. Sprinkle bacon and remaining cheese over. Garnish with deep-fried sage leaves (see Cook's Tips) and rocket. Serve immediately.

COOK'S TIPS

Pancetta (Italian bacon) is fattier than standard bacon. It can be found in major supermarkets.
For the garnish, drop a few sage leaves into a small pan of hot vegetable oil for 10 seconds. Drain on absorbent kitchen paper and use immediately.

SEAFOOD LINGUINE 'IN A BAG'

PREPARATION TIME:
30 MINUTES

COOKING TIME:
35 MINUTES

630 CALS PER
SERVING

SERVES 6

FREEZING:
UNSUITABLE

Allow your guests to 'unwrap' their parcel when it's served, releasing the glorious aroma of the seafood.

450 g (1 lb) tomatoes, preferably plum
150 ml (¼ pint) olive oil, plus extra for brushing
2 garlic cloves, crushed
400 g (14 oz) can chopped tomatoes
45 ml (3 level tbsp) sun-dried tomato paste
500 g (1 lb 2 oz) dried linguine pasta
salt and freshly ground black pepper

5 ml (1 level tsp) dried chilli flakes
700 g (1½ lb) cooked mixed seafood, such as peeled prawns, mussels and crabmeat
225 g (8 oz) can or jar clams
30 ml (2 level tbsp) chopped fresh flat-leafed parsley
flat-leafed parsley sprigs and grated toasted Parmesan cheese, to serve (see Cook's Tips)

1 Peel, de-seed and roughly chop the plum tomatoes. Heat half the olive oil in a large, heavy-based saucepan, add the garlic and cook for 30 seconds. Add the canned tomatoes, chopped fresh tomatoes and tomato paste and cook for a further 5 minutes on the BOILING PLATE.

2 Meanwhile, cook the linguine pasta in an ovenproof pan of boiling, salted water. Bring to the boil, then transfer to the SIMMERING OVEN for about 5 minutes (see Aga Tips). Drain well, place in a bowl and stir through the remaining olive oil. Add the tomato sauce, dried chilli flakes, seafood, drained clams and chopped fresh parsley. Season well.

3 Place six pieces of greaseproof paper, each about 35.5 cm (14 in) square, on a flat worksurface. Brush lightly with oil. Divide the pasta mixture among the squares of paper. Wrap up in a bundle and tie paper with string, then place on a baking sheet.

4 Cook the seafood parcels on the plain shelf on the bottom runners of the ROASTING OVEN for 20-25 minutes or until heated through. Allow your guests to open each package at the table, then sprinkle with flat-leafed parsley sprigs and toasted Parmesan cheese.

COOK'S TIP

To prepare ahead, cool the cooked tomato sauce and pasta completely. Complete the recipe to the end of step 3. Refrigerate for up to 4 hours. To use, complete recipe, cooking for 25-30 minutes or until heated through.

AGA TIPS

To toast Parmesan, sprinkle the grated cheese on to a baking sheet, then place in the ROASTING OVEN on the bottom runners for 2-4 minutes until golden brown. If you leave the door open, you will smell when the cheese is ready – it does burn very easily. Use a fish slice to scrape up the cheese from the baking sheet, then sprinkle it over pasta or salads.

Bringing the pasta to the boil then transferring it to the SIMMERING OVEN avoids pans boiling over.

MUSSEL AND SAFFRON PILAFF

PREPARATION TIME:
10 MINUTES +
SOAKING

COOKING TIME:
ABOUT 30 MINUTES

435 CALS PER
SERVING

SERVES 4

FREEZING:
UNSUITABLE

Use packets of ready cooked mussels for this recipe if you wish, but not those in jars as they often contain vinegar which would spoil the flavour of this dish.

1 large onion
1 large pinch saffron
60 ml (4 tbsp) oil
2 garlic cloves
225 g (8 oz) long-grain rice
600 ml (1 pint) light stock

1 bay leaf
salt and freshly ground black pepper
450 g (1 lb) cooked mussels in the shell (see Cook's Tip)
50 g (2 oz) dried currants

1 Finely chop the onion. Soak the saffron in 90 ml (6tbsp) boiling water for 15 minutes.

2 Heat the oil in a flameproof casserole, add the onion and cook on the SIMMERING PLATE for 4-5 minutes or until soft and golden. Crush the garlic, add to onion and cook for 30 seconds before adding the rice. Cook, stirring, for 1-2 minutes. Pour on the stock, then add the saffron and its soaking liquid. Add the bay leaf, season well with salt and black pepper and bring to boil.

3 Cover and cook on the grid shelf on the floor of the ROASTING OVEN for 15-20 minutes or until the rice is tender but still retains some bite (see Cook's Tips).

4 Add the mussels (with their sauce) and the currants to the casserole, cover and return to the oven for 10 minutes or until the mussels are hot.

COOK'S TIPS
Most supermarkets sell ready-cooked mussels, usually in a herb- or wine-based sauce.
Fish stock cubes are readily available and can be used for the stock. Saffron flavoured cubes are also available in some supermarkets.
Brown and easy-cook long grain rice takes about 20 minutes to cook; plain long grain rice takes about 12-15 minutes.

FETTUCINE WITH SPICY SEAFOOD SAUCE

PREPARATION TIME: 10 MINUTES

COOKING TIME: 1 HOUR

345 CALS PER SERVING

SERVES 4

FREEZING: UNSUITABLE

Another useful pasta dish where portions can be set aside for a vegetarian guests and prawns added to the spicy sauce for everyone else.

1 red onion
1 red pepper
1 red chilli
15 ml (1 tbsp) olive oil
1 fat clove garlic
2.5 ml (½ level tsp) ground coriander
2.5 ml (½ level tsp) ground cumin
15 ml (1 level tbsp) sun-dried tomato paste

150 ml (5 fl oz) red wine
2 x 397 g cans chopped tomatoes
salt and freshly ground black pepper
350 g (12 oz) cooked prawns
175 g (6 oz) dried tagliatelle or 350 g (12 oz) fresh fettucine
chopped fresh parsley, to garnish

1 Slice the onion. De-seed and finely chop the pepper and chilli. To make the sauce, heat the oil in a large, shallow saucepan. Add the onion, pepper, chilli and crushed garlic. Cover and cook in the SIMMERING OVEN for 20 minutes or until the onion begins to soften. Add the spices and tomato paste; cook for 1-2 minutes.

2 Pour in the wine and bring to the boil, then place on the floor of the ROASTING OVEN for approximately 5 minutes to reduce by half. Add the tomatoes, season and return to the ROASTING OVEN, uncovered, for about 30 minutes or until the sauce is reduced and thickened. Add the prawns and heat through for 1-2 minutes only. Season to taste.

3 Cook the pasta in an ovenproof pan of boiling, salted water. When the pasta has come to the boil, transfer to the SIMMERING OVEN and cook until just tender. Drain well.

4 Stir the sauce through the pasta to serve. Garnish with chopped fresh parsley.

BAKED NEW POTATOES WITH PRAWNS

PREPARATION TIME:
5 MINUTES

COOKING TIME:
1 HOUR 20 MINUTES

430 CALS PER
SERVING

SERVES 4

FREEZING:
UNSUITABLE

Although this dish takes a little while to cook in the oven, it's so quick and easy to prepare that it makes an ideal supper dish.

700 g (1½ lb) large new potatoes
60 ml (4 tbsp) olive oil
coarse sea salt and freshly ground black pepper
3 shallots or 6 spring onions
450 g (1 lb) tomatoes, preferably plum
2 garlic cloves
5 ml (1 level tsp) paprika

15 ml (1 level tbsp) tomato paste
100 g (3½ oz) goat's cheese, preferably semi-soft chevre
60 ml (4 tbsp) crème fraîche or double cream
15 ml (1 level tbsp) chopped chives
225 g (8 oz) large peeled prawns
flat-leafed parsley, to garnish

1 Wash and prick the potatoes. Place in a small roasting tin with 15 ml (1 tbsp) oil and sprinkle with sea salt. Cook on the second runners of the ROASTING OVEN for 45 minutes-1hour or until soft.

2 Meanwhile, finely chop the shallots. Peel, de-seed and roughly chop the tomatoes.

3 Heat the remaining oil in a saucepan, add the shallots and cook until soft. Crush the garlic and add to the pan with the paprika; cook for 30 seconds. Add the tomato paste and cook for 1 minute. Add the tomatoes, season and bubble for 10-15 minutes or until the mixture is thick and pulpy.

4 Crumble the goat's cheese, mix with the creme fraiche and chopped chives and season with pepper. Cut the potatoes with a cross, about three-quarters of the way through, then squeeze to open further. Mix the prawns into the tomato mixture, then put a spoonful into each potato.

5 Place the filled potatoes in an ovenproof dish, spoon the goat's cheese mixture over the top, then cook on the top or second runners of the ROASTING OVEN, pushing well to the back for maximum heat for 15-20 minutes or until hot to the centre. Serve immediately, garnished with flat-leafed parsley.

PEPPERED TUNA SALAD

PREPARATION TIME:
10 MINUTES

COOKING TIME:
1-2 MINUTES

270 CALS PER
SERVING

SERVES 4

FREEZING:
UNSUITABLE

Fresh tuna is becoming more readily available in supermarkets. Cook it quickly over a high heat, taking care not to overcook it, as it dries out quickly.

50 g (2 oz) kumquats
50 g (2 oz) radishes
75 g (3 oz) red onions
1 green apple
about 125 g (4 oz) mixed salad leaves, such as cos, red batavia and frisée
1 bunch fresh mint leaves

75 ml (5 tbsp) olive oil
30 ml (2 tbsp) light soy sauce
15 ml (1 tbsp) lime juice
350 g (12 oz) tuna, sword or shark steaks
15 ml (1 level tbsp) coarsely ground black pepper

1 Finely slice the kumquats and radishes into rounds. Finely slice the onions. Cut the apple into thin matchsticks. Wash and dry the salad leaves and tear them into bite-sized pieces. Break the mint leaves into sprigs.

2 Mix 60 ml (4 tbsp) olive oil with the soy sauce and the lime juice. Cut the fish steaks into 7.5 cm (3 in) lengths and toss in the black pepper.

3 Heat the remaining oil in a non-stick frying pan on the BOILING PLATE. Cook the fish pieces in batches for about 30 seconds on each side.

4 Toss all the salad ingredients together with the soy dressing and arrange on four serving plates with the cooked tuna pieces.

CHICKEN CAESAR

PREPARATION TIME:
20 MINUTES

COOKING TIME:
15 MINUTES

740 CALS PER
SERVING

SERVES 4

FREEZING:
UNSUITABLE

Caesar salads make popular starters, but adding chicken turns the salad into a delicious main dish with a lovely combination of textures.

6 hen's or 12 quail's eggs
200 g (7 oz) tub crème fraîche (see Cook's Tips)
4 sprigs fresh tarragon or pinch of dried
50 g (2 oz) can anchovy fillets
1 garlic clove
dash of Worcestershire sauce
dash of Tabasco sauce

75 g (3 oz) Parmesan cheese
1 cos lettuce
½ small ciabatta loaf (see Cook's Tips)
350 g (12 oz) skinless chicken breast fillets (see Cook's Tips)
salt and freshly ground black pepper
90 ml (6 tbsp) olive oil

1 Cook hen's eggs in a pan of boiling water for 9 minutes (quail's for 3 minutes) until hard-boiled. Plunge into cold water, cool and peel.

2 While eggs are cooking, process the crème fraîche in a food processor with the tarragon, three-quarters of the anchovies, garlic, Worcestershire sauce, Tabasco sauce and 50 g (2 oz) grated cheese for 5 seconds. Set aside.

3 Tear lettuce into bite-sized pieces, place in a bowl, cover and chill. Cut the bread into 2.5 cm (1 in) cubes. Slice the chicken into strips and season.

4 Stir-fry the chicken in 45ml (3tbsp) oil for 4-5minutes or until it's cooked through. Set aside.

5 Place the croutons in a small roasting tin. Toss in the remaining oil

■ ■ Cook on the floor of the ROASTING OVEN for 5-7 minutes until golden.

■ ■ ■ ■ Cook on the floor of the BAKING OVEN for 7-12 minutes until golden, then transfer the croutons to the SIMMERING OVEN until crisp and dry.

6 Toss hot chicken and bread with lettuce and dressing. Cut eggs into quarters or halves and add to salad with remaining anchovies and Parmesan. Serve immediately.

COOK'S TIPS
If you use reduced-fat crème fraîche, it reduces the calories to 642 cals per portion.
As an alternative, use chopped hot garlic bread tossed through the salad instead of ciabatta croûtons. This salad is also delicious with grilled bacon instead of chicken.

ROAST CHICKEN, APPLE AND BLUE CHEESE SALAD

PREPARATION TIME:
30 MINUTES

490 CALS PER
SERVING

SERVES 4

FREEZING:
UNSUITABLE

This is a delicious way to use up any leftover cold roast chicken and cheese.

5 ml (1 level tsp) runny honey
15 ml (1 level tbsp) Dijon mustard
**15 ml (1 tbsp) each white wine vinegar
and apple or orange juice**
salt and freshly ground black pepper
90 ml (6 tbsp) sunflower oil
225 g (8 oz) cooked roast chicken
**225 g (8 oz) crisp apples, e.g. Cox's or
Braeburn**

400 g (14 oz) mixed salad leaves
**30 ml (2 level tbsp) toasted sunflower
seeds**
**175 g (6 oz) blue cheese, such as
Roquefort or Stilton**
**small packet potato matchsticks
(optional)**

1 To make the dressing, in a large bowl whisk together the honey, mustard, vinegar, fruit juice and seasoning with the oil.

2 Shred the chicken into small pieces and stir them into the dressing. Core the apples and cut them into fine strips.

3 Toss the apples in the dressing with the chicken, salad leaves, sunflower seeds, crumbled cheese and potato matchsticks, if using. Serve immediately.

CHICKEN ENCHILADAS WITH SALSA VERDE

PREPARATION TIME:
30 MINUTES

COOKING TIME:
50 MINUTES

720 CALS PER
SERVING FOR 4; 485
CALS PER SERVING
FOR 6

SERVES 4-6

FREEZING:
UNSUITABLE

This recipe is ideal for a light lunch or a supper dish that you can have standing by in the fridge ready to pop into the Aga when entertaining friends.

225 g (8 oz) onions
125 g (4 oz) celery
50 g (2 oz) sun-dried tomatoes
**225 g (8 oz) brown-cap or shiitake
mushrooms**
450 g (1 lb) skinless chicken breast fillet
**5ml (1 level tsp) each dried oregano and
cumin seeds**
salt and freshly ground black pepper
75 ml (3 fl oz) olive oil

2 garlic cloves
250 g (9 oz) Cheddar cheese
**30 ml (2 level tbsp) chopped fresh
coriander**
30 ml (2 tbsp) lemon juice
6-8 flour tortillas (see Cook's Tips)
butter, for greasing
Salsa Verde, to serve
basil leaves, to garnish

1 Finely slice the onions. Cut the celery into matchsticks and roughly chop the sun-dried tomatoes and mushrooms. Cut the chicken into strips and place in a bowl with the oregano, cumin seeds and seasoning. Toss to coat.

2 Heat half the oil in a large frying pan. Add the onions, celery and crushed garlic and cook for 3-4 minutes (see Aga Tip). Add the sun-dried tomatoes and mushrooms and cook for a further 2-3 minutes. Remove and set aside.

3 Add the remaining oil to the pan and stir-fry the chicken in batches for 2-3 minutes. Mix together the chicken, mushroom mixture, 175 g (6 oz) grated Cheddar cheese, chopped fresh coriander and the lemon juice. Season well.

4 Divide the chicken mixture among the tortillas and roll them up. Place, seam-side down, in a greased baking dish, then sprinkle with the remaining cheese.

5 ■ ■ Cook the tortillas on the grid shelf on the floor of the ROASTING OVEN for 20 minutes or until golden and bubbling.

■ ■ ■ ■ Cook on the bottom runners of the ROASTING OVEN for 25-30 minutes.

6 Spoon the Salsa Verde over (see recipe below), then serve, garnished with basil leaves.

COOK'S TIPS

Flour tortillas are available from major supermarkets.

To prepare ahead, complete recipe to the end of step 4. Cool, cover and refrigerate for up to 4 hours. To use, complete the recipe and cook for 30-35 minutes.

AGA TIPS

If you have a large, ovenproof frying pan, cook the onions and the celery on the floor of the ROASTING OVEN.

For some dishes tortillas can be toasted directly on the SIMMERING PLATE or in the toasting rack on the BOILING PLATE.

SALSA VERDE

PREPARATION TIME:
10 MINUTES

65 CALS PER 15 ML
(1 LEVEL TBSP)

MAKES 200 ML
(7 FL OZ)

FREEZING:
UNSUITABLE

This sauce is also delicious served with cold trout, salmon or turkey.

25 g (1 oz) white breadcrumbs
75 g (3 oz) mixed basil and flat-leafed parsley
2 garlic cloves

3 anchovy fillets
30 ml (2 tbsp) lemon juice
salt and freshly ground black pepper
100ml (4 fl oz) olive oil

1 Place the white breadcrumbs, mixed basil and flat-leafed parsley, garlic cloves, anchovy fillets, lemon juice and salt and pepper in a food processor. Process for 1-2 minutes or until evenly combined. With the motor running, gradually add olive oil.

COOK'S TIP

The Salsa Verde can be stored in the fridge, covered tightly, for up to one week.

PORK, GARLIC AND BASIL RISOTTO

PREPARATION TIME:
15 MINUTES

COOKING TIME:
50 MINUTES

515 CALS PER
SERVING

SERVES 6

FREEZING:
UNSUITABLE

ILLUSTRATED OPPOSITE

A simple tomato salad is the only accompaniment you will need for this creamy risotto. It also makes an excellent vegetarian dish if you omit the pork and ham and served with sautéed mixed mushrooms.

6 thin escalopes pork, British veal or turkey
150 g (5 oz) Parma ham, about 6 slices
about 6 basil leaves
salt and freshly ground black pepper
25 g (1 oz) plain white flour
175 g (6 oz) onion
about 65 g (2½ oz) unsalted butter

2 garlic cloves
225 g (8 oz) risotto (arborio) rice
450 ml (15 fl oz) white wine
450 ml (15 fl oz) stock
45 ml (3 level tbsp) pesto sauce
50 g (2 oz) grated Parmesan cheese
60 ml (4 level tbsp) chopped fresh parsley

1 If necessary, pound the escalopes with a rolling pin until they are wafer-thin. Lay a slice of Parma ham on each escalope and place a basil leaf on top of Parma ham. Fix in place with a wooden cocktail stick. Season and dip in the flour, dusting off any excess. Finely chop the onion.

2 Melt a small knob of the butter in a large, ovenproof pan on the BOILING PLATE and quickly fry the escalopes in batches for about 1 minute on each side or until lightly golden. Melt a little more butter for each batch. You need about half the butter at this stage. Remove and set aside.

3 Melt about the remaining butter in the pan and stir in the onion. Fry for about 10minutes or until soft and golden. Add the crushed garlic with the rice and stir well. Add the stock.

4 Bring to the boil and cook, uncovered, in the SIMMERING OVEN for 10 minutes. Add the wine , stir well and bring to the boil on the BOILING PLATE.

■ ■ Cook on the grid shelf on the floor of the ROASTING OVEN for 10 minutes.

■ ■ ■ Cook on the grid shelf on the floor of the BAKING OVEN for 12 minutes..

5 Stir in the pesto, Parmesan cheese and parsley. Push the browned escalopes into the rice, cover, and return the pan to the ROASTING OVEN for a further 5 minutes or until the rice has completely absorbed the liquid and the escalopes are piping hot.

PORK CHOPS WITH MUSTARD SAUCE

PREPARATION TIME:
10 MINUTES

COOKING TIME:
30 MINUTES

540 CALS PER
SERVING

SERVES 6

FREEZING:
UNSUITABLE

A very easy supper dish. Use spare-rib chops as loin chops won't be tender enough for this recipe.

700 g (1½ lb) onions
700 g (1½ lb) trimmed leeks
6 spare-rib pork chops
25 g (1 oz) butter
1 garlic clove
900 ml (1½ pints) milk

1 bay leaf
a sprig of thyme
120 ml (8 level tbsp) double cream or crème fraîche
45 ml (3 level tbsp) made English mustard
salt and freshly ground black pepper

1 Halve the leeks lengthwise, then chop across in half. Chop the onions. Trim the fat on the pork chops.

2 Heat butter in a flameproof casserole on the BOILING PLATE. When foaming, fry the chops briskly until very light golden brown. Lay leeks on top, add crushed garlic, herbs and seasoning. Pour in milk and bring to the boil. Bake on the grid shelf on the floor of the ROASTING OVEN for 25-30 minutes. When pork and leeks are tender, remove to an ovenproof dish, sitting the pork on the leeks and keep warm in the SIMMERING OVEN.

3 Add cream and mustard to the juices in the pan, season well and simmer on the SIMMERING PLATE for 1-2 minutes until the sauce is syrupy, then pour over the chops.

ROAST LOIN OF PORK WITH PEACHES

PREPARATION TIME:
I HOUR + SOAKING

COOKING TIME:
I HOUR 50 MINUTES

730 CALS PER
SERVING (FOR 6);
540 CALS PER
SERVING (FOR 8)

SERVES 6-8

FREEZING:
UNSUITABLE

Crisp crackling, fruity stuffing and rosemary-scented potatoes make a memorable combination.

175 g (6 oz) ready-to-eat dried peaches or apricots
400 ml (14 fl oz) unsweetened apple juice
grated rind and juice of I small orange
165 ml (11 tbsp) extra-virgin olive oil
45 ml (3 level tbsp) chopped, flat-leafed fresh parsley
15 ml (1 level tbsp) chopped fresh chives

salt and freshly ground black pepper
1.1 kg (2½ lb) potatoes
1.8 kg (4 lb) loin pork, boned (see Cook's Tips)
6-8 sprigs fresh rosemary
15 ml (1 level tbsp) plain flour

1 Soak the dried peaches in half the apple juice overnight.

2 Drain peaches, reserving juice. Place peaches in a food processor and roughly chop. Add orange rind, 60 ml (4 tbsp) olive oil and herbs and mix together; season.

3 If the pork has crackling, remove it carefully with a sharp knife, lay it in a small roasting tin, rub lightly with 15 ml (1 tbsp) oil and sprinkle with salt. Set aside.

4 Place the pork, fat-side uppermost, on a chopping board, then split it almost in half by slicing horizontally through the eye of the meat towards the fatty side. Open it like a book, spread peach stuffing on the bottom half and re-shape. Tie with string; set aside.

5 Cut the potatoes into wedges; boil on the BOILING PLATE for 1-2 minutes; drain, reserving the water. Return potatoes to the SIMMERING PLATE briefly to dry them off. Toss in the remaining oil and rosemary leaves and season. Place in a large roasting tin; cook on the top runners of the ROASTING OVEN for 30 minutes. Lower the potatoes to the floor of the oven.

6 Place the pork on a rack over the potatoes and spoon the reserved apple juice over. Cook for a further 1¼-1½ hours, basting from time to time, until the pork is cooked to the centre. After the first 30 minutes, place the crackling in the small roasting tin, hang on the top runners above the pork and cook for 20-35 minutes or until crisp (see Aga Tip); tip all the fat out and place in the SIMMERING OVEN to dry well. When cooked, place the pork, crackling and potatoes on a serving plate and keep warm in the SIMMERING OVEN.

7 Add the flour to the juices in the roasting tin. On the SIMMERING PLATE, stir until smooth and cook for 1-2 minutes. Pour in the orange juice, remaining apple juice and reserved potato water, then bring to the boil and simmer for 3-4 minutes until lightly thickened.

8 Remove the string from the pork; strain the gravy; serve with the pork.

COOK'S TIPS

Ask your butcher to bone the pork loin.

Allow 20-25 minutes per 450 g (1 lb), depending on the joint's shape – a long, thin one takes less time than a short, fat one.

To prepare ahead, complete to the end of step 4 and then refrigerate overnight. To use, complete the recipe.

AGA TIP

Place the tin of crackling above the pork to prevent it over-browning. If you prefer to cook the crackling in advance, cover the joint with foil when well browned. Cut the crackling into small pieces when cooked.

ROASTED RACK OF LAMB WITH RED ONIONS AND SHERRY SAUCE

PREPARATION TIME:
10 MINUTES

COOKING TIME:
25-30 MINUTES

98 CALS PER
SERVING

SERVES 4

FREEZING:
UNSUITABLE

Serve this sauce with roasted rack of lamb (see Cook's Tip), roast potatoes and French beans. Thin strips of lamb's liver, seasoned, tossed in a little plain flour and quickly stir-fried in a small amount of oil make a good alternative.

225 g (8 oz) red onions
25 g (1 oz) butter
75 ml (3 fl oz) dry sherry
330 g can vegetable V8 juice or beef consomme

5 ml (1 level tsp) chopped fresh thyme
5 ml (1 tsp) balsamic vinegar
salt and freshly ground black pepper

1 Cut the onions into thin slices. Melt the butter in a saucepan. When foaming, add the onions and cook, stirring constantly, for about 10 minutes or until they are a deep, golden brown.
2 Add the dry sherry to the mixture, bring to the boil and bubble to reduce the liquid by half (this may be done in advance). Pour in the vegetable juice or beef consomme, bring back to the boil, add the chopped fresh thyme and simmer gently for 10 minutes. Add the balsamic vinegar and adjust the seasoning to taste. Serve immediately.

COOK'S TIP

Buy ready-prepared racks of lamb. Halve to give small joints with about three 'chops' on each one. Secure with fine string and roast in a roasting tin on the top runners of the ROASTING OVEN for 15-20 minutes.

AGA TIP

To achieve good results, it is important that the roasting oven is very hot so avoid losing heat from the Aga unnecessarily, i.e. partly prepare the sherry sauce in advance and do not cook other items in the roasting oven for 1 hour beforehand or at the same time.

SPICED BEEF WITH AUBERGINE AND ROAST TOMATO SALAD

PREPARATION TIME:
30 MINUTES +
MARINATING AND
DRAINING

COOKING TIME:
ABOUT 45 MINUTES

360 CALS PER
SERVING

SERVES 8

FREEZING:
UNSUITABLE

ILLUSTRATED OPPOSITE

Bursting with the classic Mediterranean flavours of aubergine, garlic, tomatoes and olive oil, this beef salad is sure to be a winner! This salad is wonderful for summer – serve it for lunch, supper or as part of a cold buffet. Marinating the beef before roasting makes it mouthwateringly tender.

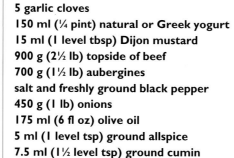

5 garlic cloves
150 ml (¼ pint) natural or Greek yogurt
15 ml (1 level tbsp) Dijon mustard
900 g (2½ lb) topside of beef
700 g (1½ lb) aubergines
salt and freshly ground black pepper
450 g (1 lb) onions
175 ml (6 fl oz) olive oil
5 ml (1 level tsp) ground allspice
7.5 ml (1½ level tsp) ground cumin

pinch of cayenne pepper
45 ml (3 level tbsp) tomato paste
25 g (1 oz) raisins (optional)
15 ml (1 level tbsp) chopped flat-leafed parsley
450 g (1 lb) red and yellow cherry tomatoes
30 ml (2 level tbsp) balsamic vinegar
fresh thyme sprigs, chives and lemon wedges, to garnish

1 Crush three garlic cloves, place them in a large bowl with the yogurt and mustard, then beat until smooth. Add the beef and coat in the marinade. Place the coated beef in a non-metallic bowl, then cover and marinate overnight in the refrigerator.

2 Halve the aubergines. Score the cut side with the point of a knife, sprinkle with salt to draw out any bitter juices and leave for about 20 minutes. Finely chop the onions. Squeeze the juices out of the aubergines, drizzle with 30 ml (2 tbsp) olive oil and place cut side down in a roasting tin. Bake on the floor of the ROASTING OVEN for 20 minutes.

3 Heat 30 ml (2 tbsp) oil in a large ovenproof pan; crush remaining garlic and add to the pan with the onions. Cook, stirring, on the BOILING PLATE for 4 minutes or until the onions begin to soften and colour. Add the spices and tomato paste and cook for another 1-2 minutes. Add 150 ml (¼ pint) water; bring to the boil and place in the SIMMERING OVEN for 10 minutes.

4 Dice the baked aubergine and add to the onion mixture with the raisins, if using, plus the chopped flat-leafed parsley. Adjust the seasoning as necessary and set aside.

5 Take the marinated beef out of the fridge and keep covered at room temperature for 30 minutes-1 hour before cooking (see Aga Tips). Place the marinated beef on a wire rack over a small roasting tin. Cook at the back of the ROASTING OVEN as high as possible (third or fourth runners) for 30 minutes for medium-rare or 45 minutes for medium. Set aside to cool.

6 Place the cherry tomatoes in a shallow roasting tin with the balsamic vinegar and the remaining olive oil and cook on the grid shelf on the floor of the ROASTING OVEN for 20 minutes. When the tomatoes are soft, set aside to cool.

7 To serve, thinly slice the cooled spiced beef and arrange on a bed of aubergine salad. Spoon the cooled roast tomato salad around the aubergine salad and beef. Garnish the roast tomato salad with tiny sprigs of fresh thyme. Grind some black pepper over the meat and salads and garnish with fresh chives and lemon wedges before serving at room temperature.

COOK'S TIP

To prepare ahead, complete the recipe to the end of step 5 up to two days ahead. When the spiced beef, the aubergine salad and the roast tomato salad are completely cool, cover and refrigerate them separately.

AGA TIPS

To ensure the Aga roasting oven remains really hot when roasting meat or cooking other large items, always allow food to reach almost room temperature immediately prior to cooking and avoid adding other cold food to the oven if you are trying to maintain a high temperature.

The oven will be at its hottest early in the day so cook the beef just after breakfast.

PHEASANT WITH SMOKED BACON AND MUSHROOMS

PREPARATION TIME:
35 MINUTES

COOKING TIME:
ABOUT 1 HOUR

420 CALS PER
SERVING

SERVES 4

FREEZING:
UNSUITABLE

This recipe 'roasts' pheasant with the addition of wine and stock to keep this naturally dry-textured bird as moist and succulent as possible. Richly flavoured dried mushrooms, garlic, juniper berries and smoked bacon add plenty of flavour to the juices.

15 g (½ oz) dried porcini or mixed dried mushrooms
1 small onion
125 g (4 oz) smoked bacon, in one piece
10 juniper berries
2 garlic cloves, crushed
2 oven-ready pheasants
25 g (1 oz) butter
10 ml (2 tsp) plain white flour
300 ml (½ pint) red wine
300 ml (½ pint) chicken or pheasant stock (see Cook's Tip)

175 g (6 oz) chestnut or brown mushrooms
30 ml (2 tbsp) redcurrant jelly

TO GARNISH
125 g (4 oz) puff pastry
15 ml (1 tbsp) finely chopped fresh rosemary
beaten egg yolk, to glaze
flat-leafed parsley

1 Rinse the dried mushrooms twice and place in a bowl with 300 ml (½ pint) warm water. Let soak for 20 minutes.

2 For the garnish, roll out the pastry to about a 5 mm (¼ in) thickness. Scatter with the rosemary, then roll out further to about a 3 mm (⅛ in) thickness. Cut out small triangular shapes and transfer to a dampened plain shelf. Brush with beaten egg yolk and bake on the third runners of the ROASTING OVEN for about 6 minutes until puffed and golden; turn the shelf round and return to the oven for a further 1-2 minutes for even colouring. Place in the SIMMERING OVEN until really crisp and dry, then set aside.

3 Meanwhile, peel and finely chop the onion. Dice the bacon. Lightly crush the juniper berries.

4 Spread the garlic over the pheasants. Melt the butter in a large flameproof casserole on the BOILING PLATE and sear the pheasants on all sides. Transfer to a plate.

5 Add the onion and bacon to the casserole and fry gently on the SIMMERING PLATE for 3-4 minutes. Stir in the flour, add the wine and stock and bring to the boil on the BOILING PLATE. Return the pheasants to the casserole, breast side down, and add the juniper. Cover and bake on the grid shelf on the floor of the ROASTING OVEN for 25 minutes.

6 Drain and rinse the dried mushrooms; halve the fresh mushrooms. Turn the pheasants breast side up and tuck the mushrooms into the sauce all around the casserole. Return to the oven and cook, uncovered, for a further 20-25 minutes. Test the pheasant by piercing the thickest part of the thigh with a skewer; the juices should run clear.

7 Transfer the pheasants and mushrooms to a serving plate, using a slotted spoon; keep warm in the SIMMERING OVEN. Add the redcurrant jelly to the cooking juices, crush with a slotted spoon and reduce on the BOILING PLATE for 1-2 minutes until syrupy. Pour a little over the pheasants and serve the rest in a sauceboat. Serve the pheasant and mushrooms garnished with the pastries and parsley, and accompanied by the sauce.

COOK'S TIP
If available, use pheasant giblets to make the stock. Simmer in sufficient water to cover with an onion, a carrot, herbs and seasoning for 1 hour; strain.

ROAST DUCK WITH ORANGE SAUCE

PREPARATION TIME:
50 MINUTES

COOKING TIME:
1 HOUR 40 MINUTES

565 CALS PER
SERVING

SERVES 4

FREEZING: FREEZE
SAUCE ONLY AFTER
STEP 4.

The quality of duck has much improved over recent years, and they are now specially bred to be meatier and less fatty.

2 large oranges
2.3 kg (5 lb) duck, preferably with giblets (see Aga Tip)
2 large sprigs fresh thyme
salt and freshly ground black pepper
60 ml (4 tbsp) oil
2 shallots
5 ml (1 level tsp) plain flour
600 ml (1 pint) home-made chicken stock
25 g (1 oz) caster sugar
30 ml (2 tbsp) red wine vinegar

100 ml (3½ fl oz) unsweetened fresh orange juice
100 ml (3½ fl oz) fruity German white wine
30 ml (2 tbsp) orange liqueur, e.g. Grand Marnier (optional)
15 ml (1 tbsp) lemon juice
mint, glazed orange quarters and deep-fried orange rind, to garnish (see Cook's Tips)

1 Using a zester, remove rind from oranges. Place rind from one orange in a pan of cold water; bring to the boil, drain and set aside. Reserve remainder. Remove pith from oranges; cut flesh into segments.

2 Remove giblets; reserve. Place thyme and reserved rind inside the duck; season. Rub the skin with 30 ml (2 tbsp) oil, sprinkle with salt and place breast-side up on a grid over a roasting tin. Roast on the third runners in the ROASTING OVEN for 1¼-1½ hours until just cooked (see Cook's Tips). Baste every 30 minutes, turning over after first 30 minutes. Turn breast-side up for last 10 minutes.

3 Meanwhile, cut the gizzard, heart and neck into pieces. Roughly chop shallots. Heat remaining 30 ml (2 tbsp) oil in a heavy-based pan, add the giblets and fry on the BOILING PLATE until dark brown. Add chopped shallots and flour; cook for 1 minute. Pour in stock, bring to the boil and bubble until reduced by half; strain.

4 Place sugar and vinegar in a heavy-based pan; place in the SIMMERING OVEN to dissolve the sugar, then cook on the SIMMERING PLATE until it forms a dark caramel. Pour in the orange juice; stir. Cool, cover and set aside.

5 Lift the duck off the grid; keep warm in the SIMMERING OVEN. Skim all the fat off the juices to leave about 45 ml (3 tbsp) sediment. Stir the wine into the sediment, bring to the boil on the BOILING PLATE and bubble for 5 minutes until syrupy. Add stock mixture and orange mixture. Return to boil; bubble until syrupy, skimming if necessary. To serve the sauce, add blanched orange rind and segments. Add Grand Marnier, if using, and lemon juice to taste.

6 Carve duck and garnish with oranges and rind. Serve with the sauce.

COOK'S TIPS
To check the duck is cooked, pierce the thigh deeply with a skewer; the juices should run clear.
To glaze the oranges, quarter them, dust with a little caster sugar and then fry in 5 ml (1 tsp) oil until caramelized.
To prepare one day ahead, complete steps 1, 3 and 4. Cover ingredients separately and chill. To use, complete the recipe.

AGA TIP
Instead of a whole duck, you could use four breast fillets, part-boned breasts or legs. Score through the skin and fat of the breasts, then oil and salt the skin. Grate rind of one orange and use to season flesh sides of the duck portions. In a heavy-based, preheated frying pan, brown the skin of the duck until golden. Transfer to a roasting tin; cook on the third runners of the ROASTING OVEN for 15 minutes, plus 15 minutes in the SIMMERING OVEN for fillets; 40 minutes for part-boned breasts and legs, plus 10 minutes in the SIMMERING OVEN. Complete sauce as in step 5.

ROASTED POUSSINS WITH PANCETTA, ARTICHOKE AND NEW POTATO SALAD

PREPARATION TIME:
20 MINUTES +
MARINATING

COOKING TIME:
I HOUR
10 MINUTES

540 CALS PER
SERVING

SERVES 6

FREEZING:
UNSUITABLE

ILLUSTRATED OPPOSITE

Roasting poussins (baby chickens) in the fruity marinade gives a deliciously light main course dish.

I lemon
5 large, fresh rosemary sprigs
60 ml (4 tbsp) white wine vinegar
150 ml (¼ pint) fruity white wine
4 garlic cloves
45 ml (3 level tbsp) chopped fresh oregano or pinch dried
290 g jar antipasto artichokes
three poussins, each weighing about 450 g (1 lb)

salt and freshly ground black pepper
2.5 ml (½ level tsp) cayenne pepper
450-600 g (1-1¼ lb) new potatoes
225 g (8 oz) pancetta or prosciutto or streaky bacon
350 g (12 oz) peppery salad leaves, such as watercress, mustard leaf and rocket, washed and dried

1 Grate the rind from the lemon and remove the leaves from the sprigs of rosemary. Place in a large bowl with the white wine vinegar, white wine, crushed garlic cloves, oregano and 60 ml (4 tbsp) oil from the antipasto artichokes. Stir well.

2 Using a fork, pierce the skin of the poussins in five or six places, then season well with ground black pepper and the cayenne pepper. Place birds, breast-side down, in the bowl and spoon the marinade over. Cover; refrigerate overnight.

3 Halve or quarter the potatoes and boil in salted water on the BOILING PLATE for 2 minutes. Drain, then toss in the remaining artichoke oil. Roughly chop the pancetta.

4 Lift the poussins from the marinade and place, breast-side up, in a large roasting tin. Scatter the potatoes, pancetta and artichokes around them and pour the marinade over.

5 Cook on the bottom runners of the ROASTING OVEN for 50 minutes, then turn the tin round to ensure even cooking, baste the birds and roast for a further 10-15 minutes or until golden and cooked through.

6 Remove the poussins and cut each in half lengthways; keep warm in the SIMMERING OVEN. Toss salad leaves with about 75 ml (5 tbsp) warm cooking juices. Arrange leaves on warm plates, then top with the potatoes, pancetta, artichokes and poussin halves. Serve immediately.

SHERRY GRAVY

PREPARATION TIME:
5 MINUTES

COOKING TIME:
15 MINUTES

300 CALS PER
SERVING

SERVES 6-8

FREEZING: SUITABLE

This gravy is particularly delicious with the lamb recipe on page 59.

45 ml (3 level tbsp) plain flour
200 ml (7 fl oz) dry sherry

1.1 litres (2 pints) home-made stock (see Aga Tip)
salt and freshly ground black pepper

1 Tilt the roasting tin and skim most of the fat off the top of the sediment, leaving 30 ml (2 tbsp).

2 Stir in the flour to make a paste. Place the tin on the SIMMERING PLATE and cook, stirring, for 2-3 minutes until golden brown.

3 Add sherry, bring to the boil and bubble for I minute. Add stock, bring back to the boil and bubble on the BOILING PLATE or on the floor of the ROASTING OVEN for 5-10 minutes or until reduced by half. Skim off any fat, season and strain into a gravy boat.

AGA TIP
To make stock, simmer giblets (or 4-5 chicken wings) in a pan with 2.3 litres (4 pints) water, seasoning and a few vegetables, such as onion, celery and leek, on the floor of the SIMMERING OVEN for 6 hours or overnight until reduced by half. Strain, cool and refrigerate.

ROAST CHICKEN WITH A DEVILLED SAUCE

PREPARATION TIME:
20 MINUTES

COOKING TIME:
ABOUT 1¾ HOURS

270 CALS PER
SERVING

SERVES 6

FREEZING:
UNSUITABLE

When roasts were the mainstay of traditional cooking, 'devilling' with a hot sauce was a popular way of reviving interest in leftovers. Here, the idea is put to better use: a hot, tangy base is used for glazing a large chicken during roasting; it also forms the basis of a delicious sauce. Accompany this dish with a crisp salad and new potatoes.

2.3 kg (5 lb) large chicken
30 ml (2 level tbsp) mango or sweet chutney
25 g (1 oz) butter
30 ml (2 tbsp) Worcestershire sauce
30 ml (2 level tbsp) grainy English mustard
5 ml (1 level tsp) paprika
45 ml (3 tbsp) freshly squeezed orange juice

salt and freshly ground black pepper
3 garlic cloves
1 large onion
450 g (1 lb) tomatoes
90 ml (3 fl oz) crème fraîche
leafy herbs, e.g. basil, lovage or lemon balm, to garnish

1 Remove the chicken from the fridge 1 hour before cooking. To make the devilled sauce, chop any large pieces in the chutney. Melt the butter in a small bowl in the SIMMERING OVEN, then add the chutney, Worcestershire sauce, mustard, paprika, orange juice and seasoning and mix together.

2 Peel and chop the garlic and onion; place in the cavity of the chicken, then place the chicken in a small roasting tin. Baste the skin all over with the devilled sauce. Roast the chicken on the grid shelf on the floor of the ROASTING OVEN, with the legs pointing towards the back of the oven for 1¾ hours or until the juices run clear when the thickest part of the thigh is pierced with a skewer. Baste the chicken every 20-30 minutes and when the skin is a deep brown set the cold plain shelf above the top runners. When the chicken is cooked through the skin should be slightly charred; if you think it is becoming slightly too brown during roasting, cover it with foil towards the end of the cooking time.

3 In the meantime, place the tomatoes in a bowl and cover with boiling water. Leave for 1 minute, then drain and peel away the skins. Scoop out the seeds, then roughly chop the tomatoes; set aside.

4 Transfer the chicken to a warmed serving platter; keep warm in the SIMMERING OVEN. Skim off the fat from the juices in the roasting tin, then stir in the tomatoes and any remaining devilled sauce. Transfer sauce to a food processor or blender and process briefly until the mixture is pulpy but still retains a little texture; return to the pan. Heat through on the SIMMERING PLATE and season to taste.

5 Meanwhile, warm the crème fraîche in a small serving bowl in the SIMMERING OVEN for about 10 minutes.

6 Garnish the chicken with plenty of herbs and serve with the devilled sauce and warmed crème fraîche.

COOK'S TIP
For a more fiery sauce, add a finely chopped chilli to the devilled mixture before basting.

BUTTER-BAKED SALMON WITH TOMATO AND CARDAMOM SAUCE

PREPARATION TIME: 40 MINUTES

COOKING TIME: 3 HOURS + STANDING

745 CALS PER SERVING

SERVES 8

FREEZING: UNSUITABLE

Take care not to overcook salmon as it will be dry instead of rich and creamy in texture. Press very firmly with your fingertips in the thickest part to check if the fish will 'flake' under pressure.

FOR THE TOMATO AND CARDAMOM SAUCE
1.8 kg (4 lb) ripe tomatoes12 garlic cloves
coarse sea salt and freshly ground black pepper
120 ml (8 tbsp) olive oil
350 g (12 oz) onions
10 ml (2 level tsp) ground turmeric
3 whole cloves
5 cardamom pods

FOR THE SALMON
2.7 kg (6 lb) salmon
50 g (2 oz) butter
1 lemon
5 cm (2 in) piece fresh root ginger
bunch parsley
about 6 bay leaves
coarse sea salt and coarsely ground black pepper
green salad leaves and herbs, to garnish

1 To make the sauce, halve the tomatoes and place cut side up in a large roasting tin. Thinly slice the garlic; scatter over the tomatoes, season well. Drizzle 60 ml (4 tbsp) oil over.

◼◼ Cook on the bottom runners of the ROASTING OVEN for 40 minutes, then transfer to the SIMMERING OVEN for a further 2 hours until shrivelled to half their size. Set aside to cool.

◼◼◼◼ Cook on the bottom runners of the BAKING OVEN for 2 hours, then transfer to the SIMMERING PLATE for 30 minutes or until shrivelled to half their size. Set aside to cool.

2 If serving the salmon whole and leaving the head and tail on, cut the latter into a 'V' shape; if serving in portions, remove head and tail. Remove fins from stomach and back with scissors then, holding the tail (fine salt on your fingers will give a better grip), scrape off the scales with a knife, working from tail to head. Rinse salmon thoroughly.

3 Use half the butter to grease a large piece of foil. Cut lemon into wedges; peel and thickly slice ginger. Place salmon on the foil; stuff its belly with parsley, bay leaves, ginger and all but one lemon wedge. Squeeze juice from remaining lemon wedge over salmon. Melt remaining butter; brush over salmon. Season, wrap salmon in foil, leaving space within the parcel but sealing edges.

◼◼ Bake on the grid shelf on the floor of the ROASTING OVEN with a cold roasting tin on the top runners for 40 minutes. If not quite cooked through, transfer to the SIMMERING OVEN for 10-20 minutes or until the flesh 'breaks' under the pressure of a finger.

◼◼◼◼ Cook on bottom runners of BAKING OVEN for 1 hour. If not cooked through, move to SIMMERING OVEN for 10-20 minutes or until the flesh 'breaks' under finger pressure.

4 Remove the cooked salmon from oven; leave in foil for 20 minutes. Meanwhile, finish the sauce. Finely chop the onions and cook in a covered pan in the remaining olive oil on the SIMMERING PLATE for 7-10 minutes or until very soft but barely coloured. Stir in the turmeric, cloves, and split cardamom pods. Using a sharp knife, scrape the tomato flesh from the skins and add to the sauce with any juices that have collected in the baking sheet.

5 Heat the sauce gently on the SIMMERING PLATE for 3-4 minutes until it is the consistency of a thin chutney. Adjust seasoning, cover and set aside. Serve the sauce either warm or cold.

6 To help remove the salmon skin, open and fold back the foil from the fish, then place in the middle of the ROASTING OVEN for 3-4 minutes or until skin turns crisp. Serve the salmon warm or cold, garnished with salad leaves and fresh herbs. Accompany with the sauce.

COOK'S TIPS
A 2.7 kg (6 lb) salmon will just fit diagonally on a baking tray. If your salmon is rounded, rather than long and thin, allow an extra 15 minutes cooking. If serving cold, leave to cool completely in the foil at step 4. To prepare ahead, complete the sauce up to two days ahead. Cool, cover and keep in the fridge. Reheat gently in the SIMMERING OVEN. The salmon can be prepared up to step 3 but should not be cooked until required. Store the wrapped fish in the fridge for up to one day before cooking.

SWEET ROASTED FENNEL

PREPARATION TIME:
10 MINUTES

COOKING TIME:
1 HOUR

190 CALS PER
SERVING FOR 4;
120 CALS PER
SERVING FOR 6

SERVES 4-6

FREEZING:
UNSUITABLE

For many this is an unfamiliar vegetable. Like celery, it is delicious raw or cooked. It can be scattered with fennel or dill seeds or splashed with vermouth to enhance its aniseed flavour.

700 g (1½ lb) fennel, about 3 bulbs
45 ml (3 tbsp) olive oil
50 g (2 oz) butter, melted
1 lemon

5 ml (1 level tsp) caster sugar
salt and freshly ground black pepper
2 large sprigs of thyme

1 Trim and quarter the fennel; place in a large roasting tin.
2 Drizzle the oil and melted butter over. Halve the lemon; squeeze the juice over. Add the lemon halves to the tin. Sprinkle with sugar and season generously. Add thyme; cover with a damp piece of non-stick baking parchment.
3 Cook on the bottom runners of the ROASTING OVEN for 30 minutes. Remove baking parchment; cook on the top runners at the back of the ROASTING OVEN for 20-30 minutes or until lightly charred and tender.

SWEET ROASTED FENNEL

SPROUTS IN HAZELNUT BUTTER

PREPARATION TIME:
30 MINUTES

COOKING TIME:
15 MINUTES

120 CALS PER
SERVING

SERVES 8-10

FREEZING:
UNSUITABLE

Chestnuts are the traditional accompaniment for Brussels sprouts, but they are quite fiddly to prepare. As an easier alternative in this recipe, use toasted hazelnuts and seasoned butter.

75 g (3 oz) hazelnuts (see Cook's Tips)
75 g (3 oz) unsalted butter, softened
salt and freshly ground black pepper
a little freshly grated nutmeg

1 garlic clove
finely grated rind of 1 lemon
1.4 kg (3 lb) Brussels sprouts

1 Toast the hazelnuts in a small roasting tin on the bottom runners at the front of the ROASTING OVEN for about 3 minutes or until golden (see Aga Tip), then roughly chop. Beat into the softened butter with salt and ground black pepper, freshly grated nutmeg, the crushed garlic and the grated lemon rind. Set aside.

2 Cook the trimmed Brussels sprouts in boiling, salted water on the BOILING PLATE for about 7-10 minutes or until tender but still retaining some of their bite. Drain well and toss in the hazelnut butter. Serve as soon as possible.

COOK'S TIPS
If you'd prefer to use fresh chestnuts, buy about 175 g (6 oz), which allows for about 50 g (2 oz) wastage. Nick the brown outer skins with a sharp knife, then cook in boiling water for 10 minutes. Drain, cool and peel off the shells and inner skins. Cover with vegetable stock and simmer in the SIMMERING OVEN for 15 minutes or until tender. Drain well. Toast, chop and use as for hazelnuts in the recipe above. Alternatively, look out for vacuum-packed chestnuts in supermarkets.
The nut butter can be prepared in advance and chilled or frozen for later use.

AGA TIP
When toasting nuts in the roasting oven, remember that they brown very quickly. Leave the door slightly open so you can smell them and set a timer as a reminder.

ROASTED ROOT VEGETABLES

PREPARATION TIME:
30 MINUTES

COOKING TIME:
1 HOUR
10 MINUTES

250 CALS PER
SERVING

SERVES 8-10

FREEZING:
UNSUITABLE

Although this recipe only uses parsnips and potatoes, many others can be used as well – carrots, swede, turnip, artichoke, garlic and onions can make mouthwatering combinations.

1.8 kg (4 lb) parsnips and old potatoes
150 ml (¼ pint) oil

coarse sea salt
125 g (4 oz) finely grated Parmesan

1 Peel the parsnips and cut them into large, even-sized chunks. Peel the potatoes if wished, and cut them into wedges. Par-boil the parsnips and potatoes in boiling, salted water on the BOILING PLATE for about 5 minutes.

2 Drain thoroughly, then roughen the potato edges using a fork, or toss them in the pan or a colander.

3 Heat the oil in a large roasting tin on the floor of the ROASTING OVEN. Spoon in the potatoes, baste with the oil and sprinkle with coarse sea salt. Roast on the top runners of the ROASTING OVEN for 15 minutes, then add parsnips, toss well and continue roasting 20 minutes. Then turn the tin round and place on the floor of the ROASTING OVEN for a further 20-25 minutes to ensure even cooking, basting occasionally.

4 Serve sprinkled with coarse salt and finely grated Parmesan cheese.

BRAISED RED CABBAGE

PREPARATION TIME:
25 MINUTES

COOKING TIME:
ABOUT 3-5 HOURS
OR OVERNIGHT

210 CALS PER
SERVING

SERVES 6

FREEZING:
SUITABLE

The longer and slower the cabbage is braised, the better it is. Placing the casserole on the grid shelf ensures it does not dry out if cooked overnight.

1.4 kg (3 lb) red cabbage
450 g (1 lb) red onions
5 cm (2 in) piece fresh root ginger
salt and freshly ground black pepper

50 g (2 oz) butter
105 ml (7 level tbsp) light soft brown (muscovado) sugar
105 ml (7 tbsp) red wine vinegar

1 Finely shred the cabbage; discard the outer leaves and stalk.

2 Layer the cabbage and onions in a casserole, seasoning as you go. Melt butter in a small pan; fry the ginger for 2-3 minutes. Off the heat, stir in the sugar and vinegar, and pour over the cabbage.

3 ■ ■ Cook at the back of the SIMMERING OVEN for 5-8 hours or, if wished, overnight. (NB Some electric Agas are too hot for slow overnight cooking and some converted Agas may be too cool.) Alternatively, cook for 2-4 hours in the SIMMERING OVEN and then for 45 minutes-1 hour on the grid shelf on the floor of the ROASTING OVEN.

■ ■ ■ ■ Cook as for the 2-oven Aga or on the grid shelf on the floor of the BAKING OVEN for 1-2 hours, then in the SIMMERING OVEN for 2-4 hours.

CRISPY-CRUMBED POTATOES

PREPARATION TIME:
20 MINUTES

COOKING TIME:
ABOUT 1 HOUR
25 MINUTES

195 CALS PER
SERVING

SERVES 5-6

FREEZING:
UNSUITABLE

These potatoes look and taste wonderfully crunchy.

1 kg (2 lb 2 oz) medium sized old potatoes
25 g (1 oz) dried white breadcrumbs
1.25 ml (¼ level tsp) ground paprika

pinch salt
about 75 ml (2½ fl oz) oil

1 Peel the potatoes and cut into quarters lengthwise into long, large chunks. Cover with water and bring to the boil; cook for 2-3 minutes. Drain, then return to pan. Cover and shake to roughen up the surfaces.

2 Stir breadcrumbs, paprika, salt and 30 ml (2 tbsp) of the oil into the potatoes until well mixed – the crumbs won't stick very well to the potatoes at this stage.

3 Heat the remaining oil in a small roasting tin just large enough to hold the potatoes. Add the potatoes, sprinkling over stray crumbs.

4 Roast on the floor of the ROASTING OVEN for 30 minutes, then place on the second or third runners for a further 30-50 minutes, shaking the potatoes in the tin as you move them. Keep warm, uncovered.

AGA TIP
For double the quantity, use a large roasting tin and turn the tin round in the oven two-thirds of the way through the cooking time to give the potatoes an even colour.

GLAZED SHALLOTS AND CRANBERRIES

PREPARATION TIME:
40 MINUTES

COOKING TIME:
30 MINUTES

95 CALS PER
SERVING

SERVES 10

FREEZING:
UNSUITABLE

A wonderful combination to serve with hot or cold turkey. Cranberries freeze beautifully so buy plenty when in season and store in the freezer.

900 g (2 lb) shallots
50 g (2 oz) butter
30 ml (2 tbsp) runny honey
30 ml (2 tbsp) Worcestershire sauce

30 ml (2 tbsp) balsamic vinegar
salt and freshly ground black pepper
175 g (6 oz) fresh or frozen cranberries

1 Peel the shallots (see Cook's Tips) and place in an ovenproof pan with enough cold water to cover. Bring to the boil, then cook in the SIMMERING OVEN for 5 minutes. Drain well.
2 Add the butter to the pan with all the remaining ingredients, except the cranberries.
3 Stir until shallots are coated with glaze. Cover and cook in the SIMMERING OVEN for 20 minutes or until tender. Remove the lid, add the cranberries and cook for a further 5 minutes on the SIMMERING PLATE.

COOK'S TIPS
For easy peeling, soak shallots in hot water for 20 minutes.
If only dried cranberries are available, pour on the hot water when draining the shallots and allow them to plump up for a few minutes. Drain then add to the pan with the shallots before cooking in the SIMMERING OVEN.

BREAD SAUCE

PREPARATION TIME:
10 MINUTES

COOKING TIME:
50 MINUTES

215 CALS PER
SERVING

SERVES 8-10

FREEZING:
UNSUITABLE

If you like bread sauce to serve with cold turkey, then make a larger quantity. Add extra milk or cream so that it is not too thick when cold.

1 onion
6 cloves
900 ml (1½ pints) milk
2 bay leaves
10 peppercorns
2 thyme sprigs

150 g (5 oz) fresh breadcrumbs (see Cook's Tips)
25 g (1 oz) butter
salt and freshly ground black pepper
nutmeg
90 ml (6 tbsp) double cream

1 Halve onion and stud with cloves. Pour milk into an ovenproof pan; add onion, bay leaves, peppercorns and thyme. Cover and place in the SIMMERING OVEN for 45 minutes
2 Strain milk into a clean pan or lift out the herbs and onion with a slotted spoon; bring to boil and add breadcrumbs. Return to boil, stirring; then cook on the SIMMERING PLATE for 2-5 minutes until thickened. Stir in butter, seasoning and grated nutmeg. Spoon into a serving dish, lightly stir in cream and sprinkle with pepper. Cover and keep warm in the SIMMERING OVEN for up to 30 minutes.

COOK'S TIPS
Use good-quality, unsliced bread. Leave breadcrumbs out at kitchen temperature for 3-4 hours to become stale.
For an extra creamy texture use 3 shallots instead of the onion. After step 1, remove the cloves from the shallots, discard the herbs and purée the shallots with the milk.
To prepare ahead, complete to end of step 1; chill for one to two days. To use, complete as in step 2.

NEW POTATOES WITH PEAS, PARSLEY AND BROAD BEANS

NEW POTATOES WITH PEAS, PARSLEY AND BROAD BEANS

PREPARATION TIME:
5 MINUTES

COOKING TIME:
30 MINUTES

275 CALS PER
SERVING

SERVES 4

FREEZING:
UNSUITABLE

A wonderful combination to serve with new season lamb when peas and beans are first in the shops. If using frozen beans, thaw, remove white skins and add to the peas for the last 5 minutes of cooking.

700 g (1½ lb) small new potatoes
salt and freshly ground black pepper
200 g (7 oz) each fresh shelled peas and broad beans

40 g (1½ oz) butter
pinch of sugar
45 ml (3 level tbsp) chopped flat-leaf parsley

1 Bring the new potatoes to the boil in an ovenproof pan with 2.5 cm (1 in) salted water, then transfer to the SIMMERING OVEN for 15-20 minutes or until tender. Drain and set aside.

2 In the meantime, place the peas and broad beans in a large pan with the butter, a pinch of sugar and 75 ml (3 fl oz) water. Bring to the boil, cover tightly and cook on the SIMMERING PLATE for 10 minutes. Remove the lid from the pan, stir in the potatoes and transfer to the BOILING PLATE until all the liquid has evaporated. Season well and stir in the parsley. Serve.

RICE AND APRICOT STUFFING

PREPARATION TIME:
15 MINUTES

COOKING TIME:
45 MINUTES

150 CALS PER
SERVING

MAKES ENOUGH
FOR A 4.5 KG
(10 LB) TURKEY

This light, fruity stuffing complements turkey beautifully.

175 g (6 oz) mixed long-grain and wild rice, or basmati rice
salt and freshly ground black pepper
150 g (5 oz) ready-to-eat dried apricots
50 g (2 oz) shelled, skinned pistachio nuts
200 g (7 oz) shallots or onions

45 ml (3 tbsp) oil
60 ml (4 level tbsp) chopped flat-leafed parsley
15 ml (1 level tbsp) chopped fresh thyme
1 large egg

1 Bring the rice to the boil in an ovenproof pan of salted water on the BOILING PLATE, then transfer to the SIMMERING OVEN for 15-20 minutes (12 minutes for basmati) or until just cooked. Drain; cool quickly. Cut apricots into strips. Chop the nuts and shallots.

2 Heat oil; add shallots or onion. Cook in the SIMMERING OVEN with the apricots for 5-7 minutes until soft. Leave to cool, then add the rice, pistachios, herbs and egg. Mix, season well and chill until required.

3 Place in a shallow, ovenproof 1-litre (¾-pint) dish and cover with foil. Bake in the SIMMERING OVEN for 15 minutes, then transfer to the ROASTING OVEN for 30 minutes when the turkey is placed in the simmering oven to rest while you make the gravy, etc.

COOK'S TIP

Do not stuff the centre cavity of the turkey with stuffing, particularly rice stuffing, when slow roasting as there is an increased risk of food poisoning.

CHESTNUT AND MUSHROOM STUFFING

PREPARATION TIME: 20 MINUTES

COOKING TIME: 40-50 MINUTES

190 CALS PER SERVING

SERVES 10

MAKES ENOUGH FOR A 4.5 KG (10 LB) TURKEY

FREEZING: PACK AND FREEZE AT THE END OF STEP 3 (ONLY FOR SAUSAGES THAT HAVE NOT BEEN PREVIOUSLY FROZEN). THAW AT COOL ROOM TEMPERATURE OVERNIGHT, THEN COOK AS IN STEP 5.

This also makes an excellent supper dish. If cooking for vegetarians, replace the Cumberland sausage with vegetarian sausagement made up according to the manufacturer's instructions.

200 g (7 oz) onions
100 g (3½ oz) celery
200 g (7 oz) brown-cap mushrooms
225 g (8 oz) Cumberland sausage
40 g (1½ oz) butter
100 g (3½ oz) fresh brown breadcrumbs
60 ml (4 level tbsp) chopped fresh parsley
20 ml (4 level tbsp) chopped thyme
1 egg
30 ml (2 tbsp) orange juice or brandy
225 g (8 oz) cooked, peeled, vacuum-packed chestnuts (see Cook's Tip)
salt and freshly ground black pepper

1 Prepare turkey for stuffing. Alternatively, you can cook stuffing separately in a small greased ovenproof dish, covered with foil.

2 Roughly chop the onions, celery and mushrooms. Skin the sausage. Heat the butter in a pan, add the onions and cook on the SIMMERING PLATE until golden and soft. Add the celery and mushrooms and cook briskly on the BOILING PLATE for 5 minutes. Allow to cool.

3 Mix sausagemeat with the breadcrumbs. Add the herbs, egg, orange juice or brandy, and the chestnuts. Season well.

4 Use to stuff the neck end of the turkey, pulling the flap of skin over and securing under the bird with skewers or cocktail sticks. If you are cooking stuffing separately, place the mixture into the prepared dish, cover with foil.

5 ▪▪ If cooking separately, place dish on the grid shelf on the floor of the ROASTING OVEN for 40 minutes or until cooked and firm to the touch.

▪▪▪▪ Place the dish on the grid shelf on the bottom runners of the BAKING OVEN for 40-50 minutes.

COOK'S TIP

Cooked, peeled chestnuts that have been vacuum-packed are now available from most good supermarkets. They save an enormous amount of time.

AGA TIP

The cooking time may vary if the oven is cooled by cooking the turkey at the same time, so allow 10-15 minutes extra cooking time if necessary. Keep the stuffing warm in the SIMMERING OVEN.

BEEF WITH CHILLI BEARNAISE SAUCE

PREPARATION TIME:
15 MINUTES

COOKING TIME:
20 MINUTES

740 CALS PER
SERVING

SERVES 4

FREEZING:
UNSUITABLE

For a faster version of this recipe, rather than making the sauce, buy some ready-made hollandaise and flavour it with a little chilli sauce, mustard and ground cumin.

125 g (4 oz) onion or shallots
1 red chilli
150 ml (¼ pint) white wine
15 ml (1 tbsp) white wine vinegar
2.5 ml (½ level tsp) ground cumin or cumin seeds
225 g (8 oz) unsalted butter

4 egg yolks (see Cook's Tips)
5 ml (1 level tsp) Dijon mustard
salt and freshly ground black pepper
4 fillet steaks, each about 175 g (6 oz)
broccoli and sauté potatoes, to serve

1 Finely chop the onions. De-seed and finely chop the chilli.

2 Put wine, vinegar, cumin, onions and half the chilli in a saucepan. Bring to the boil and bubble to reduce liquid to 30 ml (2 tbsp). Strain and reserve liquid.

3 Melt the butter in a saucepan. Process the egg yolks and mustard in a food processor for 2 minutes. When melted butter is very hot (see Cook's Tips), slowly pour it on to the eggs, running processor at full speed. Blend for 2-3 minutes or until sauce has thickened. Add reserved chilli and reduced wine. Adjust seasoning. Transfer to a heatproof bowl, cover with clingfilm and keep warm on the back or side of the Aga top. (Do not place in the simmering oven as the eggs could overheat and curdle.)

4 Season steaks with pepper and pan-fry on the BOILING PLATE for 4-6 minutes on each side, depending on thickness, for medium rare. If using a griddle plan, pre-heat for 10 minutes on the floor of the ROASTING OVEN before placing on the BOILING PLATE. Serve with the sauce, broccoli and sauté potatoes.

COOK'S TIPS

It is vital that the butter is very hot indeed and almost starting to brown when poured on to the eggs as it is this heat that cooks and thickens the sauce.

The Béarnaise sauce can be made a few hours ahead and chilled. Serve cold to melt over the hot steaks.

The young, the elderly, pregnant women and those with immune-deficiency diseases should not eat raw or lightly cooked eggs, to avoid the possible risk of salmonella.

BEEF CASSEROLE WITH BLACK OLIVES

PREPARATION TIME:
40 MINUTES

COOKING TIME:
1½-4 HOURS

835 CALS PER
SERVING

SERVES 6

FREEZING:
COMPLETE TO END
OF STEP 2, THEN
COOL QUICKLY,
WRAP AND FREEZE.
TO USE, DEFROST
OVERNIGHT AT
COOL ROOM
TEMPERATURE,
PLACE IN THE
SIMMERING OVEN
FOR 30 MINUTES,
THEN BRING
SLOWLY TO THE
BOIL ON THE GRID
SHELF ON THE
FLOOR OF THE
ROASTING OVEN
FOR 20-25 MINUTES.
COMPLETE THE
RECIPE.

This is a hearty casserole that improves if eaten the day after it is cooked, making it ideal for weekend entertaining. As an alternative to streaky bacon rashers – and to save time – look out for pre-cut bacon lardons, now sold in most major supermarkets.

450 g (1 lb) onions
225 g (8 oz) flat mushrooms
350 g (12 oz) streaky bacon rashers, preferably unsmoked
1.1 kg (2½ lb) stewing steak, preferably in one piece
90 ml (6 tbsp) oil
3 large garlic cloves
30 ml (2 level tbsp) tomato paste
100 ml (4 fl oz) brandy
15 ml (1 level tbsp) plain flour
150 ml (¼ pint) red wine
300 ml (½ pint) beef stock
bouquet garni
125 g (4 oz) black olives
sprigs of flat-leafed parsley, to garnish

FOR THE PARSLEY CROUTES
1 small ciabatta loaf
olive oil to drizzle, plus 75 ml (5 tbsp)
small handful flat-leafed parsley, about 40 g (1½ oz)
90 ml (6 level tbsp) fresh white breadcrumbs
5 ml (1 level tsp) capers
1 gherkin
30 ml (2 tbsp) lemon juice
15 ml (1 level tbsp) chopped fresh chives
salt and freshly ground black pepper

1 Roughly chop the onions. Quarter the flat mushrooms if they are large, then cover. Cut the rind from the streaky bacon and slice it into thin strips (lardons). Cut the stewing steak into 4 cm (1½ in) cubes.

2 Heat half the oil in a large, flameproof casserole. On the BOILING PLATE brown the stewing steak in batches until it is a dark chestnut brown; remove and keep warm in the SIMMERING OVEN. Add the bacon lardons to the casserole and fry until they are golden brown, then add them to the beef. Add the remaining oil and cook the chopped onions until they are golden brown. Add the crushed garlic, fry for 30 seconds, then mix in the tomato paste. Cook, stirring, for 1-2 minutes, then pour in the brandy. Bring to the boil and bubble to reduce by half.

3 Remove the pan from the heat, then add the plain flour and mix until smooth. Pour in the red wine, return to the boil and bubble for 1 minute. Return the stewing steak and bacon to the casserole, then add enough stock to barely cover the meat. Add the bouquet garni. Bring to the boil, then cover.

■ ■ Either cook on the grid shelf on the floor of the ROASTING OVEN for 30 minutes, then transfer to the SIMMERING OVEN for 1½-2 hours or cook on the floor of the SIMMERING OVEN for 4 hours or until the meat is tender. Add the mushrooms during the last 20-30 minutes.

■ ■ ■ ■ Cook on the grid shelf on the floor of the BAKING OVEN for 1¼-1½ hours or until the meat is tender. Add the mushrooms during the last 20-30 minutes.

4 To make the parsley croutes, cut the ciabatta loaf into 5 mm (¼ in) thick slices, drizzle evenly with olive oil and bake in a roasting tin on the floor of the ROASTING OVEN for 5-7 minutes until golden brown. Place all remaining ingredients, apart from the seasoning, in a food processor or blender and process until thoroughly combined; season to taste. Spoon the mixture on top of the toasted ciabatta.

5 Just before serving, remove the bouquet garni and stir in the black olives. Serve immediately, garnished with flat-leafed parsley and accompanied by the parsley croutes.

COOK'S TIPS
To prepare ahead, complete recipe to the end of step 2, cool quickly, cover and refrigerate for up to two days. Prepare the parsley topping for the croutes up to one day ahead, cover and refrigerate.
To use, bring the casserole slowly to the boil and cook on the grid shelf on the floor of the ROASTING OVEN for 15-20 minutes or until heated through. Complete the recipe.

SPICED AFRICAN LAMB

PREPARATION TIME:
30 MINUTES +
MARINATING

COOKING TIME:
1¾-2¼ HOURS

750 CALS PER
SERVING

SERVES 6

FREEZING:
UNSUITABLE

The flavour of this dish will be even better if it is cooked the day before you plan to serve it.

6 garlic cloves
45 ml (3 level tbsp) chopped fresh coriander
10 ml (2 level tsp) each ground cumin, paprika and coarse sea salt
2.5 ml (½ level tsp) saffron strands
10 ml (2 level tsp) Dijon mustard
15 ml (1 tbsp) runny honey
30 ml (2 level tbsp) sun-dried tomato paste
60 ml (4 tbsp) olive oil

1.6 kg (3½ lb) shoulder of lamb, cut into large pieces or 2 kg (4½ lb) lamb shanks (see Cook's Tips)
225 g (8 oz) each potatoes, carrots and shallots
300 ml (½ pint) white wine
2 cinnamon sticks
225 g (8 oz) can chickpeas
225 g (8 oz) sultanas
salt and freshly ground black pepper
marjoram sprigs, to garnish

1 Crush garlic, then mix with the next nine ingredients. Place in a bowl with the lamb; mix, cover and marinate overnight.

2 Cut potatoes and carrots into chunks. Peel and trim shallots (see Cook's Tips). Place the vegetables in a roasting tin with the meat, marinade, wine, 150 ml (¼ pint) water and cinnamon sticks. Cover with foil and cook on the bottom runners of the ROASTING OVEN for 1 hour (shoulder) or 1½-1¾ hours (shanks).

3 Add drained chickpeas and sultanas. Cook for 15-20 minutes, then uncover and cook for a further 20-30 minutes to brown ingredients. If using shanks, remove the bone to serve. Season, then garnish with marjoram.

COOK'S TIPS
Ask your butcher to cut the lamb shoulder into large pieces, leaving the bone in.
Don't remove the shallot root completely as this helps to keep it intact.

GLAZED LAMB

PREPARATION TIME:
30 MINUTES

COOKING TIME:
20 MINUTES +
RESTING

290 CALS PER
SERVING

SERVES 6

FREEZING:
UNSUITABLE

For a well flavoured sauce, choose tomatoes ripened on the vine. If unavailable, use three small plum tomatoes or one beef tomato.

30 ml (2 tbsp) olive oil
3 lamb fillets (taken from the best end of lamb)
2 garlic cloves
3 sprigs fresh rosemary
salt and freshly ground black pepper

2 tomatoes
400 ml (14 fl oz) red wine
60 ml (4 level tbsp) redcurrant jelly
lemon juice, to taste
fresh rosemary sprigs, to garnish

1 Heat the oil in a small roasting tin on the BOILING PLATE and brown the lamb fillets well on both sides for 3-4 minutes. Crush the garlic and add to the tin with the rosemary. Season and cook on the top runners at the back of the ROASTING OVEN for 10 minutes. Cover with foil and return to the SIMMERING OVEN to rest for a further 10 minutes.

2 Skin the tomatoes and roughly dice the flesh. Drain off the excess fat from the roasting tin, then place over a medium heat on the BOILING PLATE and stir in the wine and redcurrant jelly. Bring to the boil; bubble for 3-5 minutes or until the sauce is syrupy and reduced by half. Add

SPICED AFRICAN LAMB

lemon juice to taste; stir in the tomatoes.

3 Carve the lamb, allowing half a fillet per person. Place some potatoes and vegetables in the centre of each plate and arrange the lamb around them; garnish. Spoon a little sauce around and serve the remainder separately.

MARINATED LAMB FILLETS WITH HONEY AND LEMON COUSCOUS

PREPARATION TIME:
40 MINUTES +
MARINATING

COOKING TIME:
1 HOUR 30 MINUTES

340 CALS PER
SERVING

SERVES 12

FREEZING:
UNSUITABLE

You would never believe just how easy it is to cook couscous in the Aga until you try it for yourself. It is always free of lumps and never sticky.

4-6 best end of neck lamb fillets, about 1 kg (2¼ lb) total weight (see Cook's Tip)
2 sprigs rosemary
454 g tub thick Greek yogurt
3 garlic cloves
300 g (11 oz) soft goat's cheese
salt and freshly ground black pepper
90 ml (6 level tbsp) chopped mint
150 ml (5 fl oz) olive oil
1 aubergine, about 300 g (11 oz)

275 g (10 oz) onion
2 fennel, 300 g (11 oz) total weight
1 cucumber
275 g (10 oz) plum tomatoes
60 ml (4 tbsp) runny honey
60 ml (4 tbsp) white wine vinegar
45 ml (3 tbsp) lemon juice
225 g (8 oz) couscous
90 ml (6 level tbsp) chopped parsley

1 Trim lamb of fat; place in a bowl with the rosemary. Process yogurt, garlic and cheese until smooth, season; stir in the mint. Mix 60 ml (4 level tbsp) yogurt mixture with 90 ml (6 tbsp) oil; spread over the lamb. Marinate for at least 6 hours or overnight. Refrigerate remaining yogurt mixture. Chop the onion and fennel. Halve, de-seed and chop the cucumber. Chop the tomatoes (peel first, if wished).

2 Halve, score and sprinkle the aubergine with salt to draw out the bitter juices. Leave for 20 minutes. Squeeze out the juices and drizzle the cut side with 15 ml (1 tbsp) oil, then place cut side down in a small roasting tin. Cook on the floor of the ROASTING OVEN for 20 minutes or until soft; cool.

3 Add the fennel to a medium, ovenproof pan of 1 cm (½ in) boiling, salted water, bring back to the boil and cook for 1 minute. Drain, refresh in cold water and drain again. Add 15 ml (1 tbsp) oil to the pan and fry the onions until golden on the BOILING PLATE; cool in a bowl, then add the fennel and diced aubergines.

4 Place the honey in a small pan, bring to the boil and cook for 2 minutes, or until caramelized. Add the vinegar, bring to the boil and bubble for 1 minute; off the heat, stir in 15 ml (1 tbsp) oil, lemon juice and seasoning. Place the couscous and 10 ml (2 tsp) salt in an ovenproof bowl, add 450 ml (15 fl oz) water and leave for 15-20 minutes. Break up any lumps; stir into the aubergine mixture with honey dressing.

5 Stir the tomatoes, cucumber and parsley into the couscous; adjust the seasoning.
■■■ Place in the ROASTING OVEN for 20 minutes or until very hot.
■■■■ Place in the BAKING OVEN for 20-25 minutes.

6 Heat a large frying pan until very hot with the remaining oil. Fry the lamb (at room temperature) for 30 seconds-1 minute on each side until golden. Place in a large roasting tin on the top runners of the ROASTING OVEN for 10-15 minutes until just firm to the touch. Rest in the SIMMERING OVEN for 10 minutes. Carve in thin slices, pour over the cooking juices; serve with couscous and reserved yogurt sauce.

COOK'S TIP
If you cannot find fillet, buy 4 racks of lamb and cut out the eye of the meat in 4 long strips.

SPICED PORK WITH CRANBERRIES AND ORANGE

PREPARATION TIME:
50 MINUTES +
MARINATING
OVERNIGHT

COOKING TIME:
45-50 MINUTES

560 CALS PER
SERVING

SERVES 6

FREEZING:
COMPLETE STEP 4;
COOL, COVER AND
FREEZE THE PORK
AND SAUCE
SEPARATELY.
DEFROST
OVERNIGHT AT
COOL ROOM
TEMPERATURE.
REHEAT, AS BELOW,
FOR 15-20 MINUTES.

The richness of pork is complemented by fruity port and cranberries. This dish is good served with dauphinoise potatoes.

1.1 kg (2½ lb) pork tenderloin fillets
1 small orange
15 ml (1 level tbsp) each chopped fresh rosemary and thyme or a pinch each of dried
1 garlic clove
salt and freshly ground black pepper
300 ml (½ pint) red wine
about 24 button onions or shallots
6 large celery stalks, with leaves
125 g (4 oz) caster sugar

45 ml (3 tbsp) port
225 g (8 oz) fresh or frozen cranberries
60 ml (4 tbsp) olive oil
1 cinnamon stick
30 ml (2 level tbsp) plain flour
150 ml (¼ pint) stock
30 ml (2 level tbsp) chopped, fresh, flat-leafed parsley
25 g (1 oz) butter; preferably unsalted
grated orange rind, to garnish

1   Tie pork with string to neaten the shape. Place in a non-metallic dish with finely grated rind of the orange, herbs, crushed garlic and pepper. Squeeze juice from the orange and add to the dish, along with the red wine. Marinate overnight.

2   Peel the onions, trimming root to keep them whole. Finely chop 30 ml (2 level tbsp) celery leaves; slice stalks. Heat sugar gently on the SIMMERING PLATE until it dissolves and begins to caramelize. When golden, add port and cranberries; set aside (see Cook's Tips). If necessary, return to the SIMMERING PLATE to melt the caramel.

3   Drain pork from the marinade; dry with kitchen paper. Reserve marinade. Heat half the oil in a casserole; break cinnamon stick and add. Brown pork well on all sides on the BOILING PLATE; set aside. Add onions to pan with extra oil if necessary and fry, stirring, on the SIMMERING PLATE until brown. Stir in flour, celery leaves, reserved marinade, stock and pork; bring to boil on the BOILING PLATE. Cover.

■ ■   Cook on the grid shelf on the floor of the ROASTING OVEN for 15 minutes, then turn the meat over in the sauce and cook for a further 5-10 minutes or until the juices run clear when the pork is pierced.

■ ■ ■   Cook on the grid shelf on the floor of the BAKING OVEN for 20 minutes, then turn the meat over in the sauce and cook for a further 5-10 minutes or until the juices run clear when the pork is pierced.

4   Remove pork from oven, lift from sauce and set aside. Bring sauce to boil; bubble for 5-10 minutes on the BOILING PLATE until syrupy. Add the cranberry mixture; bring to boil; adjust seasoning.

5   Slice the pork and spoon the sauce over. Keep warm in the SIMMERING OVEN and scatter with parsley and orange rind before serving. About 10 minutes before serving, stir-fry the celery in butter for 3-4 minutes. Serve with the pork.

COOK'S TIPS

If fresh cranberries are not available, use 75 g (2½ oz) dried cranberries. Make the caramel and port sauce and add to the pork sauce after removing the pork. Add the cranberries before simmering until syrupy.

To prepare ahead, complete to end of step 4, cool quickly, then cover and refrigerate pork and sauce separately for up to two days. To use, bring casserole to the boil; ■ ■ cook in the ROASTING OVEN for 10 minutes or in the SIMMERING OVEN for 30-45 minutes; ■ ■ ■ cook in the BAKING OVEN for 10-15 minutes; complete recipe.

CIDER PORK WITH SPRING VEGETABLES

PREPARATION TIME:
1 HOUR

COOKING TIME:
1 HOUR 15 MINUTES

405 CALS PER
SERVING

SERVES 6

FREEZING:
COMPLETE STEP 3,
COOL QUICKLY,
PACK, COVER AND
FREEZE. THAW AT
COOL ROOM
TEMPERATURE
OVERNIGHT, THEN
BRING CASSEROLE
TO THE BOIL.
■■ REHEAT ON
GRID SHELF ON
FLOOR OF
ROASTING OVEN
FOR 15-20 MINUTES.
■■■■ REHEAT ON
GRID SHELF ON
FLOOR OF BAKING
OVEN FOR 20-30
MINUTES. COOK
VEGETABLES AS
STEP 4.

A classic combination of pork, apples and cider. The amount of vinegar required will depend on the sharpness of the apples you use.

1 kg (2¼ lb) shoulder pork	**salt and freshly ground black pepper**
200 g (7 oz) onions	**10 ml (2 tsp) cider vinegar**
225 g (8 oz) crisp eating apples	**125 g (4 oz) French beans**
45 ml (3 tbsp) oil	**125 g (4 oz) asparagus tips**
15 ml (1 level tbsp) plain flour	**125 g (4 oz) mangetout**
275 ml can dry cider	**2 bunches spring onions**
300 ml (½ pint) chicken stock	

1 Cut pork into 2.5 cm (1 in) cubes; chop onions; core and cut apples into wedges.

2 Heat the oil in a large, flameproof casserole. Fry apples until a light golden brown, then drain and set aside. Add pork to the pan in batches and fry over a high heat until browned; reserve. Lower heat, add onions and cook gently for 5-6 minutes.

3 Stir in the flour, pour in the cider and blend until smooth. Bring to the boil and bubble until reduced by two-thirds. Return the pork to the casserole with the stock, then season. Add the vinegar. Bring to the boil.

■■ Cook on the grid shelf on the floor of the ROASTING OVEN for 1 hour or until tender.

■■■■ Cook on the shelf on the bottom runners of the BAKING OVEN for 1¼ hours.

Add the apples to the casserole 5 minutes before the end of the cooking time. Adjust the seasoning, then reduce the juices (if necessary) by cooking fast on the BOILING PLATE.

4 Meanwhile, cut the vegetables diagonally into short lengths. Cook in boiling, salted water until just tender: French beans for 5 minutes, asparagus for 3 minutes, mangetout and spring onions for 2 minutes. Drain and season. Spoon the vegetables over the pork to serve.

COOK'S TIP

To prepare up to one day ahead, complete to the end of step 3, cool, cover and chill. Cook the vegetables as in step 4. Plunge immediately into cold, iced water, then drain, cover and refrigerate. To use, bring the casserole to the boil and reheat in the BAKING or ROASTING OVEN on the grid shelf for 20-30 minutes. Pour boiling water over the vegetables, leave for 1 minute, then drain and serve with the pork.

PORK WITH PRUNES, APPLES AND SAGE

PREPARATION TIME:
40 MINUTES

COOKING TIME:
1¾-2½ HOURS

320 CALS PER
SERVING

SERVES 8

FREEZING:
UNSUITABLE

Roast pork can be very dry, but this cooking method ensures it will be deliciously moist.

125 g (4 oz) no-soak, pitted prunes	**350 g (12 oz) each shallots and apples, such as Cox's**
45 ml (3 level tbsp) chopped fresh sage	**15 ml (1 tbsp) lemon juice**
2 garlic cloves	**45 ml (3 tbsp) oil**
75 g (3 oz) butter	**500 ml (¾ pint) apple juice**
1.6 kg (3½ lb) boned leg of pork	**150 ml (¼ pint) chicken stock**
salt and freshly ground black pepper	

CIDER PORK WITH SPRING VEGETABLES

1 Roughly chop the prunes; mix with 30 ml (2 level tbsp) sage, the crushed garlic and 50 g (2 oz) butter.

2 Remove rind from pork and set aside. Open pork out like a book, season with pepper and spread with prune mixture. Reshape pork; secure with string.

3 Brush the rind with 15 ml (1 tbsp) oil; coat in salt, cut into 1 cm (½ in) pieces with scissors. Place in a roasting tin and cook on the top runners of the ROASTING OVEN for 20-25 minutes or until very crisp; drain immediately and place in the SIMMERING OVEN until required.

4 Roughly chop the shallots. Peel, core and roughly chop the apples; toss in lemon juice. Heat the remaining oil and butter in a 2.4-litre (4½-pint) flameproof casserole on the BOILING PLATE; brown pork and set aside. Add shallots; cook, stirring, for 3-4 minutes or until soft and golden. Add apples; cook for 3 minutes. Return pork to casserole, add apple juice, bring to the boil and cover.

■ ■ Cook on the grid shelf of the ROASTING OVEN for 1¼-1½ hours. Wrap the meat in foil, then place in the SIMMERING OVEN for 30 minutes (see Aga Tip).

■ ■ ■ ■ Cook in the middle of the BAKING OVEN for 1¾-2 hours. Wrap the meat in foil and place in the SIMMERING OVEN for 30 minutes.

5 Skim juices of any fat, add the stock and remaining sage, bring to the boil and bubble on the floor of the ROASTING OVEN for 20-30 minutes or until syrupy. Season and serve with the sliced pork and crispy rind.

AGA TIP
The pork will be easier to slice if it is covered with foil and left to stand in the SIMMERING OVEN.

RABBIT CASSEROLE WITH RED WINE AND SHERRY

PREPARATION TIME: 40 MINUTES + MARINATING FOR 6 HOURS OR OVERNIGHT

COOKING TIME: 1½-3 HOURS

480 CALS PER SERVING

SERVES 6

FREEZING: COMPLETE RECIPE, COOL QUICKLY, PACK AND FREEZE. DEFROST AT ROOM TEMPERATURE OVERNIGHT; BRING THE CASSEROLE TO THE BOIL SLOWLY. COVER AND REHEAT ■■ IN SIMMERING OVEN FOR 30-35 MINUTES; ■■■■ IN BAKING OVEN FOR 20-25 MINUTES.

Pre-packed rabbit joints are now available from most supermarkets. If you are buying from your local butcher, choose the larger hind leg and saddle joints as they have more flesh on them.

4 garlic cloves
1.4 kg (3 lb) rabbit joints
2 sprigs fresh thyme
2 bay leaves
600 ml (1 pint) red wine
350 g (12 oz) onions
350 g (12 oz) carrots
350 g (12 oz) celery
1 head fennel
75 g (3 oz) streaky bacon rashers

salt and freshly ground black pepper
30 ml (2 level tbsp) plain flour, plus a little for dusting
60 ml (4 tbsp) olive oil
150 ml (¼ pint) medium-dry sherry
300 ml (½ pint) chicken stock
15 ml (1 level tbsp) redcurrant jelly
sprigs of fresh chervil or flat-leafed parsley, to garnish

1 Crush the garlic and place in a bowl with the rabbit, thyme, bay leaves and red wine. Cover, refrigerate and marinate for 6 hours or overnight.

2 Roughly chop the bacon. Drain the rabbit pieces, reserving the marinade. Pat dry with absorbent kitchen paper, season and dust lightly with flour. Heat the oil in a large, heavy-based, flameproof casserole on the BOILING PLATE, add the rabbit and fry in batches until well browned. Remove and set aside. Add the bacon, fry for 2-3 minutes, add the vegetables with more oil if necessary and cook on the SIMMERING PLATE, stirring, until the vegetables are soft and beginning to colour. Add the remaining 30 ml (2 level tbsp) flour and cook for 2 minutes.

3 Return the rabbit to the casserole with the reserved marinade, sherry and stock. Bring to the boil, cover.

■■ Cook on the floor of the SIMMERING OVEN for 2-2½ hours or until very tender.

■■■■ Cook on the grid shelf on the floor of the BAKING OVEN for 1 hour or until very tender.

4 Lift the rabbit out of the cooking liquid, then cover and keep warm in the SIMMERING OVEN. Strain the sauce, pushing as much of the vegetable mixture through the sieve as possible. Add the redcurrant jelly, bring to the boil and bubble on the BOILING PLATE for 5 minutes or until syrupy. Return the rabbit to the casserole and simmer for 5 minutes. Season to taste and serve with polenta and extra vegetables such as baby carrots and fennel; garnish with chervil or parsley.

COOK'S TIP
To prepare ahead, complete the recipe, cool quickly, cover and refrigerate for up to two days. To use, bring the casserole to the boil slowly. Cover and reheat ■■ in the SIMMERING OVEN for 30-35 minutes; ■■■■ in the BAKING OVEN for 20-25 minutes.

MUSTARD VENISON WITH HOT MUSHROOM DRESSING

PREPARATION TIME:
15 MINUTES

COOKING TIME:
25 MINUTES

510 CALS PER
SERVING

SERVES 4

FREEZING:
UNSUITABLE

When buying venison, make sure that it is suitable for roasting. If buying it in the supermarket, it will state this on the packet. If purchasing venison from a game dealer, ask for a loin of venison suitable for fast roasting. Older and less well hung venison is really only suitable for braising or slow roasting.

150 ml (5 fl oz) olive oil
550 g (1¼ lb) strip-loin venison, 6.5 cm (2½ in) diameter
15 ml (1 level tbsp) wholegrain mustard
8-10 button onions
350 g (12 oz) small shiitake or brown-cap mushrooms

30 ml (2 level tbsp) chopped fresh parsley and thyme
25 ml (5 tsp) balsamic vinegar
salt and freshly ground black pepper
lemon juice to taste
thinly cut potato chips, to accompany (optional)

1 Heat half the oil for about 10 minutes until very hot in a small roasting tin in the ROASTING OVEN. Rub venison with mustard. Roll the meat in the hot oil, then scatter the thinly sliced onions around the venison with the mushrooms. Roast on the top runners at the back of the ROASTING OVEN for 30-35 minutes for medium-rare (40 minutes well-done).

2 Roll the hot venison in the chopped fresh herbs and place on a warmed serving platter with the mushrooms and onions. Cover with foil and keep warm in the SIMMERING OVEN while you are making the dressing.

3 Add the remaining oil and vinegar to the roasting tin and warm on the SIMMERING PLATE, stirring. Season and add lemon juice to taste. Serve with the thickly sliced venison. Accompany with potato chips.

COOK'S TIP
For a spicier version of this recipe, try rolling the hot venison in crushed peppercorns rather than the chopped fresh herbs.

GAME AND HERB PIES

PREPARATION TIME:
40 MINUTES +
CHILLING

COOKING TIME:
1¾-2½ HOURS

995 CALS PER
SERVING

SERVES 8

FREEZING: SUITABLE
FOR FILLING ONLY

You can use a wide variety of game in these pies. Any you feel could be tough can be marinaded in the wine overnight before cooking.

900 g (2 lb) puff pastry
beaten egg, to seal

FOR THE FILLING
225 g (8 oz) shallots or button onions
175 g (6 oz) rindless, smoked, streaky bacon, cut in one piece if possible
225 g (8 oz) brown-cap mushrooms
700 g (1½ lb) boneless mixed game, such as rabbit and pheasant
15 ml (1 level tbsp) crushed, dried green peppercorns
25 g (1 oz) plain flour
30 ml (2 tbsp) oil

75 g (3 oz) butter
4 garlic cloves
600 ml (1 pint) dry white wine
5 ml (1 tsp) dried thyme or 15 ml (1 level tbsp) chopped fresh thyme
salt and freshly ground black pepper
450 ml (¾ pint) double cream
700 g (1½ lb) washed and prepared spinach
30 ml (2 level tbsp) each chopped fresh basil, parsley, mint and tarragon or 5 ml (1 tsp) dried tarragon
herb sprigs, dried peppercorns and garlic, to garnish (see Cook's Tips)

1 Roll out the pastry to 3 mm (⅛ in) thick and use it to line eight 7.5 cm (3 in) base-measurement brioche moulds (see Cook's Tips). Prick the bases well. Chill for 10 minutes. Line with greaseproof paper and fill with baking beans. Cook on the grid shelf on the floor of the ROASTING OVEN for 20 minutes, then remove the paper and beans, brush lightly with beaten egg to seal and return to the oven for a further 5-10 minutes or until light golden. Dry and crispen in the SIMMERING OVEN for 15-30 minutes

2 Meanwhile, make filling; peel the shallots or button onions, halving any large ones. Roughly chop the bacon; halve or slice any large mushrooms. Cut the mixed game into bite-sized pieces, season with crushed peppercorns and roll in flour. In a large flameproof casserole, heat the oil with 50 g (2 oz) of the butter on the BOILING PLATE. Add the game and bacon in batches and fry for 1-2 minutes or until golden. Remove from pan and set aside.

3 Add the onions or shallots to the pan with the crushed garlic and fry for about 3-4 minutes or until golden brown. Pour in the wine and dried thyme, if using. Bring to the boil, then bubble on the floor of the ROASTING OVEN for 10-15 minutes or until reduced to a syrupy consistency.

4 Return the game and bacon to the pan. Season and bring to the boil, then add the cream and fresh thyme, if using, and cook in the SIMMERING OVEN for 1-2 hours or until the liquid is reduced by half and the meat very tender.

5 Heat the remaining 25 g (1 oz) butter in a wide-based pan, fry the mushrooms over a high heat until golden, then set aside. In the same pan, cook the spinach for 2-3 minutes, with just the water that clings to its leaves, until just wilted and all the excess liquid has evaporated. Drain and squeeze out all the liquid. Roughly chop and season well.

6 Divide spinach among the baked pastry cases. Add chopped fresh herbs and fried mushrooms to the game mixture and spoon into the cases. Cover loosely with foil.

■ ■ Cook for 7-10 minutes in the ROASTING OVEN until piping hot to the centre.

■ ■ ■ ■ Cook for 10-15 minutes in the BAKING OVEN until piping hot to the centre. Serve pies garnished with deep-fried herb sprigs, peppercorns and garlic slices (see Cook's Tips).

COOK'S TIPS

To prepare ahead, the day before you want to serve the game pies, complete the recipe to the end of step 5. Store the pastry cases in an airtight container. Stir the fresh herbs and the mushrooms into the game mixture and chill. Cover and chill the spinach. To use, spoon the spinach into the pastries on a baking sheet. Cover loosely with foil cook as in step 6. Meanwhile, bring the game mixture to the boil. Simmer gently, adding a little cream if necessary, for 10 minutes until piping hot. Spoon the game into the pastries, then garnish to serve.

GAME AND HERB PIES

To garnish the pie, fry washed and dried sprigs of herbs and slices of garlic in hot oil for 2-3 seconds. Drain on absorbent kitchen paper. Fry extra crushed green peppercorns in a little oil. These can be made ahead and stored in an airtight container. Sprinkle over the pies to serve.
To make one large pie, use a 23 cm (9 in) base diameter, 5 cm (2 in) high fluted flan tin. Bake the pastry case as in step 1 for 40 minutes.

PINEAPPLE CHICKEN CURRY

PREPARATION TIME:
20 MINUTES

COOKING TIME:
15 MINUTES

825 CALS PER
SERVING

SERVES 6

FREEZING:
UNSUITABLE

An aromatic Thai curry with the fresh flavours of chilli, ginger and lemon grass. If only tamarind blocks are available (they are like pressed dates), soften with a little hot water, discarding the pips.

3 large red chillies
1 stalk lemon grass
5 cm (2 in) piece galangal or fresh root ginger
3 garlic cloves
50 g (2 oz) shallots
small handful fresh coriander leaves
1 small fresh pineapple, about 450 g (1 lb)
6 skinless chicken breast fillets
30 ml (2 tbsp) oil

2 x 400 ml cans coconut milk
30 ml (2 level tbsp) palm sugar or dark soft brown (muscovado) sugar
10 ml (2 level tsp) tamarind paste
30 ml (2 tbsp) Thai fish sauce
4 kaffir lime leaves (optional)
grated rind and juice of 1 lime
fresh coriander sprigs, to garnish
rice, to accompany

1 Halve and de-seed two chillies. Roughly chop lemon grass. Peel and slice galangal, garlic and shallots. Roughly chop coriander and set aside. Peel and thinly slice the pineapple. Cut chicken into short strips.

2 Heat the oil in a large frying pan on the BOILING PLATE and stir-fry the chicken strips until just turning pale golden. Remove and set aside.

3 Add chillies, lemon grass, galangal, garlic and shallots to the wok and fry for 1-2 minutes (see Cook's Tip). Stir in the coconut milk, sugar, tamarind paste, fish sauce, remaining whole chilli and kaffir lime leaves, if using. Bring to the boil and bubble for 4-5 minutes or until reduced by about one-third and lightly thickened.

4 Add chicken to the curry sauce with the pineapple and simmer gently for 3-4 minutes or until cooked through and tender. Add the lime rind and a little lime juice to taste.

5 Stir in chopped coriander, garnish with fresh coriander and serve immediately with rice.

COOK'S TIP
You can use a red or green Thai curry paste to replace chillies, lemon grass, galangal, garlic and shallots at step 3. Use 30 ml (2 level tbsp) and fry in the same way.

AGA TIP
Do not try to use a wok on an Aga. To get a high heat you always need a pan with a flat broad base – a large, deep frying pan is ideal.

PARSLEY, WALNUT AND ORANGE CHICKEN

PREPARATION TIME:
15 MINUTES

COOKING TIME:
50 MINUTES

480 CALS PER
SERVING

SERVES 6

FREEZING: SUITABLE

This chicken dish can be cooked ahead and served cold at lunch – but is just as good served hot.

125 g (4 oz) onion
75 g (3 oz) walnuts
135 ml (9 tbsp) extra-virgin olive oil
grated rind and juice of 1 large orange
90 ml (6 level tbsp) chopped fresh parsley
15 ml (1 level tbsp) cranberry sauce

1 egg
salt and freshly ground black pepper
6 chicken breast fillets, with skin
15 ml (1 level tbsp) Dijon mustard
fresh herbs sprigs, to garnish

1 Finely chop the onion and walnuts. Heat 45 ml (3 tbsp) oil in a small ovenproof pan and add the onion. Cover and cook in the SIMMERING OVEN for 20 minutes or until soft. Cool. In a bowl combine the walnuts, orange rind, parsley, cranberry sauce and beaten egg. Season well. Stir in the cooled onion mixture. Set aside.

2 Gently ease up chicken skin and push in the stuffing. Re-shape the chicken and place in a large roasting tin. Spread with the mustard and season. Drizzle over 30 ml (2 tbsp) oil and bake on the bottom runners of the ROASTING OVEN for 25-30 minutes or until cooked, basting occasionally. Set aside to cool. (See Cook's Tip.)

3 When cold, thickly slice and arrange in a serving dish. Whisk together 30 ml (2 tbsp) orange juice with the remaining olive oil and seasoning. Add the strained cooking juices, pour over the chicken, garnish with herb sprigs and serve.

COOK'S TIP
If serving hot, keep the chicken warm while making the dressing, then serve.

CHICKEN AND HAM TERRINE

PREPARATION TIME:
40 MINUTES +
CHILLING

COOKING TIME:
1-1¼ HOURS

410-310 CALS PER
SERVING

SERVES 6-8

FREEZING:
UNSUITABLE

This terrine is ideal for lunch or a late supper. Serve with small new potatoes and a large bowl of mixed green salad leaves.

125 g (4 oz) each leeks, carrots and celery
1.4 kg (3 lb) oven-ready chicken
700 g (1½ lb) piece of gammon, unsalted (see Cook's Tips)
5 ml (1 level tsp) black peppercorns
a few stalks of tarragon

150 ml (¼ pint) white wine
salt and freshly ground black pepper
60 ml (4 level tbsp) each chopped fresh tarragon and flat-leafed parsley
tarragon sprigs, to garnish
aioli mayonnaise, to serve

1 Roughly chop the leeks, carrots and celery. Place in a large ovenproof casserole with the chicken, gammon, 450 ml (¾ pint) water, black peppercorns, tarragon stalks and white wine.

2 Bring to the boil slowly on the SIMMERING PLATE, then cover.

▓ ▓ Cook on the grid shelf on the floor of the ROASTING OVEN for 1 hour or until tender.

▓ ▓ ▓ ▓ Cook on the floor of the BAKING OVEN for 1¼ hours or until tender.

Remove the chicken and gammon from the liquid, then set aside. Bring the liquid to the boil on the BOILING PLATE, bubble for 5 minutes, then strain. Cool and chill quickly in the freezer or freezer compartment of the fridge so that the liquid starts to gel a little.

3 Base-line a 20.5 cm (8 in) spring-release tin with foil. While the chicken and ham are still warm (see Cook's Tips), carve them into slices and strip the chicken meat off the legs and wings.

4 Place a layer of warm chicken in the base of the tin, season and spoon over 60 ml (4 tbsp) cooking liquor. Sprinkle with a little of the chopped tarragon and parsley. Cover with a layer of warm ham, season and spoon over another 60 ml (4 tbsp) cooking liquor. Sprinkle with some more of the herbs, then continue layering chicken, ham and cooking liquor until all the meat has been used, making the final layer a mixture of ham and chicken.

5 Cover the surface with clingfilm and a 20.5 cm (8 in) plate or the base of a flan tin. Place about 900 g (2 lb) in weight – you can use cans – evenly on the top and refrigerate for at least 24 hours.

6 To serve terrine, remove the clingfilm, turn out and cut into wedges. Garnish with tarragon and serve with aioli mayonnaise.

COOK'S TIPS
If the gammon is salted, cover it in water and leave to soak overnight. Discard the water, then continue as above.
When layering the terrine, it is important the chicken and ham are both still warm as this will help the two meats stick together.

CORONATION CHICKEN

PREPARATION TIME:
1 HOUR +
COOLING AND
SOAKING

COOKING TIME:
1 HOUR
20 MINUTES

420 CALS PER
SERVING

SERVES 8

FREEZING:
UNSUITABLE

Many variations of this disk exist. Originally served by the Cordon Bleu Cookery School to the visiting dignitaries at the coronation of the Queen, it is also known as Chicken Elizabeth.

2 celery sticks
1 onion
1.6 kg (3½ lb) chicken
bouquet garni (see Cook's Tips)
2.5 ml (½ level tsp) each salt and black peppercorns
125 g (4 oz) ready-to-eat dried apricots
2 shallots
15 ml (1 tbsp) oil
10 ml (2 level tsp) curry powder (see Cook's Tips)

10 ml (2 level tsp) tomato paste
100 ml (3½ fl oz) red wine
bay leaf
2 lemon slices
450 ml (¾ pint) home-made (see Cook's Tips), or bought thick mayonnaise
30 ml (2 level tbsp) double cream
15 ml (1 tbsp) lemon juice
pinch of cayenne, lime and coriander sprigs, to garnish
wild rice and bean salad, to accompany

1 Place chopped celery and onion in an ovenproof pan with chicken, bouquet garni, salt and peppercorns. Pour in enough cold water to just cover thighs of the chicken; cover pan. Bring slowly to the boil on the BOILING PLATE; then cook on the grid shelf in the ROASTING OVEN for 50 minutes-1 hour (see Cook's Tips). Transfer chicken to a bowl; strain hot stock over (see Cook's Tips). Sit bowl in ice-cold water; cool.

2 Place the apricots in a small pan and cover with freshly boiled water; leave to soak for 30 minutes.

3 Finely chop the shallots. Heat the oil in an ovenproof pan, add the shallots and cook on the SIMMERING PLATE for 1 minute. Add curry powder; fry for 2-3 minutes. Stir in tomato paste; fry for 1 minute. Pour in red wine and 100 ml (3½ fl oz) water. Bring to boil on the SIMMERING PLATE; add bay leaf and lemon slices. Cook for 20 minutes in the SIMMERING OVEN. Strain through a fine sieve, pressing to extract the juices; reserve curry liquid and set aside (discard contents of sieve). Bring apricots to boil, cover and simmer for 15 minutes until soft; drain and purée; set aside.

4 Remove skin and bones from chicken (see Cook's Tips); cut flesh into thick strips. Mix mayonnaise with 45-60 ml (3-4 tbsp) reserved curry liquid (see Cook's Tips), 60-75 ml (4-5 level tbsp) apricot purée and the cream. Dilute with boiling water to give a coating consistency; season. Add lemon juice and more curry liquid or apricot purée to taste. Mix chicken with some curry mayonnaise; serve the rest separately. Garnish; serve with rice and salad.

COOK'S TIPS
To check the chicken is cooked, pierce the thickest part of the thigh with a sharp knife; the juices should run clear. The chicken is more moist if it cools in stock. The chicken bones can be added to the stock and simmered again for 1 hour to make an intense stock for soups and sauces.
Use a mild, Korma-style curry powder. Freeze the remainder of the curry liquid for future use.
To prepare up to a week ahead, complete curry flavouring as step 3; refrigerate. Up to two days ahead, complete apricot purée as steps 2 and 3; refrigerate. Cook and cool chicken as step 1; refrigerate. Up to one day ahead, complete step 4; refrigerate. To use, complete the recipe.
The young, the elderly, pregnant women and those suffering from immune-deficiency diseases should not eat raw eggs, to avoid the risk of salmonella.

DUCK WITH BEETROOT AND RED ONION RELISH

PREPARATION TIME:
15 MINUTES

COOKING TIME:
30 MINUTES

640 CALS PER
SERVING

SERVES 4

FREEZING:
UNSUITABLE

A delicious and very quick dish to cook. Large vacuum-acked or frozen duck breasts can also be used – one pair will usually feed four people.

450 g (1 lb) red onions
3 oranges
2.5 cm (1 in) piece fresh root ginger
about 175 g (6 oz) vacuum-packed cooked beetroot
60 ml (4 tbsp) oil
4 duck breasts, weighing about 175 g (6 oz) each

salt and freshly ground black pepper
300 ml (½ pint) red wine
7.5 ml (1½ level tsp) light soft brown (muscovado) sugar
200 ml (7 fl oz) port
flat-leafed parsley, to garnish

1 Thinly slice the onions. Grate the rind of two oranges; squeeze juice. Peel and grate the ginger. Slice the beetroot and the remaining orange and set aside.

2 Heat the oil in a frying pan and add the onions. Cook, stirring, on the BOILING PLATE until caramelized, then place in the SIMMERING OVEN for 10-15 minutes until soft..

3 Meanwhile, sprinkle the duck with salt. Roast with the sliced orange on the top runners of the ROASTING OVEN for 12-15 minutes (see Aga Tip).

4 Add the wine and orange juice to the caramelized onions; bring to the boil on the BOILING PLATE. Bubble fast to reduce the liquid to almost nothing. Add the ginger, orange rind, sugar and port, bring to the boil and bubble again until syrupy. Add the sliced beetroot; season to taste. Serve warm with the sliced duck, garnished with parsley and orange slices.

AGA TIP
You need a very hot oven to roast the duck. If the oven has lost its heat through other cooking, fry the duck first in a frying pan, skin side down, on the BOILING PLATE for 1 minute. Turn over and fry on the other side for a further minute until golden, adding the oranges to the pan. Transfer to the small roasting tin and cook in the ROASTING OVEN for 12-15 minutes to complete the cooking.

DUCK WITH BEETROOT AND RED ONION RELISH

GARLIC POUSSINS WITH KUMQUATS

PREPARATION TIME:
20 MINUTES

COOKING TIME:
I HOUR

580 CALS PER
SERVING

SERVES 6

FREEZING:
UNSUITABLE

This impressive tasty main course contrasts a rich, creamy sauce with the tart, fruity flavour of the kumquats and cider.

3 poussins, each weighing about 700 g (1½ lb)
salt and freshly ground black pepper
225 g (8 oz) kumquats
16 garlic cloves
30 ml (2 tbsp) olive oil
25 g (1 oz) unsalted butter

2 bay leaves
450 ml (¾ pint) dry cider
200 ml (7 fl oz) apple juice
200 ml (7 fl oz) double cream
thyme sprigs, to garnish

1 Cut both sides of the backbone of the poussins with a pair of kitchen scissors and remove. Cut the poussins in half along the breast bone (see Cook's Tips). Sprinkle the skin side liberally with 10 ml (2 level tsp) salt (see Cook's Tips). Halve the kumquats. Cook the whole, unpeeled garlic cloves in a pan of boiling, salted water for 4 minutes. Drain, cool slightly and peel.

2 Heat the oil in a shallow, ovenproof casserole on the SIMMERING PLATE (see Cook's Tips), then add the butter. When the butter begins to sizzle, add the poussin halves skin-side down and cook for 4-5 minutes or until deep golden brown. Remove the poussins. Add the kumquats and garlic cloves and stir over the heat for 2-3 minutes or until golden. Return the poussins to the casserole dish, add the bay leaves, bring to the boil and cover.

3 Cook on the grid shelf on the floor of the ROASTING OVEN for 30-35 minutes or until the poussins are cooked through. With a slotted spoon, lift the poussins, kumquats and six of the garlic cloves into an ovenproof dish. Cover with foil and keep warm in the SIMMERING OVEN.

4 With a wooden spoon, crush the remaining garlic cloves in the casserole to a paste. Add the cider and apple juice, bring to the boil on the BOILING PLATE and bubble for 7-10 minutes or until syrupy. Pour in the cream (see Cook's Tips), season and bring back to the boil. Simmer for 1 minute on the SIMMERING PLATE. Return the poussins, whole garlic and kumquats to the casserole, cover and cook gently for 2-3 minutes.

5 Garnish the poussins with sprigs of thyme and serve.

COOK'S TIPS
If you are buying the poussins from a butcher, ask him to prepare them for you. Seasoning the skin of the poussins with plenty of salt makes it crisp and golden.
The casserole should be large enough for the poussin halves to fit in a single layer. If not, use a large frying pan to brown the poussins, then transfer to a casserole.
For a less rich sauce, use a 142 ml (5 fl oz) carton of double cream.
To prepare ahead, complete to the end of step 4. Cool, cover and refrigerate up to one day ahead. To use, bring to the boil, cover and reheat in the ROASTING OVEN for 15-20 minutes or until the poussins are piping hot. If the sauce becomes too thick, add a little boiling water. Garnish and serve.

GUINEA FOWL WITH PUY LENTILS, BACON AND THYME

PREPARATION TIME:
30 MINUTES +
MARINATING

COOKING TIME:
1 HOUR 20 MINUTES

525 CALS PER
SERVING

SERVES 6

FREEZING:
UNSUITABLE

Puy lentils are tiny black lentils – quick to cook with a delicious flavour which goes particularly well with game birds and other poultry.

200 ml (7 fl oz) white wine
4 garlic cloves
105 ml (7 tbsp) olive oil
6 guinea fowl or corn-fed chicken breasts with skin left on
225 g (8 oz) streaky bacon or lardons (see Cook's Tip)
350 g (12 oz) shallots or button onions
4 celery sticks

175 g (6 oz) Puy lentils
1 medium onion
2 sprigs thyme
15 ml (1 level tbsp) tomato paste
15 ml (1 level tbsp) chopped fresh thyme
15 ml (1 tbsp) balsamic vinegar
salt and freshly ground black pepper
frisée salad, to serve

1 Mix white wine with two crushed garlic cloves and 45 ml (3 tbsp) olive oil. Lay guinea fowl in a non-metallic dish and pour over wine mixture. Cover and refrigerate for 4 hours or overnight. Remove rind from bacon and cut into 1 cm (½ in) strips. Peel and quarter shallots. Cut three celery sticks into strips.

2 Place lentils in a large pan with remaining celery stick, onion and thyme sprigs. Cover with cold water, bring to boil, then cook in the SIMMERING OVEN for 40 minutes or until just tender. Drain, reserving 200 ml (7 fl oz) of cooking liquor. Discard celery, onion and thyme.

3 Lift guinea fowl from marinade and pat dry with kitchen paper. Heat 30 ml (2 tbsp) olive oil in a large ovenproof frying pan on the BOILING PLATE and brown guinea fowl, skin-side down, for 2-3 minutes. Transfer to a roasting tin and pour marinade over. Cook on the second runners of the ROASTING OVEN for 15-20 minutes.

4 Meanwhile, add shallots and bacon to the frying pan and cook on the floor of the ROASTING OVEN for 7-12 minutes until the bacon is crisp and the shallots are golden. Add tomato paste, remaining crushed garlic cloves and celery strips and cook on the SIMMERING PLATE for 3-4 minutes. Add cooked lentils, chopped thyme and vinegar.

5 Lift guinea fowl from tin. Keep warm in the SIMMERING OVEN. Add pan juices and reserved cooking liquor to lentils. Bring to boil, simmer 2-3 minutes on the SIMMERING PLATE, add remaining oil. Season. Serve with guinea fowl and frisée salad.

COOK'S TIP
Preferably buy bacon in one piece from the butcher and cut it into lardons (strips). Alternatively, buy ready-cut lardons available from major supermarkets.

COD WITH HOT POTATO AND EGG SALAD

PREPARATION TIME:
10 MINUTES

COOKING TIME:
20 MINUTES

460 CALS PER
SERVING

SERVES 4

FREEZING:
UNSUITABLE

Once the egg has been added to the potatoes, serve this salad immediately.

150 g (5 oz) butter
4 cod steaks, each about 2.5 cm (1 in)
thick and 125 g (4 oz) in weight
small bunch fresh tarragon
175 ml (6 fl oz) dry white wine

sea salt and freshly ground black pepper
225 g (8 oz) new potatoes
2 hard-boiled eggs
watercress, to serve

1 Quarter the potatoes and cook in boiling, salted water in the SIMMERING OVEN for 10 minutes. Chop the tarragon, reserving one or two sprigs; peel and finely chop the eggs.

2 Butter a shallow, ovenproof dish with a little of the butter. Add the cod, the remaining tarragon and dot with 25 g (1 oz) butter. Pour the wine over and season well with sea salt. Cook on the grid shelf on the second runners at the back of the ROASTING OVEN for 10 minutes.

3 Remove the fish from the oven and pour the liquor into a shallow sauté or frying pan. Cover the fish and return to the SIMMERING OVEN.

4 Drain the potatoes and add them to the fish liquor. Bring to the boil and bubble the potatoes in the liquid until tender and the liquid has reduced to about 60 ml (4 tbsp). Keeping the mixture hot, swirl in the remaining butter with the chopped tarragon and chopped eggs. Season to taste.

5 Place the fish on a bed of watercress, then spoon the hot potato mixture around it. Season with salt and ground black pepper and serve immediately.

BAKED MONKFISH BOULANGERE

PREPARATION TIME:
40 MINUTES

COOKING TIME:
1 HOUR

330-220 CALS PER
SERVING

SERVES 6-8

FREEZING: SUITABLE
FOR PREPARATION
OF RAW UNFROZEN
FISH ONLY.

Monkfish has a wonderful texture and with the flavour of lemony crumbs and Parma ham on a bed of roast onions and potatoes, this is a very easy dish to serve for friends.

3 lemons
50 g (2 oz) fresh white breadcrumbs
75 ml (5 level tbsp) chopped flat-leafed parsley
2 garlic cloves
30-45 ml (2-3 tbsp) olive oil
salt and freshly ground black pepper
1 kg (2¼ lb) monkfish tail, filleted into 4 pieces (see Cook's Tips)

12 slices Parma ham
350 g (12 oz) onions
900 g (2 lb) medium-sized new potatoes
75 g (3 oz) butter
5 ml (1 level tsp) dried thyme
thyme sprigs, to garnish

1 Grate rind of 2 lemons; place in a food processor with the breadcrumbs, parsley, crushed garlic, 30 ml (2 tbsp) oil and seasoning. Add remaining oil if mixture seems dry. Process for 1 minute until well combined.

2 Lay the monkfish flat-side up on a board. Sprinkle half breadcrumb mixture on one fillet; lay the other fillet on top. Repeat with remaining fish to make two parcels.

3 Wrap each parcel with the Parma ham, making sure the fish is completely covered. Tie at 5 cm (2 in) intervals with fine string (see Cook's Tips).

4 Thickly slice the onions, scrub and quarter the potatoes and quarter the remaining lemon. Use

BAKED MONKFISH BOULANGERE

25 g (1 oz) butter to grease a large roasting tin. Place the potatoes, onion and lemon in the tin, then season and sprinkle with dried thyme. Dot with remaining butter, then cook on the floor of the ROASTING OVEN for 30 minutes, then stir and place on the top runners for a further 20 minutes or until golden brown.

5 Place fish on top of the potatoes. Cover with foil and return to the bottom runners of the ROASTING OVEN for 20 minutes.

6 Garnish with thyme; serve immediately.

COOK'S TIPS
Two monkfish tails should give you this amount. The fishmonger can fillet them for you.
If you have time, refrigerate the fish for 1-2 hours at step 3, so the flavour can develop.

WARM OLIVE OIL SAUCE WITH PLAICE

PREPARATION TIME:
15 MINUTES

COOKING TIME:
7 MINUTES

565 CALS PER
SERVING

SERVES 4

FREEZING:
UNSUITABLE

A delicate sauce that's delicious when spooned over Aga-cooked fish such as plaice or salmon. Alternatively, accompany with steamed vegetables.

3 shallots or 1 small onion
100 ml (4 fl oz) dry white wine
2 large eggs (see Cook's Tips)
salt and freshly ground black pepper
cayenne pepper

300 ml (½ pint) extra-virgin olive oil
1 lemon
45 ml (3 level tbsp) chopped fresh flat-leafed parsley
15 ml (1 level tbsp) chopped fresh dill

1 Finely chop the shallots. Place in a saucepan with the wine and bring to the boil. Bubble the liquid on the BOILING PLATE to reduce to 30 ml (2 tbsp).

2 Meanwhile, place the eggs in a food processor and process with salt, pepper and a small pinch of cayenne until the mixture is well blended, fluffy and light in colour. Add the reduced wine and shallot mixture and process for 1 minute.

3 Warm the oil until hot (see Cook's Tips) and, with the processor running at full speed, pour the hot oil in a thin steady stream on to the eggs. Leave the machine running for 2-3 minutes; the sauce should be thick and creamy (see Cook's Tips). Add 15-30 ml (1-2 tbsp) lemon juice and the herbs. Adjust seasoning. Serve warm (see Cook's Tips).

COOK'S TIPS
Heat the oil in a milk pan until a finger of stale bread sizzles but doesn't brown. If the oil is too hot, the mixture will curdle.
If the sauce doesn't thicken well, transfer it to a heatproof bowl over a pan of simmering water and cook stirring continuously, for 3-4 minutes or until it thickens. Don't overheat.
Keep the sauce warm for 5-10 minutes by placing it in a heatproof bowl and sitting it at the back of the Aga.
The young, the elderly, pregnant women and those who suffer from immune-deficiency diseases should not eat raw or lightly cooked eggs, in order to avoid the possible risk of salmonella.

TO COOK PERFECT FISH ON THE AGA
For fillets of white fish such as sole or plaice, instead of grilling or streaming, season and sandwich in oiled foil. For fillets and escalopes of oily fish such as trout or salmon, season and sandwich in plain foil. Either cook directly on the BOILING PLATE for about 1 minute on each side; or cook on the floor of the ROASTING OVEN for 70-90 seconds on each side; or cook on a baking tray in the middle of the SIMMERING OVEN for 12-15 minutes (or up to 20 minutes for thick steaks of fish) or until just turning colour.

SALMON WITH BRIOCHE CRUST AND CREAMY LEEKS

PREPARATION TIME:
15 MINUTES

COOKING TIME:
20 MINUTES

680 CALS PER
SERVING

SERVES 4

FREEZING:
UNSUITABLE

This dish is particularly suitable for a casual kitchen supper so you can keep an eye on the creamy leeks while they cook. Pop the fish in the oven as you sit down to your starter.

700 g (1½ lb) leeks
50 g (2 oz) butter
75 g (3 oz) frozen broad beans
2 small brioche rolls or about 75 g (3 oz) brioche loaf
30 ml (2 level tbsp) chopped parsley
15 ml (1 level tbsp) chopped fresh thyme

4 salmon fillets, each weighing about 175 g (6 oz)
30 ml (2 tbsp) white wine
200 g (7 oz) tub crème fraîche (see Cook's Tip)
5 ml (1 level tsp) wholegrain mustard
one lime

1 Melt half the butter in a wide saucepan. Place the brioche in a food processor with the herbs and process into rough crumbs. Add the melted butter and continue to blend for 1 minute. Press the mixture on to the top of each salmon fillet.

2 Place the salmon on a baking sheet and cook on the bottom runners of the ROASTING OVEN for 7-8 minutes or until cooked through.

3 Meanwhile, finely chop the leeks. Melt the remaining butter in the pan; fry the leeks on the SIMMERING PLATE for 10 minutes, stirring occasionally. Stir in the beans. Continue to cook for 1 minute. Add the white wine to the leeks and bring to the boil, then bubble on the BOILING PLATE to reduce to almost nothing. Stir in the crème fraîche and mustard. Squeeze the lime juice over the salmon and serve with the leeks.

COOK'S TIP
Using reduced-fat crème fraîche reduces the calories to 575 cals per serving.

SKATE WITH TOMATOES, COURGETTES AND CAPERS

PREPARATION TIME:
10 MINUTES

COOKING TIME:
10 MINUTES

300 CALS PER
SERVING

SERVES 4

FREEZING:
UNSUITABLE

Lemon, capers, olives and thyme combine wonderfully with fish. This dish is also excellent made with salmon instead of skate.

1 lemon
225 g (8 oz) tomatoes, preferably plum
50 g (2 oz) black olives, pitted
125 g (4 oz) courgettes, preferably baby ones
4 skate wings, skinned, about 1.4 kg (3 lb) total weight

salt and freshly ground black pepper
30 ml (2 level tbsp) flour
100 ml (4 fl oz) oil
3 garlic cloves
125 g (4 oz) capers, drained
15 ml (1 level tbsp) chopped fresh thyme

1 Finely grate the lemon, squeeze and reserve the juice. De-seed and roughly chop the tomatoes. Halve the olives and finely slice the baby courgettes.

2 Lightly coat the skate with seasoned flour. Heat 30 ml (2 tbsp) oil in a large frying pan and cook the fish on the BOILING PLATE for 1-2 minutes on each side or until golden brown. Remove from the heat and place in the SIMMERING OVEN .

3 Place the remaining oil in a frying pan, add the crushed garlic, chopped tomato, courgettes and the lemon rind. Stir for 2-3 minutes on the BOILING PLATE. Add the lemon juice, capers, thyme and black olives. Season.

4 Spoon the courgette mixture over the fish and return to the SIMMERING OVEN for 4-5 minutes or until just tender.

PAN-FRIED SOLE WITH FOAMING HERB AND LEMON SAUCE

PREPARATION TIME:
20 MINUTES

COOKING TIME:
10 MINUTES

420 CALS PER
SERVING

SERVES 6

FREEZING:
UNSUITABLE

This light sauce, based on a hollandaise, makes a mouthwatering combination with sole.

1 lemon
salt and freshly ground black pepper
12 sole fillets, about 50 g (2 oz) each
25 g (1 oz) plain flour
3 eggs (see Cook's Tips)
pinch of cayenne pepper
30 ml (2 tbsp) white wine vinegar

225 g (8 oz) butter
30 ml (2 level tbsp) chopped fresh
tarragon or a large pinch of dried
30 ml (2 level tbsp) chopped chives
mixed salad and lemon wedges, to serve
chopped fresh chives and grated lemon
rind, to garnish

1 Grate the rind and squeeze the juice of the lemon. Season the sole, then dip each fillet in the flour. Shake off any excess, then cover and set aside.

2 Separate eggs. Place the yolks in a food processor with a pinch of salt and cayenne pepper and process for 2 minutes.

3 Place the vinegar and 45 ml (3 tbsp) lemon juice in a small saucepan and heat until it just simmers. With the processor at full speed, add the hot liquid to the yolks a little at a time.

4 Melt 175 g (6 oz) of the butter in a pan until just bubbling and almost starting to brown (see Cook's Tips). With the processor at full speed, add the foaming butter steadily to the egg yolks. Blend until the butter is incorporated and the sauce is the consistency of very lightly whipped cream. Fold in the chopped tarragon and chives.

5 Whisk the egg whites until they form soft peaks; fold in the hot sauce. Adjust the seasoning; cover the bowl and place on the back of the Aga to keep warm (or on the warming plate of a four-oven Aga).

6 Melt remaining butter in a non-stick frying pan. Fry the sole on the BOILING PLATE for 1 minute on each side or until golden brown. Keep warm in the SIMMERING OVEN until all the fillets are cooked.

7 Serve the sole with a little of the warm sauce. Serve with salad and lemon wedges, and garnish with chopped chives and grated lemon rind. Spoon remaining sauce into a bowl and hand round separately.

COOK'S TIPS
It is important to get the butter really hot in step 4 as it cooks and thickens the yolks lightly.
The young, elderly, pregnant women, young children and people with immune-deficiency diseases should not eat raw or lightly cooked eggs, due to the possible risk of salmonella.

SEAFOOD PIE WITH LEEKS AND BLUE CHEESE

PREPARATION TIME:
40 MINUTES

COOKING TIME:
1¼ HOURS

675 CALS PER
SERVING

SERVES 4

FREEZING: SUITABLE

This pie will satisfy the largest appetite! You can use different fish, vegetables and cheese, but keep the quantities in the proportions stated in the recipe.

700 g (1½ lb) floury potatoes
salt and freshly ground black pepper
450 g (1 lb) cod, haddock or whiting fillet
350 ml (12 fl oz) milk
350 g (12 oz) leeks
25 g (1 oz) butter
freshly grated nutmeg
225 g (8 oz) large peeled prawns

FOR THE CHEESE SAUCE
50 g (2 oz) butter
45 ml (3 level tbsp) plain white flour
125 g (4 oz) blue Stilton cheese
60 ml (4 tbsp) single cream

1 Peel the potatoes and cut into 5 mm (¼ in) slices. Bring a large saucepan containing 1 cm (½ in) of salted water to the boil. Add the potato slices, bring to the boil and cook in the SIMMERING OVEN for 10-15 minutes until partially softened. Drain thoroughly in a colander.

2 Place the fish in the pan. Pour 50 ml (2 fl oz) of the milk over. Season lightly.

▓ ▓ Cover and poach in the ROASTING OVEN with the grid shelf on the floor of the oven for about 15 minutes or until the fish flakes easily.

▓ ▓ ▓ ▓ Cover and poach in the BAKING OVEN with the grid shelf on the floor of the oven for about 15 minutes or until the fish flakes easily.

3 Drain the fish, reserving the cooking liquor. Flake the fish, discarding skin and bones.

4 Trim and slice the leeks. Melt the butter in the same pan and fry the leeks for 3 minutes on the SIMMERING PLATE, adding plenty of freshly grated nutmeg. Lightly butter the sides of a 1.7-litre (3-pint) pie dish. Toss the fish, prawns and leeks in the pan and tip into the dish.

5 To make the cheese sauce, melt the butter in the same saucepan on the SIMMERING PLATE. Add the flour and cook, stirring, for 1 minute. Remove from the heat and blend in the remaining milk and the reserved fish poaching liquor.

6 Return the pan to the heat and cook the sauce, stirring, until thickened and smooth. Remove from the heat. Crumble in the cheese, then add the cream and season to taste.

7 Spoon half of the cheese sauce over the fish mixture in the dish. Layer the cooked potato slices over the filling, then pour the remaining sauce over the potatoes. Place the dish on a baking sheet and bake on the grid shelf on the floor of the ROASTING OVEN for 40-45 minutes or until bubbling and golden and the potatoes are tender. Serve with green vegetables.

AGA TIP
If you use the same pan for each stage of the recipe, you will only have one pan to wash up at the end, rather than four!

SPICED MOROCCAN SEAFOOD PILAFF

PREPARATION TIME:
30 MINUTES +
MARINATING

COOKING TIME:
I HOUR

695 CALS PER
SERVING

SERVES 8

FREEZING:
UNSUITABLE

A wonderful combination of flavours makes this a very robust and colourful dish which looks particularly good in a large, shallow cast iron casserole.

FOR THE MARINADE
3 medium red chillies
75 ml (5 level tbsp) chopped fresh coriander
22.5 ml (4½ level tsp) ground cumin
5 ml (I level tsp) saffron strands
9 garlic cloves
150 ml (¼ pint) olive oil
100 ml (4 fl oz) lemon juice
22.5 ml (4½ level tsp) ground mild paprika
10 ml (2 level tsp) salt

FOR THE PILAFF
450 g (I lb) skinless, boned chicken thighs
450 g (I lb) fresh or frozen raw shellfish and seafood, e.g. squid, prawns and scallops

225 g (8 oz) skinless cod or haddock fillet
750 g (I½ lb) raw mussels in shells
225 g (8 oz) onion
125 g (4 oz) celery
2 red peppers
175 g (6 oz) piece chorizo sausage
30 ml (2 tbsp) oil
275 g (10 oz) long-grain white rice
900 ml (I½ pints) chicken stock
400 g can chopped tomatoes
salt and freshly ground black pepper
coriander sprigs and lemon quarters, to garnish

I De-seed and roughly chop the chillies. Place them in a food processor with all the remaining marinade ingredients. Process for I minute or until smooth. Place the chicken thighs in a bowl and mix with half the marinade. Cover for at least 2 hours or overnight. Prepare the shellfish and seafood mix: cut the squid into 5 mm (¼ in) rings, shell the prawns, trim and halve the scallops. Cut the cod or haddock into bite-size pieces. Place the fish and shellfish in a bowl with the remaining marinade. Cover for 2 hours or overnight. Scrub the mussels, pull off the beards and discard any open ones, then cover and refrigerate.

2 Chop onion. Cut celery, red peppers and chorizo sausage into finger-length strips. Heat oil in a large 5-6 litre (8-10 pint) flameproof casserole. Fry celery, red pepper and chorizo for 2-3 minutes on the BOILING PLATE. Set aside.

3 Drain the chicken and all the seafood, reserving the marinade. Cover the seafood and return to the fridge. Add the chicken pieces to the pan in batches and fry them for 2-3 minutes or until they are lightly golden on each side. Set aside.

4 Add the onion to the pan, cook for 10 minutes in the SIMMERING OVEN. Add the marinade and bring to the boil. Bubble on BOILING PLATE for I minute. Add the rice and stir on the SIMMERING PLATE for I minute. Add the chicken stock and the chopped tomatoes.

5 Bring to the boil, stirring all the time to prevent sticking. Return the chicken to the rice mixture and season well. Cover tightly with foil or the pan lid and cook at in the ROASTING OVEN with the grid shelf on the floor for 30 minutes.

6 Return celery, pepper and chorizo sausage to pan. Place the marinated seafood, fish and mussels on top. Cover and bring to the boil on the BOILING PLATE, shaking the pan occasionally. Return to the ROASTING OVEN for 10-20 minutes or until mussels have opened (discard any closed ones). Leave to stand, covered, in the SIMMERING OVEN for 10 minutes. Adjust seasoning, garnish with coriander and lemon.

SPICED MOROCCAN SEAFOOD PILAFF

FRESH TUNA NIÇOISE

PREPARATION TIME:
30 MINUTES

COOKING TIME: 10
MINUTES

375 CALS PER
SERVING

SERVES 4

FREEZING:
UNSUITABLE

A treat for the eyes as well as the taste buds! This dish is a colourful combination of summery ingredients that evoke Mediterranean days in the sun.

125 g (4 oz) shallots
90 ml (6 tbsp) lemon juice
100 ml (4 fl oz) extra-virgin olive oil
salt and freshly ground black pepper
450 g (1 lb) fresh tuna steaks
1 lemon
10 ml (2 level tsp) chopped fresh thyme

30 ml (2 tbsp) olive oil
cherry tomatoes, cucumber, French beans, hard-boiled eggs and pitted olives, to serve
rouille or mayonnaise with saffron and garlic, to accompany
lemon, to garnish

1 Finely chop the shallots; mix them with the lemon juice and extra-virgin olive oil; season.
2 Cut tuna into 5 cm (2 in) strips, coat in juice of the lemon and thyme; season. Heat the olive oil in a frying pan, add the tuna and cook in batches on the BOILING PLATE for 2-3 minutes.
3 Serve the warm tuna and shallot dressing on a salad of cherry tomatoes, cucumber, lightly cooked French beans, hard-boiled eggs and pitted olives. Accompany with rouille or mayonnaise that has been flavoured with a little saffron and garlic. Garnish with lemon wedges.

BAKED STUFFED PUMPKIN

PREPARATION TIME:
45 MINUTES

COOKING TIME:
1¼-1½ HOURS +
STANDING

430-285 CALS PER
SERVING

SERVES 4-6

FREEZING:
UNSUITABLE

A Crown Prince squash can be substituted in this recipe when pumpkins are unavailable.

1 pumpkin, about 1.4-1.8 kg (3-4 lb)	**5 ml (1 level tsp) turmeric**
2 leeks	**125 g (4 oz) long-grain rice**
30 ml (2 tbsp) olive oil	**2 tomatoes**
2 garlic cloves	**50 g (2 oz) cashew nuts**
30 ml (2 level tbsp) chopped fresh thyme	**125 g (4 oz) Gruyère or Cheddar cheese**
10 ml (2 level tsp) paprika	**salt and freshly ground black pepper**

1 Cut a 3-5 cm (1½-2 in) slice from the top of the pumpkin and set aside for the lid. Scoop out and discard the seeds. Using a grapefruit knife and a spoon, cut out most of the pumpkin flesh, leaving a thin shell. Cut the pumpkin flesh into small pieces and set aside.

2 Trim and chop the leeks. Heat the olive oil in a large pan, add the pumpkin with the crushed garlic, thyme, paprika and turmeric, and fry for 2-3 minutes on the SIMMERING PLATE. Add the leeks and fry for a further 4-5 minutes until golden, stirring frequently to prevent sticking.

3 In the meantime, cook the rice according to the packet directions until just tender. Skin, de-seed and dice the tomatoes. Toast the cashew nuts carefully in the ROASTING OVEN for 2-4 minutes (see Aga Tip), cool, then roughly chop.

4 Drain the rice. Add the pumpkin mixture with the tomatoes, cashews and cheese. Fork through to mix and season to taste. Spoon the stuffing mixture into the pumpkin shell, top with the lid.

5 ▨ ▨ Bake at the front of the ROASTING OVEN on the grid shelf on the floor for 45 minutes. After the first 30 minutes, turn the pumpkin round and place the cold shelf on the top runners to ensure even cooking. Transfer to the SIMMERING OVEN for a further 30 minutes or until tender and the skin is browned.

▨ ▨ ▨ ▨ Bake on the grid shelf on the floor of the BAKING OVEN for 45 minutes until tender and golden.

6 Remove from the oven and leave to stand for 10 minutes. Cut into wedges to serve.

AGA TIP
Be very careful when browning nuts in the oven. It may help to leave the oven door slightly open so that you can smell when they are ready.

NUT AND CRANBERRY TERRINE

PREPARATION TIME:
45 MINUTES +
COOLING

COOKING TIME:
45-50 MINUTES

490 CALS PER
SERVING FOR 8, 395
CALS IF SERVING 10

SERVES 8-10

FREEZING: SUITABLE

A lovely combination of nuts and cheese in a hot water crust pastry that is as easy to handle as children's play dough!

FOR THE FILLING
125 g (4 oz) long-grain rice
I onion
I leek
4 celery sticks
60 ml (4 tbsp) olive oil
60 ml (4 level tbsp) chopped mixed fresh herbs, such as sage, parsley and thyme
40 g (1½ oz) walnuts
125 g (4 oz) dolcelatte cheese
I large egg
40 g (1½ oz) fresh white breadcrumbs
125 g (4 oz) fromage frais or crème fraîche
salt and freshly ground black pepper

FOR THE PASTRY
225 g (8 oz) plain flour
pinch of salt
45 g (1½ oz) white vegetable fat
15 g (1 oz) butter

FOR THE TOPPING
125 g (4 oz) redcurrant jelly
5 ml (1 tsp) lemon juice
125 g (4 oz) cranberries or redcurrants, thawed if frozen
bay leaves, to garnish

1 Cook the rice in boiling, salted water, according to the packet instructions, in the SIMMERING OVEN until just tender; refresh under cold water, drain thoroughly and set aside. Peel and finely chop the onion; trim and thinly slice the leek and celery.

2 Heat the oil in a frying pan, add the onion, leek, celery and herbs and fry gently on the SIMMERING PLATE for 5 minutes until softened; transfer to a bowl. Carefully toast the walnuts for 3-5 minutes in the ROASTING OVEN, then roughly grind. Crumble the cheese and lightly beat the egg. Add the walnuts, cheese and egg to the fried mixture with the rice and remaining filling ingredients, seasoning generously. Stir until evenly combined.

3 For the pastry, sift the flour and salt into a bowl; make a well in the middle. Heat 100 ml (3½ fl oz) water, fat and butter in a saucepan until the liquid comes to the boil. Pour into the flour and gradually work together, using a wooden spoon.

4 When cool enough to handle, bring the dough together and knead lightly until smooth. Roll out to a 25 x 20 cm (10 x 8 in) rectangle and use to line a 1 kg (2 lb) loaf tin, pressing the dough into the corners; trim the overhanging pastry and reserve.

5 Spoon the filling into the pastry case; smooth the surface. Divide the pastry trimmings in half, roll each piece into a long thin rope and plait together.

6 Dampen the pastry edges and top with the pastry plait, pressing down gently. Bake on the grid shelf on the floor of the ROASTING OVEN for 30-35 minutes, then place on the floor of the ROASTING OVEN for 10 minutes to ensure the base is crisp. The top should be golden and a skewer inserted into the centre should come out hot; cool.

7 For the topping, heat the redcurrant jelly in a small pan with the lemon juice and 15 ml (1 tbsp) water until melted, then simmer for 3 minutes. Remove from the heat and stir in the fruit.

8 To unmould the pie, upturn and tap gently, then set on a board. Spoon the topping over and leave to set. When cold, garnish with bay leaves. Cut into generous slices to serve.

ROASTED VEGETABLE TATIN

PREPARATION TIME:
10 MINUTES

COOKING TIME:
40 MINUTES

495 CALS PER
SERVING

SERVES 4

FREEZING:
UNSUITABLE

The classic upside-down apple tart of the Tatin sisters has inspired this delicious vegetable version.

175 g (6 oz) each celeriac, carrot and swede
175 g (6 oz) shallots
3 garlic cloves
125 g (4 oz) leeks
75 g (3 oz) ready-to-eat dried apricots
5 ml (1 level tsp) each coriander and fennel seeds

45 ml (3 tbsp) olive oil
salt and freshly ground black pepper
225 g (8 oz) puff pastry
50 g (2 oz) butter
10 ml (2 level tsp) sugar
15 ml (1 tbsp) lemon juice

1 Peel and cut the celeriac, carrot and swede into chunks. Peel the shallots and cut in half, if large. Peel the garlic cloves and leave whole. Cut the leeks into rough pieces. Roughly chop the apricots. Finely grind the coriander and fennel seeds in a bowl with the end of a rolling pin.

2 Place the celeriac, carrot, swede and shallots in a roasting tin with the ground spices, 30 ml (2 tbsp) olive oil and seasoning. Cook on the top runners on the ROASTING OVEN for 20 minutes, then add the garlic cloves and toss well. Toss the leeks in the remaining oil and place at the front of the roasting tin. Continue cooking for 10 minutes..

3 Roll out pastry and cut into a 22.5 cm (10 in) circle. Prick with a fork and chill for 10 minutes.

4 Melt the butter with the sugar, lemon juice and 50 ml (2 fl oz) water in a heavy-base, ovenproof frying pan or cake tin (not loose-bottomed), about 20 cm (8 in) diameter base, on the floor of the ROASTING OVEN for 10 minutes. When the sugar has dissolved, transfer to the SIMMERING PLATE and bubble until the mixture turns a light caramel colour.

ROASTED VEGETABLE TATIN

5 Mix the apricots into the vegetables and place on top of the butter and sugar mixture; cook on the floor of the ROASTING OVEN for 10 minutes.

6 Quickly place the chilled pastry on top of the vegetables and cook on the grid shelf on the third runners of the ROASTING OVEN for 15-20 minutes or until the pastry is golden. Cool for 5 minutes, then turn out on to a serving plate pastry side down. Serve immediately.

COOK'S TIP

To prepare ahead, complete up to the end of step 5. Leave the vegetable mixture in the frying pan: cool, cover and chill in the fridge for up to 6 hours. To use, place the pan in the SIMMERING OVEN for 20 minutes to reheat the vegetables, then complete step 6.

CLAY POT STEW

PREPARATION TIME:
20 MINUTES +
OVERNIGHT
SOAKING

COOKING TIME:
3-8 HOURS OR
OVERNIGHT

190 CALS PER
SERVING

SERVES 6

FREEZING:
UNSUITABLE

To cook this dish and many other Aga recipes, you need a traditional earthenware deep casserole with a tight fitting lid. It is well worth treating yourself to one of these casseroles.

50 g (2 oz) dried chickpeas
50 g (2 oz) haricot beans
900 ml (1½ pints) vegetable stock, or water and 2 vegetable stock cubes
1 onion
2 carrots
2 parsnips
2 tomatoes
50 g (2 oz) bulgur wheat
60 ml (4 tbsp) olive oil
4 red chillies

15 ml (1 level tbsp) chopped fresh thyme
15 ml (1 level tbsp) chopped fresh mint
10 ml (2 level tsp) dried oregano
5-10 ml (1-2 level tsp) ground cumin
5-10 ml (1-2 level tsp) ground coriander
5 ml (1 level tsp) ground cinnamon
30 ml (2 level tbsp) tomato paste
salt and freshly ground black pepper
30 ml (2 level tbsp) chopped fresh parsley and extra-virgin olive oil, to serve

1 Soak the chickpeas and haricot beans separately in cold water overnight. Drain the chickpeas and haricot beans and place in a saucepan. Pour in the vegetable stock or water (see Cook's Tips) and bring to the boil. Cover and boil steadily for 10 minutes.

2 Peel and dice the onion, carrots, parsnips and tomatoes into 1.5 cm (¾ in) pieces.

3 Transfer the pulses and stock to a large 2¼ litre (4 pint) clay pot or casserole dish. Add the bulgur wheat, diced vegetables, tomatoes, olive oil, whole chillies, herbs and spices. Cover with a tight-fitting lid.

4 ■ ■ Cook in the SIMMERING OVEN for 5-8 hours or overnight if wished (some electric ovens are too hot for overnight cooking and some converted ones are cooler than average).

■ ■ ■ ■ Cook in the BAKING OVEN for 2 hours with the grid shelf on the floor of the oven.

5 Remove the lid and stir in the tomato paste and stock cubes if used. Re-cover the casserole and return to the grid shelf on the floor of the ROASTING or BAKING OVEN for a further 20-45 minutes until the beans and vegetables are tender.

6 Remove the stew from the oven and season generously with salt and pepper to taste. Allow to stand for 10 minutes before serving, sprinkled with chopped fresh parsley and drizzled with extra-virgin olive oil.

COOK'S TIPS

If possible, make this stew a day ahead to give the flavours time to develop.

If using stock cubes, delay adding these until the end of the cooking time. Crumble them in when adding the tomato paste.

Pulses should always be cooked without salt until tender. If using stock cubes, remember that these are also high in salt.

SPRING VEGETABLES IN TARRAGON DRESSING

PREPARATION TIME:
10 MINUTES

COOKING TIME:
25 MINUTES

110 CALS PER
SERVING

SERVES 6

FREEZING:
UNSUITABLE

Always snap off the end of the asparagus stalks to get rid of any inedible stringy ends and leave just the tender stalks and tips.

15 ml (1 tbsp) wine or cider vinegar
60 ml (4 tbsp) oil
15 ml (1 level tbsp) chopped fresh tarragon

salt and freshly ground black pepper
275 g (10 oz) small new potatoes
150 g (5 oz) asparagus tips
150 g (5 oz) mangetout

1 In a small bowl whisk together the vinegar, oil, tarragon and seasoning. Cover and set aside.

2 Cook the potatoes in an ovenproof pan of boiling, salted water. Bring to the boil, then transfer to the SIMMERING OVEN for 10-20 minutes or until just tender. Drain and plunge into a bowl of iced water and cool.

3 Bring a pan half-full of salted water to the boil. Add the asparagus spears and cook on the SIMMERING PLATE for 2-3 minutes until just beginning to soften. Drain and cool in iced water. Repeat this process with the mangetout, with just a cupful of water in the pan.

4 To serve, drain the vegetables well and toss in the dressing.

GREEN COUSCOUS WITH LEMON DRESSING

PREPARATION TIME:
15 MINUTES

COOKING TIME:
7-10 MINUTES

515 CALS PER
SERVING

SERVES 6

FREEZING:
UNSUITABLE

Couscous and bulgar wheat were the first instant dried foods ever invented. Dating back thousands of years in Middle Eastern cooking, they are just as popular with busy cooks today.

125 g (4 oz) rocket or watercress
2 bunches spring onions
1 cucumber
100 ml (4 fl oz) lemon juice

300 ml (½ pint) olive oil
salt and freshly ground black pepper
450g (1 lb) couscous

1 Remove any tough stalks from the rocket or watercress, then roughly chop. Chop the spring onions; halve, de-seed and roughly chop the cucumber. Set aside the vegetables. For the dressing, mix together the lemon juice, olive oil and seasoning; set aside.

2 Place the couscous in a bowl and cover with 1 litre (1¾ pints) warm water. Leave for 10-15 minutes to allow the grains to swell (see Aga Tip). Lightly rake the grains to remove any lumps.

3 Place the couscous in a large, shallow ovenproof dish, lightly greased. Cover with oiled foil. Bake on the grid shelf on the floor of the ROASTING OVEN for 7-10 minutes until hot.

4 Stir in the rocket or watercress, spring onions, cucumber and lemon dressing, then serve immediately (see Cook's Tip)

COOK'S TIP
This could also be served as a cold salad. As step 4, stir in the lemon dressing. Allow to cool, then add rocket, spring onions and cucumber before serving.

AGA TIP
Pre-soaking couscous allows it to cook more quickly. Couscous is usually steamed for 20-25 minutes, but this oven method is much more suitable as it conserves Aga heat and is much easier. The couscous is less likely to stick in lumps.

SUMMER VEGETABLES WITH LIME DRESSING

PREPARATION TIME:
5 MINUTES

COOKING TIME:
4 MINUTES

190-125 CALS PER
SERVING

SERVES 4-6

FREEZING:
UNSUITABLE

Choose a variety of green vegetables for this fresh, warm summer vegetable salad. The different textures and unusual dressing make this a memorable dish.

**700 g (1½ lb) summer vegetables
(see Cook's Tips)**
salt and freshly ground black pepper
**15 ml (1 tbsp) Japanese rice vinegar
(see Cook's Tips)**
1 lime
**5 ml (1 level tsp) light soft brown
(muscovado) sugar**

60 ml (4 tbsp) grapeseed oil
**60 ml (4 level tbsp) coconut cream
(see Cook's Tips)**
**30 ml (2 level tbsp) chopped coriander
coriander sprigs, to garnish**

1 Trim vegetables. Cut courgettes into batons. Cook broad beans in boiling, salted water for 1 minute. Drain; refresh in cold water. Cook the rest of vegetables for 3 minutes. Drain, refresh; drain all vegetables again.

2 Whisk vinegar, lime rind, 10 ml (2 tsp) juice, seasoning and sugar, then add the oil and cream. Pour over vegetables. Toss in coriander. Garnish and serve immediately.

COOK'S TIPS
Use a mixture of fine green beans, mangetout, sugar-snap peas, podded broad beans and courgettes.
If the broad beans are tough, remove the outer casing after blanching for fresh beans, or for frozen, thaw and remove.
If you cannot find Japanese rice vinegar, dilute white wine vinegar with a little water.
Spoon the thicker, creamy top off a can of coconut milk for this dressing. Use the remainder for soups.

ROSEMARY AND GORGONZOLA MASH

PREPARATION TIME:
15 MINUTES

COOKING TIME:
25 MINUTES

355 CALS PER
SERVING

SERVES 6

FREEZING:
UNSUITABLE

Everyone loves mashed potatoes. They never need to be dull with all the many possibilities of herbs, spices, cheeses and other flavourings that can be added.

1.4 kg (3 lb) old, floury potatoes
salt and freshly ground black pepper
3 sprigs fresh rosemary
100 ml (4 fl oz) warm milk

75 g (3 oz) butter, preferably unsalted
**125 g (4 oz) Gorgonzola, crumbled (see
Cook's Tip)**
fresh rosemary, to garnish

1 Peel and roughly chop the potatoes, bring to the boil in salted water with the rosemary, then cover and cook in the SIMMERING OVEN for 15-25 minutes or until very tender. Warm the milk in the SIMMERING OVEN.

2 Drain the potatoes; discard the rosemary. Return potatoes to the pan and, using a potato masher or ricer, mash them over a gentle heat for 2-3 minutes. Beat in warm milk and butter, then season well with pepper.

3 Stir the Gorgonzola into the potatoes; garnish with chopped fresh rosemary and sprigs.

COOK'S TIP
Gorgonzola is a blue-veined sharp-flavoured Italian cheese. If you prefer, you could substitute milder Dolcelatte.

RUSTIC POTATOES NORMANDE

PREPARATION TIME:
10 MINUTES

COOKING TIME:
2 MINUTES + 40-50
MINUTES

SERVES 4–6

340-225 CALS PER
SERVING

FREEZING:
UNSUITABLE

Many sliced, baked potato dishes have to be prepared and baked immediately, and served straight away to prevent discolouring and losing their creamy texture. This makes the timing inconvenient when entertaining. By parboiling the potatoes in advance they can be left ready for the oven later in the day.

1 kg (2 lb 3 oz) potatoes
350 ml (12 fl oz) milk
2 bay leaves
4 cloves garlic, sliced
50 g (2 oz) butter

5 ml (1 tsp) rosemary
5 ml (1 tsp) salt
2.5 ml (½ tsp) ground nutmeg
freshly ground black pepper

1 Peel and slice the potatoes 5 mm (½ in) thick. Place in a pan with the remaining ingredients.

2 Bring to the boil on the SIMMERING PLATE without a lid and simmer for 2 minutes, giving the occasional stir so that the loose potato starch gives the milk a creamier texture.

3 Turn into a 1.25 litre (2 pint) ovenproof dish and leave to cool. If prepared well in advance, cover the dish with foil and place in the refrigerator until cold.

4 Bake uncovered on the grid shelf on the second set of runners in the ROASTING OVEN for 30 minutes until golden and almost cooked, then transfer to the SIMMERING OVEN for 10-20 minutes until cooked and the milk still creamy. If kept too hot for too long, the potatoes may become dry.

COOK'S TIP
The top of the potato dish is not neatly arranged in overlapping rings, but left uneven and rustic in style, looking most appetising when golden brown.

CARROT AND PARSNIP PUREE WITH CORIANDER

PREPARATION TIME:
10 MINUTES

COOKING TIME:
20-25 MINUTES

130 CALS PER
SERVING

SERVES 4

FREEZING: SUITABLE

A wonderfully colourful purée that can be completed in a food processor for a velvety smooth texture.

450 g (1 lb) carrots
450 g (1 lb) parsnips
salt and freshly ground black pepper
15 ml (1 level tbsp) ground coriander

45 ml (3 level tbsp) reduced fat crème fraîche
60 ml (4 level tbsp) chopped fresh coriander

1 Peel and slice the vegetables. Place in a pan of cold, salted water. Bring to the boil; cover and cook in the SIMMERING OVEN for 20-25 minutes until soft. Drain well.

2 Purée the vegetables, coriander and crème fraîche (this may be done in a food processor). Season, stir in fresh coriander and serve.

BAKED BABY BEETROOT

PREPARATION TIME:
15 MINUTES

COOKING TIME:
1¼-1½ HOURS

90 CALS PER
SERVING

SERVES 6

FREEZING:
UNSUITABLE

This is a method of cooking beetroot with almost no mess. You may wish to wear rubber gloves to rub off the skins to avoid staining your fingers.

1.25 kg (2¾ lb) baby beetroot
15 g (½ oz) butter
salt and freshly ground black pepper

1 Trim the beetroot and carefully rinse in cold water, making sure you do not tear the skin.

2 Rub the butter over one side of a large piece of foil. Place the beetroot on the buttered foil, season and wrap well to form an airtight parcel.

3 Cook in an earthenware dish on the grid shelf on the floor of the ROASTING OVEN for 1¼-1½ hours or until soft and the skin comes away easily.

4 Allow to cool a little, rub off the skin and serve hot.

STIR-FRY GARLIC CABBAGE

PREPARATION TIME:
15 MINUTES

COOKING TIME:
5 MINUTES

40 CALS PER
SERVING

SERVES 8

FREEZING:
UNSUITABLE

This recipe is for Savoy cabbage, but you will find it also works well with spring cabbage, spring greens and shredded sprouts.

one small Savoy cabbage
30 ml (2 tbsp) olive oil
2 garlic cloves

salt and freshly ground black pepper
chopped parsley

1 Quarter and shred cabbage. Heat the olive oil in a heavy-based saucepan on the BOILING PLATE, add crushed garlic cloves and cook for 30 seconds.

2 Add the cabbage; cook, stirring, for 5 minutes. Season, stir in the chopped parsley and serve.

COOK'S TIP
Shred the darker, coarser leaves of the cabbage finely and the paler ones more broadly to even out the cooking time.

GRANDMOTHER'S CHRISTMAS PUDDING

PREPARATION TIME:
40 MINUTES +
MATURING FOR AT
LEAST 6 WEEKS FOR
OPTIMUM FLAVOUR

COOKING TIME:
8-10 HOURS +
2 HOURS

790 CALS PER
SERVING

SERVES 10

FREEZING:
SUITABLE, BUT
DOES KEEP ALMOST
INDEFINITELY IN A
COOL, DARK PLACE.

The joy of cooking Christmas pudding in the simmering oven of the Aga is the lack of anxiety that the steamer may boil dry and ruin the pudding.

butter, for greasing
finely grated rind of 1 lemon
75 g (3 oz) chopped mixed peel
225 g (8 oz) each seedless raisins, currants and sultanas
225 g (8 oz) suet (see Cook's Tips)
225 g (8 oz) fresh breadcrumbs
225 g (8 oz) soft light brown (muscovado) sugar

75 g (3 oz) plain flour
2.5 ml (½ level tsp) mixed spice
1.25 ml (¼ level tsp) salt
4 large eggs
150 ml (¼ pint) brandy, dark rum or medium sherry
100 ml (4 fl oz) milk
Brandy Butter or cream, to serve

1 Grease and baseline a 1.6-litre (2¾-pint) pudding basin (see Cook's Tips).
2 Place the finely grated lemon rind in a bowl with the mixed peel, raisins, currants and sultanas, suet, breadcrumbs, brown sugar, plain flour, mixed spice and salt. Whisk together the eggs, 100 ml (4 fl oz) brandy, rum or sherry and the milk. Stir the egg mixture into the fruit mixture until well blended, then spoon into the greased and lined pudding basin. Press the mixture down, cover with greaseproof paper and foil and secure with string. Cook within 24 hours.
3 Lower the basin into a large pan. Pour in enough boiling water to come halfway up the side of the basin. Cover tightly, bring to the boil and simmer gently for 15 minutes on the SIMMERING PLATE, then transfer to the SIMMERING OVEN for 8-10 hours (overnight is ideal, except some electric Agas with hotter simmering ovens where 5-6 hours will be sufficient).
4 Lift out the basin; allow to cool. Re-cover with fresh greaseproof paper and foil and secure with string. Store for at least six weeks in a cool, dark place.
5 To reheat, follow step 3, but allow the pudding to cook in the SIMMERING OVEN for only 2-3 hours, or simply place the bowl in the SIMMERING OVEN for 1-2 hours. Lift the pudding out of the pan, remove the covering, run a palette knife around the inside of the bowl and turn the pudding out on to a warmed serving plate. Warm the remaining brandy, rum or sherry in a pan or ladle and ignite it. While still flaming, pour it over the Christmas pudding and serve.

COOK'S TIP
When making this pudding, you can use beef or vegetarian suet or melted butter. If you're concerned about the calorie count or want to make a lighter pudding, use half the quantity of fat.

AGA TIPS
If short of space in your Aga, place the pudding directly in the SIMMERING OVEN for 1-2 hours, then on the back of the Aga to keep warm while the turkey is resting in the simmering oven. Return the pudding to the simmering oven while you are eating the turkey, then turn out just before serving.
In the simmering oven it is not usually necessary to top up the pan with boiling water during the cooking time to prevent it from boiling dry.
Slices of pudding may be reheated wrapped in foil in the SIMMERING OVEN for 30-40 minutes.

PLUM AND GINGER CRISP

PREPARATION TIME:
10 MINUTES

COOKING TIME:
ABOUT 30 MINUTES

345 CALS PER
SERVING

SERVES 8

FREEZING:
COMPLETE TO THE
END OF STEP 4,
COVER AND
FREEZE. THAW
OVERNIGHT AT
COOL ROOM
TEMPERATURE AND
COOK AS IN STEP 5.

A delicious version of the traditional fruit crumble and custard. Try it also with apricots, rhubarb or cooking apples.

3 pieces stem ginger, plus 45 ml (3 tbsp) syrup
1 lemon
1.1 kg (2½ lb) plums, such as Victoria
200 g (7 oz) light soft brown (muscovado) sugar

125 g (4 oz) plain flour
100 g (3½ oz) butter
375 ml carton fresh custard (see Cook's Tip)
double cream, to serve

1 Finely chop the ginger. Grate the lemon rind. Halve and stone the plums.

2 Place plums in a single layer, skin side down, in a shallow pan. Add the syrup and 75 g (3 oz) sugar. Cover and place in the SIMMERING OVEN until the juices begin to run. Bring to the boil and simmer for 3-5 minutes. Remove the lid, transfer to the BOILING PLATE and bubble for another 5 minutes or until most of the juice has evaporated; cool.

3 Place flour and remaining sugar in a food processor blend for 2-3 seconds. Add the diced butter and process until mixture resembles breadcrumbs. Add the stem ginger and lemon rind. Blend for 2-3 seconds.

4 Spoon custard into eight 150 ml (5 fl oz) ramekins or ovenproof dishes. Cover with a layer of the plums. Sprinkle crumbs over the plums, pressing lightly and evenly.

5 Place dishes in a large roasting tin with 1 litre (1¾ pints) cold water. Cook on the bottom runners of the ROASTING OVEN for 10 minutes, then turn the roasting tin round to ensure even cooking and cook for a further 5-10 minutes or until the crumbs form a golden crust. Cool slightly, then serve with double cream.

COOK'S TIP
You can use Crème Anglaise (see page 111) instead of custard if you wish.

BLACKBERRY GRANITA

PREPARATION TIME:
15 MINUTES +
FREEZING

COOKING TIME:
2 MINUTES

100 CALS PER
SERVING

SERVES 6

FREEZING:
COMPLETE TO THE
END OF STEP 2 AND
FREEZE FOR UP TO
A MONTH. TO USE,
COMPLETE THE
RECIPE.

A wonderfully refreshing dessert which can also be made with blackcurrants. Try also pale fruits like apricots with a sweet white wine and schnaps to replace the red wine and cassis.

350 g (12 oz) blackberries
75 g (3 oz) caster sugar
150 ml (¼ pint) red wine

50 ml (2 fl oz) creme de cassis
extra blackberries, to serve

1 Place the blackberries in a saucepan with the sugar, wine, cassis and 150 ml (¼ pint) water. Bring to the boil and bubble on the SIMMERING PLATE for 1-2 minutes or until the fruit has softened.

2 Allow the mixture to cool for a few minutes, then strain the blackberries, reserving the juice. Place the blackberries in a blender or food processor and pulse until well broken down. Sieve the cooled fruit and mix the purée with the reserved juice. Pour into a shallow, non-reactive metal container and freeze for at least 2½-3 hours or until the mixture is just firm. Stir after the first 2 hours to break up the ice crystals. Cover.

3 To serve, place in the fridge for 15 minutes before needed. Use a spoon to break down the mixture, then serve in chilled glasses with extra berries.

PEACH AND CARDAMOM PUDDING

PREPARATION TIME:
20 MINUTES +
INFUSING

COOKING TIME:
ABOUT I HOUR

590-395 CALS PER
SERVING

SERVES 4-6

FREEZING:
UNSUITABLE

There is a wide range of exotic dried druits now available in larger supermarkets. Some are drier in texture than others so to make sure the fruit is really soft, cook for slightly longer if necessary.

225 g (8 oz) dried, ready-to-eat peaches
150 ml (¼ pint) fresh orange juice
60 ml (4 tbsp) dessert wine or orange liqueur, such as Grand Marnier
2 green cardamom pods
100 ml (4 fl oz) milk
142 ml (5 fl oz) carton double cream

4 eggs
125 g (4 oz) caster sugar
25 g (1 oz) plain flour
butter, for greasing
pared orange rind, to decorate
warm apricot jam, to glaze (optional)

1 Bring the peaches to the boil in the orange juice in an ovenproof pan on the BOILING PLATE, then place in the SIMMERING OVEN for 30 minutes. Add liqueur; cool.
2 Split the cardamom pods to expose the black seeds, then place in a small ovenproof pan with the milk and double cream. Bring to the boil on the BOILING PLATE, then leave to infuse in the SIMMERING OVEN for about 15 minutes.
3 Meanwhile, with an electric whisk, whisk the eggs and sugar until thick and pale. Gradually whisk in the flour. Strain the cream mixture, then gradually whisk into egg mixture.
4 Drain the peaches, reserving any liquid, then fold liquid into the cream mixture. Spoon peaches into the base of a 3 cm (1¼ in) deep, 1.7-litre (3-pint) buttered ovenproof dish. Pour the cream mixture over the peaches.
5 ▨ ▨ Bake in a small roasting tin containing 500 ml (¾ pint) boiling water set on the grid shelf on the floor of the ROASTING OVEN. Place a cold roasting tin on the second runners. After 30 minutes, pour 500 ml (¾ pint) cold water into the top tin and cook for a further 10-20 minutes until lightly set and golden brown.
▨ ▨ ▨ Bake in the middle of the BAKING OVEN in a roasting tin for 45-50 minutes.
6 Decorate with pared orange rind and brush with warmed apricot jam, if using. Serve immediately.

COOK'S TIP
To prepare ahead, complete to the end of step 4 up to 4 hours ahead.

STICKY TOFFEE PUDDINGS

PREPARATION TIME:
20 MINUTES

COOKING TIME:
25-30 MINUTES +
RESTING

570 CALS PER
SERVING

SERVES 4

FREEZING: SUITABLE

One of the most popular puds ever! The moulds are widely available in cook shops, or use large ramekins instead.

15 ml (1 tbsp) golden syrup
15 ml (1 tbsp) black treacle
150 g (5 oz) butter, softened
25 g (1 oz) pecan nuts or walnuts
75 g (3 oz) self-raising flour

125 g (4 oz) caster sugar
2 large eggs
custard, cream or Crème Anglaise, to serve

1 Put the syrup, treacle and 25 g (1 oz) of the butter into a bowl. Warm in the SIMMERING OVEN for 5-10 minutes and stir until smooth. Divide the mixture between four 150 ml (¼ pint) greased timbales or ramekins and set aside.
2 Put the remaining butter, caster sugar, nuts and eggs into a food processor and blend well. Add the flour; blend again for 10 seconds.
3 Spoon the sponge mixture into the timbales or ramekins, covering the syrup mixture.
4 ▨ ▨ Place in a small roasting tin and set on the grid shelf on the floor at the front of the ROASTING OVEN with the cold plain shelf on the third runners above for 20-25 minutes until risen and golden.

STICKY TOFFEE PUDDINGS

■ ■ ■ ■ Place in a small roasting tin on the middle runners of the BAKING OVEN for 25-30 minutes.

5 Remove the puddings from the oven and leave to rest for 5 minutes, then unmould on to warmed serving plates. Serve immediately with custard, cream or Crème Anglaise.

CREME ANGLAISE

PREPARATION TIME:
20 MINUTES +
INFUSING

COOKING TIME:
15 MINUTES

115 CALS PER
SERVING

SERVES 4

FREEZING:
UNSUITABLE

This classic custard forms the base of many traditional desserts, as well as making an excellent accompaniment to all sponge puddings and tarts.

1 vanilla pod
300 ml (½ pint) milk

3 large egg yolks (see Cook's Tips)
15 ml (1 level tbsp) caster sugar

1 Split the vanilla pod to reveal the seeds. Pour the milk into a heavy-based saucepan, add the vanilla pod, cover and place in the SIMMERING OVEN to infuse for 20 minutes. Remove the vanilla pod and store for re-use.

2 Whisk the egg yolks and sugar together in a bowl until thick and creamy. Gradually whisk in the hot milk, then strain back into the pan. Cook on the SIMMERING PLATE, stirring constantly with a wooden spoon, until the custard thickens enough to coat the back of the spoon lightly; don't allow the custard to boil or it may curdle (see Cook's Tips).

3 Pour into a jug and serve hot or cold with the Sticky Toffee Puddings.

COOK'S TIPS
To rescue a custard that's beginning to separate and curdle, strain immediately into a cold bowl, add a few ice cubes and whisk vigorously to reduce the temperature; the custard should become smooth.
The young, the elderly, pregnant women and those with immune-deficiency diseases should not eat raw or lightly cooked eggs, to avoid the risk of salmonella.

BAKED APPLE AND LEMON TARTLETS

PREPARATION TIME:
40 MINUTES +
CHILLING

COOKING TIME:
30-50 MINUTES

625 CALS PER
SERVING

SERVES 8

FREEZING:
COMPLETE TO THE
END OF STEP 6.
COOL, WRAP AND
FREEZE. TO USE,
RETURN TO THE
TINS, THEN THAW
OVERNIGHT AT
COOL ROOM
TEMPERATURE.
REHEAT IN THE
ROASTING OVEN
FOR 5-10 MINUTES.

You can also bake this recipe as one large tart in a 25 cm (10 in) tin if you do not have small, individual tartlet tins.

3 eggs
pinch of salt
300 g (11 oz) plain flour
75 g (3 oz) icing sugar
300 g (11 oz) butter
2 lemons

700 g (1½ lb) Bramley or Granny Smith apples
225 g (8 oz) caster sugar
5 ml (1 level tsp) arrowroot
caster sugar and cinnamon, for dusting
clotted cream, to serve

1 Beat one egg with a pinch of salt; set aside 15 ml (1 tbsp). Process the flour, icing sugar and 175 g (6 oz) of the butter in a food processor until the mixture resembles fine crumbs. Add the remaining beaten egg with 45 ml (3 tbsp) water; pulse until pastry comes together. Divide into eight balls; chill for 30 minutes.

2 Roll out pastry and line eight 8 cm (3⅓ in) base-measurement 3 cm (1¼ in) deep, fluted, loose-bottomed tartlet tins. Prick the bases and chill for 20 minutes. Line the tins with greaseproof paper or muffin cases and baking beans. Place in a large roasting tin and set on the grid shelf on the floor of the ROASTING OVEN and bake for 15 minutes. Remove greaseproof paper and baking beans; brush the inside of the pastry with reserved beaten egg to seal. Return to the oven for a further 2-3 minutes, turning the tray round to ensure even cooking; set aside.

3 Grate rind and squeeze the lemon juice. Peel, core and thinly slice the apples. Toss them in 30 ml (2 tbsp) lemon juice, then fry in 25 g (1 oz) melted butter for 1-2 minutes. Spoon into the pastry cases.

4 Soften the remaining 125 g (4 oz) butter by placing in an ovenproof bowl on the back of the Aga for 5-10 minutes; process with the caster sugar for 3 minutes or until soft, well combined and pale. Add the lemon rind, arrowroot and remaining two eggs; blend for 2 minutes or until well combined.

5 With the food processor running, add remaining lemon juice (see Cook's Tip). Blend for 1 minute or until combined. Pour over the apples. Dust with caster sugar.

6 ■ ■ Set the roasting tin of tarts on the grid shelf on the floor of the ROASTING OVEN and bake for 25-30 minutes. After 10-15 minutes, turn the tin around for even cooking and return the tin to the oven with the cold plain shelf above on the third runners for the remaining cooking time or until pastry is golden and apples start to caramelize. The filling will puff up during cooking and sink on cooling.

■ ■ ■ ■ Cook in the middle of the BAKING OVEN for 40-50 minutes, turning the tin round after 30 minutes to ensure even cooking.

Remove from tins and serve warm or cold with clotted cream, dusted with cinnamon.

COOK'S TIP
The lemon juice is added at the last minute to prevent the mixture curdling.

CREAMY RICE PUDDING WITH HOT TIPSY PINEAPPLE

PREPARATION TIME:
15 MINUTES

COOKING TIME:
40 MINUTES

570 CALS PER
SERVING

SERVES 6

FREEZING:
UNSUITABLE

For the best results serve this rice pudding well chilled, almost iced.

I lemon
I vanilla pod (see Cook's Tips)
175 g (6 oz) arborio rice
25 g (1 oz) butter
I cinnamon stick

one 405g can condensed milk
284 ml (10 fl oz) carton double cream
soft dark brown sugar, to decorate

1 Grate the zest from the lemon and squeeze the juice. Split the vanilla pod in half lengthways. Thoroughly wash the arborio rice under cold water until the water runs clear.

2 Melt the butter in a large saucepan, then add the rice and stir well until all the grains are coated. Add the zest and the juice of the lemon, the split vanilla pod, cinnamon stick and about 150 ml (5 fl oz) boiling water and cook on the SIMMERING PLATE, stirring all the time, for I minute, then place on the floor of the SIMMERING OVEN for 2-3 minutes, covered, until all the liquid has been absorbed. Continue adding boiling water, in the same amounts and cooking on top and then in the oven as before, until the rice is tender and cooked through. In all, you should use about 600 ml (1 pint) of boiling water.

3 Stir in the condensed milk and continue to cook on top and then in the SIMMERING OVEN as before until mixture has lightly thickened and all the excess liquid has evaporated. Pour into a bowl and cool quickly (the rice should be soft and the mixture should resemble a creamy risotto).

4 Remove the vanilla pod and the cinnamon stick. Whip the double cream to soft peaks and fold it into the cold rice (see Cook's Tips). Cover and chill thoroughly.

5 Serve the ice-cold pudding with Hot Tipsy Pineapple (see below), sprinkled with soft dark brown sugar to decorate.

COOK'S TIPS
If you are unable to find a vanilla pod, stir in about ¼ level tsp vanilla extract or essence to taste at the end of step 3.
If you find that the rice has become very thick and stiff on cooling, stir in a little milk to soften the mixture before folding in the double cream.

HOT TIPSY PINEAPPLE

PREPARATION TIME:
15 MINUTES

COOKING TIME:
15 MINUTES

370 CALS PER
SERVING

SERVES 6

FREEZING:
UNSUITABLE

I medium pineapple, about 1.4 kg (3 lb)
125 g (4 oz) butter
75 g (3 oz) soft dark brown sugar

200 ml (7 fl oz) white rum
juice of I small orange

1 Remove all the skin from the pineapple and cut the fruit into thin slices (see Cook's Tip).

2 In a large frying pan, melt the butter and add the sugar, rum and orange juice. When the sugar has dissolved, bring to the boil and bubble vigorously for 2-3 minutes on the BOILING PLATE.

3 Add the pineapple in 2 batches; cook each batch for about 1 minute.

4 While still hot, serve with the buttery rum sauce and spoonfuls of the chilled Creamy Rice Pudding.

COOK'S TIP
To remove the core easily from the pineapple, use an apple corer.

CHOCOLATE ROULADE

PREPARATION TIME:
30 MINUTES +
CHILLING

COOKING TIME:
25 MINUTES

325 CALS PER
SERVING

SERVES 10

FREEZING:
COMPLETE TO END
OF STEP 7, WRAP
AND FREEZE. THAW
AT COOL ROOM
TEMPERATURE
OVERNIGHT, THEN
COMPLETE THE
RECIPE.

Chocolate Roulade is a baked chocolate mousse mixture that should melt in the mouth. Like Coronation Chicken, it was part of the menu for the coronation for Elizabeth II.

175 g (6 oz) plain chocolate (see Cook's Tips)
6 large eggs
175 g (6 oz) caster sugar, plus 5 ml (1 level tsp) and extra for dusting
284 ml (10 fl oz) carton whipping cream

2.5 ml (½ tsp) vanilla extract (see Cook's Tips)
cocoa, for sprinkling
chocolate shavings, for decorating

1 Base-line the large roasting tin with non-stick baking parchment.
2 Break up the chocolate and place in a small heatproof bowl with 150 ml (¼ pint) boiling water. Melt at the front of the SIMMERING OVEN for 7-10 minutes, then stir until smooth.
3 Meanwhile, separate eggs. Place yolks in a bowl with 175 g (6 oz) caster sugar and beat with an electric whisk until light in colour and thick. Beat in the warm, liquid chocolate until blended.
4 In a large bowl, whisk the egg whites until they just hold a soft peak (see Cook's Tips). Beat a quarter of the egg white into the chocolate mixture to loosen it, then carefully fold into the remaining egg white in the bowl with a large metal spoon or plastic spatula- do not over-fold. Pour immediately into the prepared tin.
5 ■■ Bake on the grid shelf on the floor of the ROASTING OVEN with the cold plain shelf on the third runners for 22-25 minutes (see Cook's Tips).
■■■■ Bake on the middle runners of the BAKING OVEN for 25 minutes (see Cook's Tips). To ensure even cooking, turn the tin round after the first 15 minutes. Allow the roulade to cool a little in the tin, then cover with clingfilm and a clean, damp cloth. Once cold, cover cloth with clingfilm; refrigerate for at least 6 hours or overnight.
6 Whip the cream until it just begins to thicken, add 5 ml (1 level tsp) caster sugar and the vanilla extract. Continue to whip until it just holds its shape.
7 Lightly dust a large sheet of greaseproof paper with caster sugar. Remove clingfilm and cloth from the roulade; carefully turn out on to greaseproof paper. Cut 5 mm (¼ in) off two short

sides of the roulade to neaten. Spread cream over the roulade and roll up tightly from the long side, using greaseproof paper to help (don't worry if the sponge cracks).

8 Transfer to a serving dish, sprinkle with cocoa and decorate with chocolate shavings.

COOK'S TIPS

Use chocolate with 60-70% cocoa solids. Pure vanilla extract has a much better flavour than essence. Ensure the whisk is absolutely clean and free of any trace of fat before whisking the egg whites. Whisk the whites in a metal or glass bowl rather than a plastic or earthenware one to make them less rubbery in texture. Don't whisk whites too stiffly otherwise they will be difficult to incorporate. A crust develops while baking, so it is hard to see if the roulade is cooked. Press with your fingertips or use a skewer – the sponge should spring back.

To prepare ahead, complete step 7 up to 6 hours ahead or overnight, then cover and refrigerate.

LEMON AND LIME PAVLOVA PIE

PREPARATION TIME:
1 HOUR + CHILLING

COOKING TIME:
ABOUT 1 HOUR
20 MINUTES

815 CALS PER
SERVING

SERVES 6

FREEZING:
UNSUITABLE,
ALTHOUGH THE
RAW PASTRY MAY
BE FROZEN

An updated recipe for addicts of the old favourite, Lemon Meringue Pie!

9 eggs (or 6 eggs plus 3 yolks)
225 g (8 oz) plain flour
200 g (7 oz) butter
175 g (6 oz) caster sugar, plus 15 ml (1 level tbsp)
5 limes

2 large lemons
65 ml (4 level tbsp, plus 1 level tsp) cornflour
5 ml (1 tsp) distilled vinegar
275 g (10 oz) icing sugar, plus extra for dusting

1 Lightly beat one egg. In a food processor, blend the flour with 150 g (5 oz) of the butter, 15 ml (1 level tbsp) of the caster sugar and the grated rind of one of the limes until mixture resembles fine breadcrumbs. Reserving 10 ml (2 tsp) beaten egg, add remainder to pastry mixture with 15 ml (1 tbsp) water. Pulse until the pastry comes together; chill for 30 minutes.

2 Roll out pastry and line a 23 cm (9 in) base, 4 cm (½ in) deep, loose-bottomed flan tin. Prick base; chill for 30 minutes. Line pastry with greaseproof paper and baking beans; bake blind on the floor of the ROASTING OVEN for 10-12 minutes. Remove paper and beans; cook for a further 7-10 minutes until golden. Brush with reserved egg to seal cracks, then return to the oven for 1 minute; cool.

3 Finely grate rind from remaining four limes and the lemons. Place in a pan with juice of lemons and all five limes. Make up to 600 ml (21 fl oz) with water; add the remaining caster sugar and butter; heat gently on the SIMMERING PLATE until sugar dissolves.

4 Separate the remaining eggs. Whisk 60 ml (4 level tbsp) cornflour with 90 ml (6 tbsp) water and all the egg yolks. Pour into a pan, bring to boil slowly on the SIMMERING PLATE, stirring. Cook for 1-2 minutes until slightly thickened. Cool; pour into pastry case.

5 Place five egg whites, vinegar, remaining 5 ml (1 level tsp) cornflour and the icing sugar in a bowl over a pan of barely simmering water. With an electric whisk, whisk for 10 minutes until thick and shiny. Off the heat, whisk on lowest setting for 5-10 minutes or until bowl feels cool.

6 Pile the meringue on to the filled pastry case, covering the filling but leaving the meringue in rough peaks (see Cook's Tip). Place on the floor at the back of the SIMMERING OVEN and cook for 50 minutes-1 hour or it resembles a firm marshmallow in texture, then place on the grid shelf on the floor of the ROASTING OVEN with the cold plain shelf on the third runners for 1-2 minutes until golden. Cool for 20 minutes; dust with icing sugar and serve.

COOK'S TIP

Five egg whites, 50 ml (10 level tsp) cornflour, 5 ml (1 tsp) distilled vinegar and 275 g (10 oz) icing sugar will cover filling generously. The remaining egg whites can be poured into a screw-top jar and frozen for up to 6 months. For a truly extravagant topping, use all eight egg whites with 450 g (1 lb) icing sugar (cornflour and vinegar quantities remain the same).

AUTUMN ALMOND PANCAKES

PREPARATION TIME:
40 MINUTES +
STANDING

COOKING TIME:
40 MINUTES-
I HOUR 25 MINUTES

275 CALS PER
SERVING

SERVES 8

FREEZING:
COMPLETE TO THE
END OF STEP 5,
WRAP AND FREEZE.
TO USE FROM
FROZEN, CONTINUE
AS IN STEP 5,
COVERING THE
PANCAKES WITH
THE COLD PLAIN
SHELF ON THE
SECOND RUNNERS
AFTER 20-30
MINUTES AND
COOKING FOR
50 MINUTES MORE,
UNTIL HOT
THROUGH.

A delicious 'cake' of wafer thin layers of pancakes with a hot almond soufflé mix in between, served with autumn fruits.

FOR THE BATTER
125 g (4 oz) plain white flour
I egg, plus I egg yolk
15 ml (I tbsp) oil
300 ml (½ pint) milk

FOR THE FILLING
300 ml (½ pint) milk
75 g (3 oz) ground almonds
2 eggs, separated
50 g (2 oz) caster sugar

20 ml (4 level tsp) plain white flour
25 ml (5 level tsp) cornflour
almond essence
30 ml (2 tbsp) double cream
oil and butter, for greasing
a little melted butter
icing sugar, for dusting
poached plums and blackberries, to accompany

I Blend the flour, egg yolk, oil and milk in a processor until the batter is the thickness of single cream. Cover, set aside in a cool place for at least 30 minutes.

2 Meanwhile, make the filling. Bring the milk and ground almonds slowly to the boil on the SIMMERING PLATE, cover and set aside for 15 minutes. Beat the egg yolks with 25 g (I oz) sugar until fluffy. Beat in the flours, then blend in the milk mixture. Return to the rinsed-out pan and stir slowly to the boil on the SIMMERING PLATE. Add a few drops of almond essence and float the cream on the top to prevent a skin forming. Cover and cool.

3 Whisk the egg whites until stiff, then whisk in the remaining sugar to make a stiff, shiny mixture; carefully fold into the cooled almond custard. Cover and set aside.

4 Heat and lightly oil a 18 cm (7 in) base pancake pan. Fry paper-thin pancakes and set aside (see Aga Tips).

5 Lightly butter a 18-20.5 cm (7-8 in) round ovenproof dish. Lay a pancake in the bottom, spread about 30 ml (2 tbsp) custard on the pancake and lay a second pancake on top. Continue until all the filling is used. Finish with a pancake – you will probably use 8 in all (see Cook's Tip). Brush the top with melted butter.

6 Dust heavily with icing sugar and cook on the grid shelf on the floor of the ROASTING OVEN for 40-45 minutes or until hot to the centre. Cover pancakes with the cold plain shelf on the second runners if they are becoming too brown. Cut into wedges and serve immediately with poached plums and blackberries.

COOK'S TIP
Leftover pancakes freeze well without a filling; interleave with greaseproof paper so you can defrost as many as needed.

AGA TIP
Lightly oil the SIMMERING PLATE or a second frying pan by the pancake pan. After frying the first side of the pancake on the BOILING PLATE, flip it onto the SIMMERING PLATE or second pan to cook the second side, then fry another. It'll take half the time.

GRAND MARNIER SOUFFLE PARCELS

PREPARATION TIME:
45 MINUTES +
RESTING

COOKING TIME:
I HOUR

490 CALS PER
SERVING

SERVES 8

FREEZING:
COMPLETE STEP 5.
WRAP AND FREEZE
PANCAKES, ORANGE
SEGMENTS AND
SAUCE SEPARATELY.
COOK PANCAKES
FROM FROZEN AS
STEP 6 FOR 15-17
MINUTES. THAW
ORANGE SEGMENTS
AND SAUCE FOR 2-3
HOURS AT COOL
ROOM
TEMPERATURE.

A stunning pudding with a special orange and caramel sauce which is perfect when cooked straight from the freezer.

225 g (8 oz) plain flour
150 g (6 oz) caster sugar
salt
7 eggs
30 ml (2 tbsp) oil
750 ml (1¼ pints) milk
25 g (1 oz) butter
I large lemon
4 large oranges

125 ml (5 fl oz) Grand Marnier
icing sugar for dusting, gold thread to decorate

FOR THE ORANGE SAUCE
75 g (3 oz) butter
75 g (3 oz) sugar
300 ml (½ pint) orange juice
50 ml (2 fl oz) Grand Marnier

1 Mix 175 g (6 oz) flour, 25 g (1 oz) caster sugar, a pinch of salt, three eggs and the oil with 450 ml (¾ pint) milk to make a smooth batter. Cover; set aside for at least 30 minutes.

2 Melt butter in a small bowl in the SIMMERING OVEN; brush a little on to a 23 cm (9 in) non-stick crêpe pan. Heat the crêpe pan on the BOILING PLATE until very hot; pour in a small ladleful of batter (tilt pan to give a thin, even layer). Cook until well browned; flip over onto the SIMMERING PLATE for 30 seconds, then cool on a folded tea towel. Make about 12 pancakes (store the extra, interleaved with greaseproof paper and wrapped in foil, in the fridge for up to two days or in the freezer). Cover; set aside.

3 Infuse zest of the lemon and one orange with the remaining milk and the Grand Marnier for 30 minutes in the SIMMERING OVEN. Peel the oranges, removing the pith. Cut the flesh into segments; set aside.

4 Separate remaining eggs. Beat yolks with 25 g (1 oz) sugar until thick; stir in remaining flour. Bring infused milk to the boil; strain on to egg-yolk mixture, stirring all the time. Return to pan; bring to the boil on the SIMMERING PLATE, stirring continuously. Place custard immediately in a bowl, cover with clingfilm; leave to cool.

5 Meanwhile, make the sauce. Place the butter and sugar in a pan and cook on the SIMMERING PLATE, stirring, for 15 minutes or until golden caramel. Off the heat, stir in the orange juice. Return to the boil, then bubble gently for 15 minutes until syrupy. Remove from the heat and stir in the Grand Marnier.

6 Whisk egg whites until stiff; whisk in remaining caster sugar until stiff. Whisk a quarter of the mixture into the custard until smooth then fold in the rest. Place 45-60 ml (3-4 level tbsp) in the centre of each pancake, bring edges together and tie with string (see Cook's Tip).

7 Dust with icing sugar; cook on a non-stick baking on the third runners of the ROASTING OVEN for 7 minutes, then turn the tray round and cook for a further 3 minutes. Remove string; tie with gold thread. Dust with icing sugar. Serve immediately with orange segments and sauce.

COOK'S TIP
To fill pancakes easily, line a small, wide bowl or teacup with a pancake, fill, shape and tie. Don't overfill or it may burst.

117

CINNAMON CUSTARD TART WITH CARAMELIZED FRUITS

PREPARATION TIME: 50 MINUTES + CHILLING FOR 1 HOUR AND STANDING FOR 20-30 MINUTES

COOKING TIME: 1½ HOURS

655 CALS PER SERVING

SERVES 8

FREEZING: COMPLETE STEP 4, COOL, PACK AND FREEZE. DEFROST AT COOL ROOM TEMPERATURE OVERNIGHT. COMPLETE THE RECIPE (SEE AGA TIP).

ILLUSTRATED OPPOSITE

You can use any fruit to accompany this traditional tart, but make sure you spoon the fruit over at the last moment – or serve the fruit separately in a shallow serving dish.

250 g (9 oz) plain flour, plus extra for dusting
100 g (3½ oz) butter
100 g (3½ oz) icing sugar
4 large eggs
450 ml (¾ pint) milk

248 ml (10 fl oz) carton double cream
1 vanilla pod
1 large cinnamon stick
275 g (10 oz) caster sugar
1 mango, 1 small pineapple, 2 clementines and 125 g (4 oz) kumquats, to accompany

1 Place the flour, butter and icing sugar in a food processor and process until the mixture forms fine crumbs. Lightly beat one egg and add to the flour mixture with 15 ml (1 tbsp) water. Process until the crumbs just come together to make a dough. Wrap the pastry in clingfilm and refrigerate if necessary until firm enough to roll.

2 Roll the pastry out on a lightly floured worksurface and use to line a deep 23 cm (9 in) loose-bottomed tart tin. Prick the base well and line with greaseproof paper and baking beans. Refrigerate for 30 minutes. Place on a baking tray and bake on the floor of the ROASTING OVEN for 7-8 minutes, then remove the paper and baking beans and cook for a further 5-7 minutes or until the base of the pastry is cooked and looks dry. Lightly whisk the three remaining eggs. Use 15 ml (1 tbsp) beaten egg to brush over the base and sides of the pastry case to seal, then return to the oven for a further 1-2 minutes.

3 Place the milk, cream, split vanilla pod and crumbled cinnamon stick in a large pan. Bring slowly to the boil on the SIMMERING PLATE, then infuse for 20 minutes in the SIMMERING OVEN. Mix the remaining whisked egg with 150 g (5 oz) sugar. Stir the hot milk into the egg mixture, strain through a fine sieve into a jug and pour into the tart (see Cook's Tips).

4 ■ ■ Place in the roasting tin on the bottom runners of the ROASTING OVEN and set the cold plain shelf on the third runners above. Cook for 20 minutes until beginning to set, then transfer to the top runners of the SIMMERING OVEN for 10-15 minutes or until the filling has just set in the middle (see Cook's Tips).

■ ■ ■ ■ Place in the roasting tin on the bottom runners of the BAKING OVEN and set the cold plain shelf on the top runners. Bake for 30 minutes or until the filling has just set in the middle (see Cook's Tips).

Transfer the tart to the SIMMERING OVEN for 15 minutes before taking it out and setting aside to cool. Leave in the tin for 20-30 minutes before transferring to a rack to cool completely.

5 To decorate, cut thick slices of mango, pineapple, clementines and kumquats and spread over two non-stick baking sheets. Place remaining sugar in a small, heavy-based saucepan. Cook on the SIMMERING PLATE until the sugar begins to dissolve and cook to a pale caramel. Cool a little and drizzle over the fruit with a fork. Allow to set (see Cook's Tips). Cut the tart into portions and spoon the fruit over the top just before serving.

COOK'S TIPS
It may be easiest to fill the flan case without taking it out of the oven completely. This will avoid the custard spilling as you put it back. The custard will firm further on cooling.
The caramel will stay brittle for 1-2 hours. If you use strawberries, clementine segments or kumquats with a dry surface it will stay brittle for 3-4 hours, so choose these if making well in advance.
To cook ahead, complete step 4; store in an airtight container in fridge for up to three days.

AGA TIP
To crisp the pastry after it has been prepared or frozen ahead, place in the SIMMERING OVEN while you have your main course and serve just warm.

GLAZED BRANDIED PRUNE TART

PREPARATION TIME:
25 MINUTES +
SOAKING, CHILLING
AND INFUSING

COOKING TIME:
50 MINUTES

450 CALS PER
SERVING

SERVES 8

FREEZING:
UNSUITABLE,
ALTHOUGH RAW
PASTRY CAN BE
FROZEN

Choose the best and biggest prunes you can to make this French dessert. You can use Armagnac instead of brandy if you wish.

FOR THE FILLING
250 g (9 oz) no-soak dried pitted prunes
75 ml (5 tbsp) brandy
1 vanilla pod
142 ml (5 fl oz) carton double cream
142 ml (5 fl oz) carton single cream
25 g (1 oz) caster sugar
2 large eggs

FOR THE PASTRY
175 g (6 oz) plain white flour
75 g (3 oz) lightly salted butter
75 g (3 oz) caster sugar
3 large egg yolks
60 ml (4 level tbsp) apricot jam and
30 ml (2 tbsp) brandy, to glaze
crème fraîche, to serve

1 For the filling, put the dried prunes into a small bowl or jam jar, add the brandy, then cover and leave to soak in the SIMMERING OVEN for about 1 hour until the brandy is absorbed.

2 To make the pastry, sift the flour into a bowl, then rub in the butter until the mixture resembles fine breadcrumbs. Stir in the caster sugar, add the egg yolks and mix to a soft dough. Knead lightly.

3 Roll out the pastry on a lightly floured worksurface and line a 23-24 cm (9-9½ in) diameter, 2.5 cm (1 in) deep, loose-based flan tin. Refrigerate for 20 minutes.

4 Meanwhile, split the vanilla pod to reveal the seeds and place in an ovenproof pan with the double cream. Bring just to the boil on the BOILING PLATE, then cover and place in the SIMMERING OVEN to infuse for 20 minutes.

5 Prick the pastry base with a fork, then line with greaseproof paper and baking beans. Place on the floor at the front of the ROASTING OVEN with the cold baking sheet set on the third runners and bake blind for 7-10 minutes until the pastry is coloured around the edge. Remove the greaseproof paper and beans and return to the oven with the darkest edge towards the front for a further 5 minutes until the pastry is pale golden.

6 Remove the vanilla pod, wipe and store for re-use. Pour the infused cream into a bowl, then add the single cream, sugar and eggs. Beat well. Scatter the prunes in the pastry case, then pour the cream mixture around them.

7 ■ ■ Cook in a roasting tin on the grid shelf on the floor of the ROASTING OVEN with the cold plain shelf on the third runners above for 15 minutes, then remove the top baking tray and allow to brown and set for a further 5-10 minutes.
■ ■ ■ ■ Cook in a roasting tin on the bottom runners of the BAKING OVEN for 30 minutes until the custard is just set in the centre.

8 Meanwhile, sieve the jam into a bowl, warm in the SIMMERING OVEN for 10-15 minutes, add the brandy and beat gently until smooth. Brush the glaze over the tart and serve warm or cold with crème fraîche.

AGA TIP
To remove the tight lid of a jam jar, place the jar upside-down on the SIMMERING PLATE for 4-6 seconds then, wearing a rubber glove, unscrew.

PECAN STREUSEL CHEESECAKE WITH MAPLE SAUCE

PREPARATION TIME:
40 MINUTES +
CHILLING

COOKING TIME:
45 MINUTES-1 HOUR
20 MINUTES

745 CALS PER
SERVING

SERVES 8

FREEZING: SUITABLE

Cheesecakes are one of the all-time great American desserts. This version is partnered by another delicious American invention – maple sauce.

200 g (7 oz) shortbread-style biscuits
90 g (3 oz) butter
3 x 200 g (7oz) packets half-fat soft cheese
275 g (10 oz) light soft brown sugar
3 eggs
150 ml (5 fl oz) carton double cream
15 ml (1 tbsp) vanilla essence

125 g (4 oz) chopped pecan nuts
icing sugar, for dusting

FOR THE MAPLE SAUCE
50 g (2 oz) butter
25 g (1 oz) caster sugar
60 ml (4 level tbsp) maple syrup
150 ml (5 fl oz) double cream

1 Grease and base-line a 23 cm (9 in) spring-release cake tin with non-stick baking parchment. Place biscuits in a food processor and process until mixture resembles fine crumbs. In an ovenproof bowl, melt 30 g (1 oz) of the butter in the SIMMERING OVEN and stir into 125 g (4 oz) of the biscuits. Press on to the base of the spring-release cake tin. Refrigerate for 30 minutes.

2 Place the cheese and 225 g (8 oz) light soft brown sugar in a food processor and process until evenly combined. Add the eggs, 50 ml (2 fl oz) double cream and the vanilla essence. Blend for about 1 minute or until mixture is well mixed (see Cook's Tips). Pour the filling over the chilled biscuit base.

■ ■ Cook on the grid shelf on the floor of the ROASTING OVEN with the cold plain shelf on the top runners for 45 minutes until just set.

■ ■ ■ ■ Cook in the middle of the BAKING OVEN for about 45 minutes, then transfer to the floor of the SIMMERING OVEN for 15-20 minutes until just set (see Cook's Tips).

Cool, then refrigerate for at least 6 hours.

3 Melt 50 g (2 oz) of the remaining butter in a non-stick frying pan, add the pecan nuts and fry on the SIMMERING PLATE for about 2 minutes. Add the remaining biscuit crumbs and the remaining 50 g (2 oz) light soft brown sugar, then fry for about 3 minutes or until the biscuit crumbs are beginning to turn golden. Add 75 ml (3 fl oz) of the double cream and, stirring constantly, cook for about 2 minutes or until the mixture thickens. Remove from the heat, spoon on to a foil-lined baking sheet and cool. Break into pieces, then pile on top of the cheesecake. Dust with icing sugar.

4 For the maple sauce, melt the butter with the caster sugar, maple syrup and the double cream. Bring to the boil on the SIMMERING PLATE and cook until lightly golden. Serve the sauce warm with the cheesecake.

COOK'S TIPS
Don't worry if the mixture looks a little buttery at this stage of step 2 – it will be absorbed by the biscuit-crumb base as it cooks.
During cooking the top of the cheesecake puffs up and may crack slightly, but when shaken gently it shouldn't wobble. Don't worry about any cracks as they'll be covered by the streusel topping.

SPICED NUT STRUDEL

PREPARATION TIME:
20 MINUTES

COOKING TIME:
30 MINUTES

365-290 CALS PER
SERVING

SERVES 8-10

FREEZING:
UNSUITABLE

With all the flavours of dried fruits, spice and nuts, this is a lovely Christmas dessert if you would like a change from traditional mince pies.

FOR THE FILLING
50 g (2 oz) glacé cherries
200 g (7 oz) mixed chopped nuts, such as walnuts, hazelnuts and almonds
50 g (2 oz) soft white breadcrumbs
25 g (1 oz) dark soft brown (muscovado) sugar
25 g (1 oz) chopped candied peel
50 g (2 oz) raisins
5 ml (1 level tsp) ground cinnamon

5 ml (1 level tsp) ground ginger
50 g (2 oz) unsalted butter
90 ml (6 tbsp) maple syrup
1 large egg

8 large sheets filo pastry
25 g (1 oz) unsalted butter
a little extra maple syrup to drizzle
cream or ice cream, to serve

1 To make the strudel filling, chop the glacé cherries and place them in a bowl with the chopped nuts, breadcrumbs, muscovado sugar, candied peel, raisins, cinnamon and ginger. Add the melted butter, maple syrup and egg to the mixture and mix together well.

2 Lay one sheet of the filo pastry on a clean teatowel, then brush it lightly with melted butter. Take a second sheet of filo pastry and position it on the long side so that it overlaps the first sheet by 5 cm (2 in). Brush this second sheet of filo pastry lightly with melted butter.

3 Spoon half of the strudel filling over the filo pastry, leaving a 5 cm (2 in) border all around the edges.

4 Lay another two sheets of filo pastry over the filling, again overlapping them slightly. Brush lightly with butter.

5 Spoon the remaining filling on top. Fold the two short opposite edges of the pastry over the edge of the filling.

6 Loosely roll up like a Swiss roll to enclose the filling. Carefully transfer the strudel to the large plain shelf, placing it seam-side down. Brush lightly with melted butter. Tear the remaining filo pastry into broad strips. Crumple the filo strips and arrange them on top of the strudel. Brush with remaining melted butter.

7 Place on the grid shelf on the floor of the ROASTING OVEN with the cold large roasting tin on the second runners above. Bake for 15 minutes, then turn the strudel round to ensure even colouring and bake for a further 7-12 minutes or until the pastry is a deep golden brown. Drizzle a little extra maple syrup over and serve warm with cream or ice cream.

SPICED NUT STRUDEL

CHOCOLATE AND CHERRY GATEAU

PREPARATION TIME:
1 HOUR +
MARINATING FOR
6 HOURS OR
OVERNIGHT,
COOLING, AND
CHILLING FOR 2
HOURS

COOKING TIME:
45 MINUTES

625-520 CALS PER
SERVING

SERVES 10-12

FREEZING:
COMPLETE STEP 6,
PACK AND FREEZE.
DEFROST
OVERNIGHT AT
COOL ROOM
TEMPERATURE.
COMPLETE THE
RECIPE.

A magical combination of chocolate and cherries. If fresh cherries are not available, use a 400 g can of pitted cherries instead.

350 g (12 oz) cherries
45 ml (3 tbsp) dark rum
butter, for greasing
50 g (2 oz) almonds (blanched)
50 g (2 oz) plain flour
350 g (12 oz) plain chocolate, preferably with 70% cocoa solids
3 large eggs, separated

125 g (4 oz) butter, softened
125 g (4 oz) caster sugar
450 ml (¾ pint) double cream
chocolate curls and cocoa powder to decorate (see Cook's Tips)
pouring cream and cherries to accompany (optional)

1 Stone the cherries and place in a bowl with 30 ml (2 tbsp) rum (see Cook's Tips). Cover and leave to marinate for 6 hours or overnight.

2 Grease and base-line a 23 cm (9 in) diameter deep loose-bottomed cake tin. Place the almonds in a small roasting tin and bake for 3-4 minutes on the grid shelf on the floor of the ROASTING OVEN, then leave the oven door slightly open and check every minute until pale golden brown. Cool; process with flour until finely ground.

3 Melt 125 g (4 oz) chocolate with 45 ml (3 tbsp) boiling water in a bowl on the floor of the SIMMERING OVEN for 5 minutes. Then add the remaining rum and the egg yolks and beat until smooth.

4 Place butter and sugar in a food processor and beat until light and fluffy. Briefly work in the chocolate mixture. Whisk the egg whites to a soft peak in a large bowl, fold in the flour and almonds and the chocolate mixture. Pour into the prepared tin.

▓ ▓ Bake on the grid shelf on the floor of the ROASTING OVEN with the cold plain shelf on the third runners for 25-30 minutes or until the cake is cooked.

▓ ▓ ▓ ▓ Bake in the middle of the BAKING OVEN for 30-35 minutes or until the cake is cooked.

Leave to cool in the tin for 10 minutes, pour over the cherry juices while still warm, then turn onto a serving plate.

5 Roughly chop remaining chocolate. In a small pan bring the cream to the boil. Remove from the heat and add the chocolate, allow to stand for 5 minutes, then stir until melted. Pour into a bowl and cool completely. Using an electric whisk, beat until lighter in colour and thick. Chill slightly if the mixture is slow to thicken.

6 Clean cake tin and slip the sides around the cake (do not use the base). Spoon cherries over the cake. Spoon the chocolate cream on top, smooth the surface, then cover and refrigerate for at least 2 hours.

7 Decorate with chocolate curls and dust heavily with cocoa powder. Serve in thin slices with cream and cherries, if wished.

COOK'S TIPS

To make chocolate curls, use dark chocolate with at least 70% cocoa solids. Melt the chocolate and spread a thin layer over a clean, smooth worksurface, marble slab or baking sheet. When it has just set, push a large knife across it at an angle of about 25 degrees. Scrape off the remaining chocolate and repeat the process. Chill or freeze the curls in an airtight container between leaves of greaseproof paper for up to one week.

If using canned cherries, drain the juice before marinating.

To prepare ahead, complete to the end of step 6; store in an airtight container in the fridge for up to three days. You may need to take the cake out of the fridge 30-45 minutes before serving to allow the chocolate topping to soften slightly.

CHOCOLATE AND HAZELNUT MERINGUES

PREPARATION TIME: 25 MINUTES + SOFTENING

COOKING TIME: 2 HOURS

500 CALS PER SERVING

SERVES 6

FREEZING: SUITABLE, UP TO THE END OF STEP 4 (BUT DO NOT LEAVE IN THE FRIDGE FOR 2 HOURS)

Mini versions of these meringues are lovely to serve with after-dinner coffee. Allowing them to stand after filling ensures they melt in the mouth.

125 g (4 oz) hazelnuts, toasted
125 g (4 oz) caster sugar
75 g (3 oz) good-quality plain chocolate
2 egg whites
284 ml (10 fl oz) carton double cream

redcurrants, blackberries, kumquats, Cape gooseberries dipped in caramel (see Aga Tip) and shavings of chocolate, to serve

1 Line two baking sheets with non-stick baking parchment. Place nuts in a food processor with 45 ml (3 level tbsp) caster sugar. Process to fine powder. Add chocolate and pulse until chopped.
2 In a large, grease-free bowl, whisk the egg whites until stiff; whisk in remaining caster sugar a spoonful at a time until mixture is stiff and shiny. Fold in nut mixture.
3 Place spoonfuls of the mixture in six small rough mounds, about 9 cm (3½ in) in diameter, on the baking sheets. Cook on the top runners and the floor of the SIMMERING OVEN for about 1 hour, changing the shelves over after 45 minutes, or until the meringues will just peel off the paper. Gently push in the base of each meringue to form a deep hollow; return to the oven for 1-2 hours or until crisp and dry. Allow to cool; store in an airtight container for up to one week.
4 Whisk cream until it just holds its shape; spoon three-quarters on to the meringues. Leave in the fridge to soften for up to 2 hours.
5 Decorate each meringue with the remaining cream, fruits and chocolate; serve immediately.

AGA TIP
To make the caramel, dissolve 125 g (4 oz) caster sugar in a small, heavy-based pan on the SIMMERING PLATE. Bring to the boil and bubble until a golden caramel colour. Dip each Cape gooseberry into the caramel, then place on an oiled baking sheet until cool.

PEARS, FIGS AND BLUEBERRIES IN WINE

PREPARATION TIME: 10 MINUTES + CHILLING

COOKING TIME: ¾-1 HOUR

194 CALS PER SERVING

SERVES 8

FREEZING: SUITABLE FOR PEARS ONLY

To give the pears a crimson glow, use a full-bodied red wine such as a French Syrah, ideally from the Rhone valley, Australian Shiraz or any red wine made from the Cabernet Sauvignon grape.

1 lemon
4 pears
300 ml (½ pint) red wine
175 g (6 oz) caster sugar

1 stick cinnamon
2 bay leaves
125 g (4 oz) fresh blueberries
8 figs, preferably fresh (see Cook's Tips)

1 Pare the rind of the lemon. Halve but don't peel or core the pears.
2 Place wine, 150 ml (¼ pint) cold water, sugar, cinnamon, bay leaves and lemon rind in a non-metallic pan. Place on the SIMMERING PLATE. Once sugar has dissolved, add pears, cut side down. Cover the pan, bring to the boil and place on the floor of the SIMMERING OVEN for ¾-1 hour or until tender (see Cook's Tips). Remove pan from heat, add blueberries and halved or quartered figs. Cool in syrup, cover and chill before serving.

COOK'S TIPS
Choose a large, shallow enamelled or stainless steel pan.
Cooking time depends on the pears' ripeness. If using dried figs, cook them with the pears.

TROPICAL FRUITS WITH ORANGE AND CARDAMOM SAUCE

PREPARATION TIME:
10 MINUTES

COOKING TIME:
15 MINUTES

290 CALS PER
SERVING

SERVES 4

FREEZING:
UNSUITABLE

Fragrant parcels of hot fruit i buttery sauces.

2 large oranges	**1 small papaya**
1 lemon	**2 passion fruit**
5 whole cardamom pods	**1 star fruit**
60 ml (4 level tbsp) light soft brown sugar	**1 banana**
50 g (2 oz) unsalted butter	**caramel 'bark', to decorate (see Aga Tip)**
1 small ripe pineapple	

1 Squeeze the juice of the oranges and the lemon. Split open the cardamom pods and scrape the seeds into a shallow saucepan with 150 ml (5 fl oz) orange juice, 45 ml (3 tbsp) lemon juice and the sugar and butter. Bring to the boil, stirring, and bubble on the BOILING PLATE until syrupy. Set aside.

2 Remove skin and core from the pineapple – there should be about 450 g (1 lb) flesh. Peel, halve and remove seeds from the papaya. Remove pulp from the passion fruit. Thickly slice all the fruit; divide among four 20.5 cm (8 in) squares of foil. Spoon some of the passion fruit pulp and 45-60 ml (3-4 tbsp) sauce over each serving, reserving the remainder.

3 Seal the parcels; cook in a roasting tin on the bottom runners of the ROASTING OVEN for 7-10 minutes until hot. Open the parcels; serve with remaining sauce and decorate with 'bark'.

AGA TIP
For an easy caramel 'bark' decoration for bought flans, ice cream or creme brulee, sprinkle caster sugar in a thin, even layer over a lightly oiled cold roasting tin. Set on the bottom runners of the ROASTING OVEN and cook for 3-4 minutes or until golden brown and liquid. Carefully tilt the tin to make caramel run into a thin sheet, allow to cool and set. Lift off with a knife, break into fine pieces.

GINGER AND ROSEMARY-BAKED BANANAS

PREPARATION TIME:
20 MINUTES

COOKING TIME:
ABOUT 45 MINUTES

240 CALS PER
SERVING

SERVES 6

FREEZING:
UNSUITABLE

The fruits can also be divided among six pieces of foil, wrapped into parcels and cooked separately. To save time, scoop the ice cream into portions and place on a foil-lined tray in the freezer 24 hours in advance, ready to serve.

5 mm (¼ in) piece of fresh root ginger	**5 spears of fresh rosemary**
3 large oranges	**50 g (2 oz) butter**
200 ml (7 fl oz) dark rum	**4 bananas**
20 ml (4 level tsp) sugar	**ginger or vanilla ice cream, to serve**
juice of 1 lemon	

1 Peel and grate the ginger. Peel the oranges and cut into slices. Place the ginger, rum, sugar, lemon juice and rosemary in a large non-stick frying pan. Bring to the boil and simmer on the BOILING PLATE for 1-2 minutes or until syrupy. Add 25 g (1 oz) butter and set aside in a bowl at the back of the Aga to keep warm.

2 Slice the bananas lengthways. Melt the remaining butter in the frying pan. Fry the bananas on the BOILING PLATE for 1-2 minutes, turning from time to time, until golden brown. Place in a shallow ovenproof dish with the oranges. Pour the warm rum syrup over the top, cover and cook on the grid shelf on the floor of the ROASTING OVEN for 20 minutes if still hot or for 25-30 minutes in prepared a little in advance and cooked from cold.

3 Serve immediately with the ice cream.

LEMON FUDGE TART

PREPARATION TIME:
1 ¼ HOURS +
COOLING,
REFRIGERATING
AND STANDING

COOKING TIME:
40-50 MINUTES

350 CALS PER
SERVING

SERVES 8

FREEZING:
COMPLETE TO END
OF STEP 5; WRAP
AND FREEZE. THAW
AT COOL ROOM
TEMPERATURE FOR
4 HOURS.
COMPLETE THE
RECIPE.

ILLUSTRATED OPPOSITE

A delicious lemon curd-like filling in an easy-to-slice long tart.

25 g (1 oz) ground almonds
grated rind of ½ a lemon
150 g (5 oz) plain flour
65 g (2 ½ oz) caster sugar
75 g (3 oz) butter, diced
1 egg
few drops almond or vanilla essence

FOR THE FILLING
25 g (1 oz) butter
3 large lemons

5 eggs
150 g (5 oz) caster sugar

FOR THE DECORATION
1 egg white
lemon balm or mint leaves
caster sugar
fresh fruits, such as redcurrants and blackberries
rose petals

1 First make the pastry. Bake the almonds by placing on a baking tray on the grid shelf on the floor of the ROASTING OVEN. Cook carefully for 1-2 minutes until pale golden, leaving the oven door slightly open so you can smell them; cool. Place the grated lemon rind in a food processor with the flour, caster sugar and butter. Process until the mixture resembles fine crumbs. Add the cooled ground almonds, then process for 2-3 seconds only (see Cook's Tips). Whisk the egg and set aside 10 ml (2 tsp). Add the almond essence to the remainder with 15 ml (1 tbsp) cold water, then pulse into the flour mixture. Process until the mixture just comes together, then turn out on to a lightly floured worksurface and knead lightly. Wrap and refrigerate for at least 2 hours. Roll the pastry out thinly.

2 Line a 10 x 33.5 cm (4 x 13¼ in) rectangular, loose-bottomed tart tin with the chilled pastry, pinching up the edge all around to make it stand up 1 cm (½ in) above the top edge of the tin (see Cook's Tips), then refrigerate for 30 minutes. Line the pastry with greaseproof paper and baking beans. Bake blind on the floor of the ROASTING OVEN for 10-12 minutes. Remove the paper and baking beans, turn the tin round to ensure even browning and return to the oven for 3-5 minutes. Brush the inside of the pastry case with the reserved 10 ml (2 tsp) beaten egg to seal up any cracks, then return the tin to the oven for 1 minute.

3 To prepare the filling for the tart, melt the butter in a medium sized bowl on the floor of the SIMMERING OVEN for 10-15 minutes. Grate the rind from all the lemons and squeeze the juice – you will need about 175 ml (6 fl oz) in total.

4 Add the eggs, lemon rind, lemon juice and caster sugar to the melted butter. Whisk together quickly until the mixture is smooth and well combined.

5 Place the tart tin in a roasting tin. Pour the lemon filling immediately into the warm pastry case (see Cook's Tips).

■ ■ Bake on the grid shelf on the floor of the ROASTING OVEN with the cold plain shelf above on the third runners for 20-30 minutes or until just set.

■ ■ ■ ■ Bake on bottom runners of the BAKING OVEN for 30-40 minutes or until just set. Allow the tart to stand for 15 minutes before carefully removing from the tin on to a cooling rack or serving tray.

6 To decorate, whisk the egg white lightly. Dip lemon balm leaves into it; shake off the excess. Dip leaves in caster sugar to coat then repeat with berries. Leave in a dry atmosphere (not the fridge) until crisp. Decorate the tart with leaves, berries and rose petals.

COOK'S TIPS
Avoid over-processing the almonds as this will release too much of their oil.
Don't worry if the pastry breaks as it's easy to patch. Once melted butter has been mixed with the filling ingredients, bake the tart immediately or the butter will start to solidify.
To prepare ahead, complete to end of step 5 up to one day ahead. Store in an airtight container. To use, complete the recipe.

LEMON AND SUMMER BERRY CRUNCH CAKE

PREPARATION TIME:
40 MINUTES +
COOLING

COOKING TIME:
1 HOUR

575-435 CALS PER
SERVING

SERVES 6-8

FREEZING:SUITABLE.
COMPLETE TO END
OF STEP 5

For an unusual summer birthday cake, this recipe can also be cooked in a 20 cm (8 in) round tin.

butter, for greasing
1 lemon
150 g (5 oz) self-raising flour
2 eggs, plus 1 egg yolk
pinch of salt
150 g (5 oz) butter, softened
150 g (5 oz) caster sugar
125 g (4 oz) raspberries and blueberries

FOR THE LEMON CRUNCH TOPPING
25 g (1 oz) rough white sugar cubes
25 ml (1 fl oz) bottled lemon juice (see Cook's Tips)
225 g (8 oz) caster sugar
icing sugar, to dust
whitecurrants, blackcurrants, wild strawberries and crème fraîche or Greek yogurt, to accompany

1 Grease and base-line a 1.1-litre (2-pint) loaf tin. Finely grate zest and squeeze the juice of the lemon. Sift the flour. Lightly beat the eggs and egg yolk with the salt.

2 Place butter, lemon zest and sugar in a bowl; beat until light and fluffy (see Cook's Tips). Slowly add the eggs, beating as you do so; this should take 10 minutes (see Cook's Tips). Fold in flour with 30 ml (2 tbsp) of the lemon juice (reserve remainder). Fold in fruit. Spoon into the tin.

3 ■ ■ Cook at the front of the grid shelf on the floor of the ROASTING OVEN with the cold roasting tin containing 1 litre (2 pints) cold water on the second runners for 45-55 minutes.

■ ■ ■ ■ Cook at the front of the grid shelf on the floor of the BAKING OVEN with the cold baking tray on the third runners for 50 minutes-1 hour.

Leave in the tin for 5 minutes; cool on a wire rack.

4 Lightly crush sugar cubes. Mix together reserved fresh lemon juice, bottled lemon juice and caster sugar. Spoon over the warm cake; sprinkle with crushed sugar. Leave for 1 hour until set.

5 Dust the cake with icing sugar, slice and serve with berries and crème fraîche or yogurt.

COOK'S TIPS
Bottled lemon juice as it gives a more intense lemony flavour than fresh juice.
If using a food processor to beat butter and sugar, use the beater attachment and process very well before adding eggs. The more the mixture is beaten between additions of egg, the lighter the cake will be. The mixture will curdle if eggs are added too quickly. Add a little flour if this happens.
The weight of the fruit may make it sink towards the bottom of the cake, but it will still taste delicious. Other berries such as blackberries, loganberries and blackcurrants can be used in the cake.

AGA TIP
To defrost frozen raspberries, place them on a plate in the SIMMERING OVEN for 10 minutes until almost thawed.

SORBET IN BISCUIT BASKETS WITH RASPBERRY SAUCE

PREPARATION TIME:
20 MINUTES

280 CALS PER
SERVING

SERVES 8

FREEZING: SUITABLE
FOR THE SORBET

Sorbets always make an elegant, refreshing desert and are particularly good after a filling main course.

FOR THE SAUCE
450 g (1 lb) fresh or frozen raspberries
225 g (8 oz) caster sugar
30 ml (2 tbsp) lemon juice

500 ml (15 fl oz) blackcurrant or cassis sorbet
12 Biscuit Baskets (see right)
whitecurrants, raspberries and mint sprigs to decorate

1 To make the sauce, puree the raspberries with the sugar in a food processor until smooth, then put through a sieve to remove the seeds. Stir in lemon juice to taste

2 Chill baking sheets in the freezer. Place about 24 scoops of the sorbet in single layers on the sheets, then return to the freezer for at least 10 minutes.

3 Flood serving plates with 30-45 ml (2-3 tbsp) sauce. Add scoops of sorbet to baskets; place one on each plate. Decorate with fruit and mint sprigs (see Cook's Tip).

COOK'S TIP
The baskets may be frozen with the scooped sorbet in them. Allow 5 minutes at room temperature before serving.

BISCUIT BASKETS

PREPARATION TIME:
15 MINUTES +
CHILLING

COOKING TIME:
15 MINUTES

60 CALS PER
SERVING

SERVES 8

These baskets are made from a brandy snap-type mixture and are quite robust,

**40 g (1½ oz) each butter, sugar, flour and
liquid glucose (see Cook's Tip)**

1 Warm the butter, sugar and glucose in a bowl in the SIMMERING OVEN for 5-10 minutes until soft. Stir in the flour until smooth.

2 Place 1 rounded teaspoon of the mixture per basket, wide apart, on silicone parchment-lined baking trays, 2-3 per tray. Cook one tray at a time.

■ ■ Place on the grid shelf on the floor of the ROASTING OVEN for 6 minutes, then turn the tray round for even colouring and cook for a further minute until pale golden.

■ ■ ■ ■ Place in the middle of the BAKING OVEN for 7 minutes, then turn the tray round for even colouring and cook for a further minute until pale golden.

3 Leave for a few seconds until cool and firm enough to lift with a palette knife, then mould over the base of an upturned tea-cup or ramekin to make baskets. Cool; store in an airtight container for 2-3 days.

COOK'S TIP
Liquid glucose is like a stiff syrup. You will find it at most chemists.

VANILLA-SCENTED CREAMS

PREPARATION TIME:
35 MINUTES +
CHILLING

COOKING TIME:
5 MINUTES

365 CALS PER
SERVING

SERVES 8

FREEZING: SUITABLE

These delicate creams can be cooked in just a few minutes.

sunflower oil, for brushing
10 ml (2 level tsp) powdered gelatine
568 ml (20 fl oz) carton double cream

75 g (3 oz) caster sugar
2 vanilla pods

1 Lightly brush eight 100 ml (4 fl oz) dariole moulds or ramekins with oil. Pour 45 ml (3 tbsp) cold water into a heatproof bowl, sprinkle gelatine over and soak for 5 minutes. Place cream, sugar and split vanilla pods in a heavy-based saucepan. Bring to the boil on the SIMMERING PLATE then add the soaked gelatine immediately and stir well to dissolve; set aside to cool. Strain into the dariole moulds. Cover and refrigerate the moulds for at least 6 hours or overnight to set.

2 To serve, dip the moulds into warm water for a few seconds, then turn out on to individual serving plates.

COOK'S TIP
Vanilla pods can be rinsed and re-used.

129

GINGER CREAMS

PREPARATION TIME:
30 MINUTES +
INFUSION

COOKING TIME:
I HOUR 50
MINUTES

640 CALS PER
SERVING

SERVES 8

FREEZING:
UNSUITABLE

ILLUSTRATED BELOW

This is a delicious variation on the classic creme caramel. These creams are excellent made up to two days ahead and kept in the fridge, ready to serve.

350 g (12 oz) caster sugar
I cm (½ in) piece fresh root ginger or 5 ml (I level tsp) ground ginger
375 ml (13 fl oz) double cream
300 ml (½ pint) milk

100 ml (4 fl oz) ginger wine
3 eggs, plus 4 egg yolks
desiccated or sliced coconut, to decorate

I Melt 225 g (8 oz) caster sugar with 50 ml (2 fl oz) water in the SIMMERING OVEN without stirring for 20-30 minutes until clear and liquid. Bring to the boil and bubble on the SIMMERING PLATE for 5-6 minutes or until a golden caramel colour.

2 Add 1.25 ml (¼ tsp) water to the pan (see Cook's Tips). Carefully swirl the caramel around the base and sides of eight 150 ml (5 fl oz) heatproof moulds. Set aside (see Cook's Tips).

3 Peel and grate root ginger, if using, then whisk together with cream, milk and ginger wine. Pour into a small pan and warm on the SIMMERING PLATE for 2-3 minutes (it should barely simmer). Whisk together the eggs, yolks and remaining 125 g (4 oz) sugar (adding ground ginger here, if using).

4 Pour the flavoured milk slowly on to the whisked egg mixture, stirring constantly, then strain the mixture into a large jug. Meanwhile, toast the desiccated or sliced coconut on a baking tray in the ROASTING OVEN for 2-3 minutes or until it turns golden brown. Keep the door of the oven slightly open so you can smell when the coconut is ready.

5 Pour custard into moulds set in a roasting tin. Add hot water to come halfway up sides.

■ ■ Place on the grid shelf on the floor of the ROASTING OVEN with the cold plain shelf on the bottom runners for 30 minutes, then transfer to the floor of the SIMMERING OVEN for a further 30 minutes or until lightly set.

■ ■ ■ ■ Place on the grid shelf on the floor of the BAKING OVEN with the cold plain shelf on the bottom runners for 40 minutes, then transfer to the floor of the SIMMERING OVEN for a further 30 minutes or until lightly set.

Remove the custards from the tin. When cool, cover with clingfilm and refrigerate for at least 4 hours and up to two days.

6 To serve, run a finger lightly around the edge of the creams to loosen, then turn out on to serving plates. Decorate with toasted desiccated coconut or coconut slices dipped in caramel (see Cook's Tips).

COOK'S TIPS
Adding a tiny bit of water to the caramel helps to release the custards with their sauce from the moulds once cooked.
To make the optional caramel for dipping slices of coconut in, follow step I, melting 125 g (4 oz) caster sugar with 25 ml (I fl oz) water.

AGA TIP
To clean the caramel pan, put some hot water in the pan and place it in the SIMMERING OVEN for about 10 minutes.

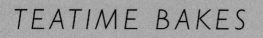

TEATIME BAKES

LIGHT GINGER SPONGE WITH STICKY RUM AND RAISIN TOPPING

LIGHT GINGER SPONGE WITH STICKY RUM AND RAISIN TOPPING

PREPARATION TIME:
15 MINUTES

COOKING TIME:
45 MINUTES-1 HOUR

275 CALS PER SLICE

MAKES 24 SLICES

FREEZING: SUITABLE

This sponge freezes beautifully, so make a large batch and keep a few slices in the freezer for unexpected guests.

180 g (6 oz) butter
300 g (10 oz) dark muscovado sugar
60 ml (4 tbsp) golden syrup
6 eggs
10 ml (2 tsp) bicarbonate of soda
600 ml (1 pint) milk
500 g (1 lb 2 oz) self-raising flour
30 ml (2 tbsp) ground ginger

45 ml (3 tbsp) fresh ginger, grated
extra butter, for greasing

FOR THE TOPPING
90 ml (6 tbsp) rum
300 g (10 oz) raisins
120 ml (8 tbsp) ginger or lime marmalade
30 ml (2 tbsp) fresh ginger, grated
juice of 1 lemon

1 Line a large roasting tin with foil and brush with melted butter.

2 Warm the butter in a large ovenproof bowl in the SIMMERING OVEN for 2-3 minutes, then beat in the sugar, golden syrup and eggs to a smooth consistency. Stir well and add all the remaining cake ingredients, beating all to a smooth batter. Pour cake batter in to the prepared tin.

3 ■ ■ ■ Bake on the bottom runners of the ROASTING OVEN with the cold plain shelf on the third set of runners. Bake for 20 minutes or until the back of the cake is golden. Turn the roasting tin round and bake for a further 5-10 minutes. Complete the cooking by placing the roasting tin on the hot plain shelf on the second set of runners in the SIMMERING OVEN for a further 5-15 minutes, until springy in the centre.

■ ■ ■ ■ Cook on the bottom runners of the BAKING OVEN for 30 minutes, then turn the tin round and cook for a further 15-25 minutes.

4 Meanwhile, place the topping ingredients in a covered ovenproof bowl, and place in the SIMMERING OVEN for 30 minutes for the raisins to plump. Stir well and spoon over the hot cake as soon as it is cooked. Cool and cut into squares.

COOK'S TIP
This cake is also delicious served warm with vanilla or lemon ice-cream as a dessert.

APRICOT AND ALMOND ROULADE

PREPARATION
25 MINUTES +
COOLING

COOKING 13-20
MINUTES
FREEZING: FREEZE
AT THE END OF
STAGE 10. THAW
OVERNIGHT IN THE
FRIDGE AND DUST
WITH ICING SUGAR
TO SERVE.

525 CALS PER
SERVING

SERVES 6-8

This irresistible, moist roulade is flecked with grated marzipan to give a superb almond flavour with chopped fresh apricots and whipped cream encased inside. You will probably find that the roulade cracks as you roll it – but this is part of its charm!

25 g (1 oz) flaked almonds
5 eggs, separated
150 g (5 oz) caster sugar
5 ml (1 tsp) vanilla essence
75 g (3 oz) white marzipan, coarsely grated or finely chopped
45 ml (3 tbsp) plain white flour

TO ASSEMBLE
300 ml (½ pint) double cream
25 g (1 oz) caster sugar
275 g (10 oz) ripe apricots, stoned and chopped
icing sugar, for dusting

1 Spread the flaked almonds on a baking sheet and toast on the grid shelf on the floor of the ROASTING OVEN for 3-4 minutes or until golden brown.

2 Lightly grease a 33 × 23 cm (13 × 9 in) Swiss roll tin and line with non-stick baking parchment. Scatter the toasted almonds evenly over the paper.

3 Put the egg yolks and 125 g (4 oz) of the caster sugar into a bowl and whisk, using an electric beater, until pale and thick. Fold in the vanilla essence and grated marzipan. Sift the flour over the mixture, then lightly fold in using a large metal spoon.

4 Whisk the egg whites in another bowl until stiff, but not dry. Whisk in the remaining 25 g (1 oz) caster sugar, a spoonful at a time. Using a large metal spoon, carefully fold a quarter of the egg whites into the almond mixture to lighten it, then gradually fold in the rest. Turn the mixture into the prepared tin and spread evenly, gently easing it into the corners.

5 ▦ ▦ Place the tin on the grid shelf on the floor of the ROASTING OVEN with the cold plain shelf on the third set of runners. Bake for 13-15 minutes until well risen and firm to the touch, carefully turning the tin around after 8 minutes to ensure even cooking.

▦ ▦ ▦ ▦ Place the tin on the grid shelf on the fourth set of runners in the BAKING OVEN. Cook for 17-20 minutes, until well risen and firm to the touch, carefully turning the tin around after 10 minutes.

6 Leave to stand for 5 minutes, then cover the sponge with a sheet of non-stick baking parchment and a damp tea-towel and leave until cold.

7 Remove the tea-towel and invert the sponge with the covering paper onto the work surface. Peel off the lining paper and trim the long edges to neaten.

8 For the filling, lightly whip the cream in a bowl until soft peaks form, then fold in the caster sugar. Spread the cream over the sponge and scatter the chopped pineapple evenly on top. Carefully roll up the sponge from one of the narrow ends, using the paper to help. Transfer to a serving plate and dust with icing sugar.

AGA TIP
For a decorative effect, place a long metal skewer directly on the BOILING PLATE, close the lid and leave until it is red hot. Protecting your hand with an oven glove, use the skewer to mark lines diagonally along the length of the roulade.

LEMON CURD SPONGE WITH CRUNCHY LIME AND GINGER TOPPING

LEMON CURD SPONGE WITH CRUNCHY LIME AND GINGER TOPPING

PREPARATION TIME:
20 MINUTES

COOKING TIME:
35-40 MINUTES

MAKES 8 SLICES

425 CALS PER SLICE

FREEZING:
COMPLETE UNTIL
MIDDLE OF STEP 6;
FREEZE BEFORE
SPLITTING AND
FILLING WITH
LEMON CURD.

If you do not have time to make your own lemon curd filling, many delicatessens stock good quality lemon curd which can be used instead.

2 lemons
180 g (6 oz) butter
180 g (6 oz) caster sugar
3 large eggs
2.5 ml (½ tsp) baking powder

30 ml (2 tbsp) milk
200 g (7 oz) self-raising flour
1 lime
100 g (3½ oz) granulated sugar
10 ml (2 tsp) fresh ginger, finely grated

1 Base-line, grease and flour a 20 cm (8 in) spring clip cake tin. Grate the lemons finely. Save the lemon juice for use in the topping.

2 Cream the lemon rind, butter and sugar with a hand whisk or in the food processor. Add the eggs one at a time and beat well between each addition, then beat in the baking powder and the milk.

3 Carefully fold in the flour with a plastic spatula or using the pulse button in brief bursts in the food processor to incorporate the flour. Do not stir more than essential, or the cake will rise in a peak when baked. Turn into the prepared tin.

4 ■ ■ Bake at the front of the grid shelf on the floor of the ROASTING OVEN with the cold plain shelf on the bottom runners above for 35-40 minutes, checking the cake after the first 25-30 minutes and turning the tin round to ensure even colouring. Remove the cake from the oven when just firm to the fingertips when pressed in the centre.

■ ■ ■ Bake in the middle of the BAKING OVEN with the grid shelf on the third runners for 40-45 minutes, checking cake after the first 30-35 minutes and turning the tin round to ensure even colouring. Remove the cake from the oven when just firm to the fingertips when pressed in the centre.

5 Meanwhile, make needle shreds or grate rind of lime. Squeeze juice and make up to 60 ml (4 tbsp) with lemon juice. Combine rind, granulated sugar and ginger. Pour juice over the hot cake immediately it comes out of the oven and sprinkle on the sugar mixture. Cover the tin with an upturned plate to keep the steam in for 5 minutes maximum. Then uncover and leave in the tin until just warm.

6 Remove the tin and allow the cake to cool completely. When cold, remove the paper under the cake, split and fill with lemon curd (see recipe right).

134

LEMON CURD

46 CALS PER 15 ML
(1 TBSP)

1 large lemon
90 g (3 oz) caster sugar

50 g (2 oz) butter
1 large egg

1 Finely grate the lemon rind and squeeze the juice. Place in a pan with sugar and butter and melt, stirring occasionally, on the SIMMERING PLATE.
2 Whisk the egg well in a small bowl. Allow the lemon mixture to come just to the boil then pour slowly onto the egg, whisking constantly. Return the mixture to the pan and place on the floor at the front of the SIMMERING OVEN for 7-10 minutes until just set. Stir well and allow to cool and chill before use.

COOK'S TIP
Lemon curd will keep for up to 2 weeks in the refrigerator. You may wish to make double or triple the quantity to serve with bread or toast, or to give as a present. Pour the lemon curd into warm, clean jam jars while hot, then cover, cool and chill. Larger quantities will need slightly longer in the SIMMERING OVEN to thicken, so stir well after 10 minutes and return to the oven for 3-5 minutes or until set.

WALNUT CAKE

PREPARATION TIME:
15 MINUTES +
COOLING

COOKING TIME:
25-35 MINUTES

400 CALS PER SLICE

MAKES ABOUT
10 SLICES

FREEZING: FREEZE
CAKES AT STEP 5,
BEFORE FILLING.
THAW AND FILL
TO SERVE.

A lovely cake to keep in the freezer, ready to bring out and fill with cream and raspberries, strawberries or apricots.

175 g (6 oz) butter, plus extra for greasing
2 eggs
225 g (8 oz) caster sugar
2.5 ml (½ level tsp) vanilla essence
225 g (8 oz) self-raising flour
2.5 ml (½ level tsp) salt

10 ml (2 level tsp) baking powder
150-175 ml (5-6 fl oz) milk
50 g (2 oz) chopped walnuts
apricot jam, fresh fruit and whipped cream
icing sugar, to dust

1 Grease and base-line two 20.5 cm (8 in) Victoria sandwich tins.
2 Separate the eggs. Cream together the butter, sugar, egg yolks and vanilla essence until light and fluffy. In a separate bowl, sieve together flour, salt and baking powder. Beat flour mixture and milk into creamed mixture, a little at a time.
3 Place the egg whites in a medium bowl and, using an electric whisk, beat until they form soft peaks. Fold into the cake mixture with the chopped walnuts. Turn mixture into the prepared tins.
4 ▨ ▨ Bake on the grid shelf on the floor of the ROASTING OVEN with the cold plain shelf on the second runners for 20-25 minutes or until golden and nearly cooked. Reverse the cake tin in the oven to ensure even cooking and bake for a further 5-10 minutes or until a skewer inserted into the centre comes out clean.
▨ ▨ ▨ ▨ Bake on the grid shelf on the bottom runners of the BAKING OVEN for 20-25 minutes until golden and nearly cooked. Reverse the cake tin in the oven to ensure even cooking and bake for a further 5-10 minutes or until a skewer inserted into the centre comes out clean.
5 Cool in the tins for 5-10 minutes, then transfer to a wire rack to cool completely (see Cook's Tip). Spread one of the cakes with a little warmed apricot jam; top with fruit and cream. Top with second cake and dust with sieved icing sugar.

FRUIT CAKE

PREPARATION TIME:
40 MINUTES +
SOAKING; MATURE
FOR SIX WEEKS

COOKING TIME:
4-5 HOURS

883 CALS PER
SERVING

SERVES 12

FREEZING: SUITABLE

A fantastic, moist cake full of flavour - the perfect recipe for a Christmas cake. If you don't have a food mixer with a beater attachment, use an electric hand whisk. If short of time, leave the mixture in a cool place until the next day to bake (this will also ensure the cake has a flat top). Brush very lightly with cold water before baking to prevent a hard crust forming.

75 g (3 oz) candied peel
75 g (3 oz) glacé cherries
150 g (5 oz) seeded raisins
150 g (5 oz) large seedless raisins
200 g (7 oz) sultanas
225 g (8 oz) currants
200 ml (7 fl oz) brandy, plus 60 ml (2 fl oz) for spooning over
butter, for greasing
300 g (11 oz) plain white flour
5 ml (1 level tsp) ground cinnamon
salt
a little freshly grated nutmeg

150 g (5 oz) softened butter, preferably unsalted
150 g (5 oz) soft dark brown (muscovado) sugar
4 large eggs, separated
5 ml (1 level tsp) cocoa powder
pinch bicarbonate of soda

TO DECORATE
90 ml (6 level tbsp) honey or apricot jam
cornflour, for dusting
450 g (1 lb) white marzipan
about 225 g (8 oz) ready-to-roll fondant icing

1 Finely chop the peel; halve the cherries. Place in a bowl with all the dried fruit and 200 ml (7 fl oz) brandy. Cover and place in the SIMMERING OVEN for 45 minutes, then leave to cool. Grease and double-line a 20.5 cm (8 in) deep cake tin with greaseproof paper (see Cook's Tips). Sift flour with cinnamon, a pinch of salt and a little nutmeg.

2 Place softened butter in a food mixer and, with the beater attachment, beat until creamy. Add sugar gradually, beating well between each addition, until light and fluffy. With the machine at full speed, beat in egg yolks one at a time. Reduce speed; add 150 g (5½ oz) flour mixture, the fruit and its soaking liquid, then add remaining flour. In a separate bowl, whisk egg whites to a foam. Add to mixture with cocoa and bicarbonate of soda, mixing well. Turn the cake mixture into the prepared tin and smooth the top.

3 ■ ■ Bake on the grid shelf on the floor at the front of the ROASTING OVEN with the cold plain shelf on the bottom runners for about 1 hour, turning the cake round to colour evenly after the first 35-40 minutes. Then place the hot plain shelf on the second runners in the SIMMERING OVEN and bake for a further 3-4 hours until a skewer inserted comes out clean.

■ ■ ■ ■ Bake on the grid shelf on the floor of the BAKING OVEN for 55-60 minutes until the cake is golden. Have the plain shelf heating in the ROASTING OVEN. Then place the hot shelf on the runners of the SIMMERING OVEN and transfer the cake, pushing it to the back of the oven. Bake for a further 2½-3¼ hours until a skewer inserted into the centre comes out clean. Cool for 30 minutes in the tin, then transfer to a rack to cool completely. Wrap in greaseproof paper and foil, and store in a cool place for up to six weeks (see Cook's Tips).

4 Warm the honey and brush a layer over the cake. On a worksurface dusted with cornflour, roll out the marzipan to a 30 cm (12 in) circle, place over the top and sides of the cake, press down and trim any excess. Cover with greaseproof paper; leave in a cool place for two days.

5 To ice, place the cake on a board. Warm remaining honey and brush over the marzipan. On a worksurface dusted with cornflour, thinly roll out 225 g (8 oz) fondant icing and cover in the same way as with the marzipan. Re-roll fondant trimmings and use to decorate the cake.

COOK'S TIPS
To prepare the tin, lightly grease the base, then cover with a disc of greaseproof paper. Halve a double thickness of greaseproof paper 12.5 cm (5 in) wide and 72 cm (28 in) long. Fold up 2.5 cm (1 in) along the open edge and cut diagonally at 1 cm (1/2 in) intervals. Curl the strip of paper around the inside of the tin, placing the snipped edge on the base. Place a second disc of greaseproof paper in the base of the tin.

The minimum time between cooking and decorating is one week. Every week for the first two weeks, prick the cake base and spoon 30 ml (2 tbsp) brandy over the top. Wrap until ready to decorate.

GUGELHOPF

PREPARATION TIME: 45 MINUTES + CHILLING FOR ABOUT 24 HOURS AND RISING FOR ABOUT 3 HOURS

COOKING TIME: 45-55 MINUTES

390-330 CALS PER SERVING

SERVES 12-14

FREEZING: COOL, WRAP TIGHTLY AND FREEZE BEFORE DECORATING IN STEP 5. THAW AT ROOM TEMPERATURE AND PLACE IN THE SIMMERING OVEN FOR 10 MINUTES TO SERVE WARM, THEN DECORATE.

Instead of traditional Christmas cake, try this wonderfully light Gugelhopf. Eaten at Christmas in Austria and Germany, the cake is made with yeast so is best eaten within two days. Freeze the cake in slices if you have any left over — it's good toasted or used for making a bread and butter pudding.

200 g (7 oz) raisins, preferably black seedless

45 ml (3 tbsp) light rum

1 sachet easy-blend yeast (see Cook's Tips)

300 g (11 oz) plain white flour

4 large eggs

100 ml (4 fl oz) milk

225 g (8 oz) unsalted butter, plus extra for greasing

75 g (3 oz) caster sugar

generous pinch of salt

finely grated rind of 1 lemon

flour, for dusting

100 g (3½ oz) split blanched almonds

icing sugar, for dusting

whole glacé fruits, nuts and dragees, to decorate

1 Place the raisins in a small bowl or jam jar, pour the rum over, cover and leave in a cool place overnight. Place the yeast in a food processor with the flour. Mix well. With the machine running on a slow speed, pour in the eggs and milk and mix for about 10 minutes or until the dough is very smooth, shiny and elastic (see Cook's Tips).

2 Meanwhile, place 225 g (8 oz) butter in an ovenproof bowl and soften in the SIMMERING OVEN for 10 minutes. Beat in the caster sugar, salt and the grated lemon rind. With the machine running, add the butter and sugar mixture to the dough, spoonful by spoonful, until evenly incorporated. Turn the mixture into a large, lightly floured bowl, then cover with clingfilm and refrigerate overnight.

3 Lightly toast the almonds for 2-3 minutes on the grid shelf on the floor of the roasting oven (see Cook's Tips). Heavily butter a 2-litre (3½-pint) Gugelhopf ring mould. Take a third of the cold almonds and press on to the sides of the mould (see Cook's Tips); refrigerate. Roughly chop the remaining almonds and mix by hand into the chilled dough, along with the raisins and rum. Carefully place the dough in the prepared mould, then cover and leave in a warm, draught-free place near but not on the Aga until the dough feels spongy and has risen to within 2 cm (¾ in) of the top of the mould.

4 ▨ ▨ Bake on the grid shelf on the floor of the ROASTING OVEN for 10 minutes, then cover with the cold plain shelf and cook for a further 35-40 minutes or until the Gugelhopf sounds hollow when you tap the mould.

▨ ▨ ▨ ▨ Bake on the grid shelf on the floor of the ROASTING OVEN for 10 minutes, then transfer to the centre of the BAKING OVEN for 40-45 minutes or until the Gugelhopf sounds hollow when you tap the mould.

5 Allow to cool in the tin for 15 minutes, then turn on to a cooling rack to cool completely. Serve the cake dusted with icing sugar and decorated with glacé fruits, nuts and dragees.

COOK'S TIPS

If using dried active baking yeast, mix 10 ml (2 level tsp) yeast with 75 ml (3 fl oz) warm water and 5 ml (1 level tsp) caster sugar; leave until frothy. Mix into the flour with 30 ml (2 tbsp) double cream. If using fresh yeast, take 25 g (1 oz) and proceed as for dried active baking yeast.

If you don't have a beater attachment, use a food processor with a flat plastic blade and mix for 1 minute at full speed.

When browning the nuts, leave the oven door slightly open so you can smell the nuts and catch them before they burn. If the almonds won't stay in place, use soft butter on each nut to help them stick.

MANGO AND APRICOT CHELSEA BUNS

PREPARATION TIME:
20 MINUTES + 2-3
HOURS RAISING

COOKING TIME:
15-18 MINUTES

330 CALS PER BUN

MAKES 12 BUNS

FREEZING: SUITABLE

This is a wonderful variation on the classic Chelsea bun recipe, using just two of the interesting variety of dried fruits now available in many supermarkets.

150 g (5 oz) butter
90 ml (6 tbsp) milk
400 g (14 oz) plain strong white flour
2.5 ml (½ tsp) salt
1 sachet easy-blend dried yeast
3 eggs
75 g (2½ oz) caster sugar

60 ml (4 tbsp) pale muscovado sugar
7.5 ml (1½ tsp) ground cinnamon
125 g (4 oz) dried, ready-to-eat mangos, chopped
200 g (7 oz) dried, ready-to-eat apricots, chopped
30 ml (2 tbsp) icing sugar

1 Warm half the butter and 60 ml (4 tbsp) of the milk in a small ovenproof bowl in the SIMMERING OVEN for 5 minutes until just tepid.

2 Combine the flour, salt and dried yeast in a food processor (using the dough blade) or in a large bowl. Mix well, then add the eggs and caster sugar. With the food processor running, pour in the tepid milk and the butter and work to a smooth, elastic dough in about 1-2 minutes. If mixing by hand, knead the dough in the bowl for 5-7 minutes.

3 Place a thick folded towel on the lid of the SIMMERING PLATE and set the unopened processor bowl on top or cover the mixing bowl with clingfilm and place it on top of the towel. Leave the dough until it is doubled in size (1-1½ hours).

4 Grease and base-line a small roasting tin. Tip the dough out onto a floured worksurface and roll or pat the dough out into an oblong measuring about 25 × 40 cm (10 × 15 in).

5 Spread the dough oblong with the remaining butter. Sprinkle with the muscovado sugar and cinnamon and scatter with the chopped mango and apricots. Roll up the dough like a long Swiss roll, mark into 12 even slices and cut with an oiled sharp knife. Arrange the slices, cut side up and evenly spaced in the prepared tin. Cover with clear plastic film and place on the folded towel on the SIMMERING PLATE lid until the buns have doubled in size and the tin is well filled.

6 Place the tin on the bottom runners at the front of the ROASTING OVEN for 10 minutes or until golden brown, then set the cold plain shelf on the third runners and cook for a further 5-8 minutes. Combine the remaining milk with the icing sugar and brush on the buns as soon as they come out of the oven to give a sticky glaze.

COOK'S TIP
Make sure you spread the butter and scatter the fruit right to the edges of the dough so that the first and last buns are well filled.

AGA TIP
Whether fresh or frozen, you can always serve the buns warm by placing them briefly in the SIMMERING OVEN.

DROP SCONES

PREPARATION TIME:
10 MINUTES +
STANDING TIME

COOKING TIME:
1 MINUTE

40-30 CALS PER
SCONE

MAKES 24-30

FREEZING: NOT
SUITABLE

For ease, have your batter ready mixed with only the final ingredients to add just before cooking. Serve hot and freshly made.

150 ml (¼ pint) milk
1 large egg
100 g (3 ½ oz) plain flour
1.25 ml (¼ tsp) salt

5 ml (1 tsp) sugar
50 g (2 oz) butter
10 ml (2 tsp) baking powder
cooking oil, for greasing

1 Measure the milk in a 1 litre (1¾ pint) jug and add the egg, flour, salt and sugar to the jug. Stir together and leave to stand in the jug for 30 minutes or overnight in the refrigerator.

2 Warm the butter to melt in a small ovenproof bowl or ramekin in the SIMMERING OVEN or on the side of the Aga.

3 Just before cooking, wipe the SIMMERING PLATE sparingly with kitchen paper dipped in a little cooking oil. Stir the butter and baking powder into the batter and pour 6-8 puddles of batter approximately 5 cm (2 in) in diameter directly onto the SIMMERING PLATE. When bubbles appear on the surface, flip over with a palette knife or fish slice and allow to brown on the other side.

4 Stack the cooked drop scones on a folded napkin on a plate. Repeat, making more drop scones to use up the batter. Serve immediately with butter.

AGA TIP
If any leftover drop scones need reheating, then put them briefly on the SIMMERING PLATE with the lid down for 10-15 seconds. Tiny drop scones are as an excellent substitute for blinis; serve topped with sour cream, dill and smoked salmon for canapés.

139

CHOCOLATE BROWNIES

PREPARATION TIME:
20 MINUTES

COOKING TIME:
35-40 MINUTES

300 CALS PER
BROWNIE

MAKES 24

FREEZING: SUITABLE

An all-time favourite for all the family. For the best results, use good quality chocolate.

550 g (1¼ lb) plain chocolate
225 g (8 oz) butter
3 eggs
30 ml (2 tbsp) freshly made strong coffee
225 g (8 oz) caster sugar

75 g (3 oz) white self-raising flour
1.25 ml (¼ tsp) salt
175 g (6 oz) walnut pieces
5 ml (1 tsp) vanilla essence

1 Turn a small roasting tin upside-down and cover with foil, moulding it over the corners. Lift the foil off and place inside the tin. Place 5 ml (1 tsp) butter in the tin for greasing. Place the tin in the SIMMERING OVEN just to melt the butter, then brush it over the base and sides.

2 Break up 325 g (12 oz) of the chocolate and melt with the butter in an ovenproof bowl in the SIMMERING OVEN for 15-20 minutes. Stir until completely melted, then leave to cool slightly. Using a sharp knife, roughly chop the remaining chocolate and the walnuts and set aside (see Cook's Tip).

3 Mix the eggs, coffee and sugar together in a large bowl until smooth, then gradually beat in the melted chocolate mixture. Fold in the flour, salt, walnuts, vanilla essence and chopped chocolate.

4 Pour into the prepared tin and bake on the bottom runners at the front of the ROASTING OVEN with the cold plain shelf on the second runners for 35-40 minutes or until just firm to the touch. Leave to cool in the tin, then lift out. Trim the edges if wished and cut into squares.

COOK'S TIP
Place a small chopping board inside the large roasting tin when chopping the nuts and chocolate to prevent them scattering all around the kitchen.

CRANBERRY AND RAISIN TEA BREAD

PREPARATION TIME:
10 MINUTES + 30
MINUTES SOAKING

COOKING TIME:
1 HOUR

180 CALS PER SLICE:

MAKES 12 SLICES

FREEZING: SUITABLE

Dried cranberries are now available in larger supermarkets. If you cannot find them, raisins make a very good substitute.

75 g (2½ oz) dried cranberries
150 g (5 oz) raisins
300 ml (½ pint) strong cold tea
100 g (3½ oz) caster sugar
250 g (9 oz) self-raising flour

2.5 ml (½ tsp) baking powder
2.5 ml (½ tsp) mixed spice
1 egg
25 g (1 oz) flaked almonds

1 Place the cranberries, raisins, tea, butter and sugar in an ovenproof bowl and place in the SIMMERING OVEN for 20-30 minutes, until you can smell the fruit and the sugar and butter have melted. Cool until hand-hot.

2 Grease and base-line a loaf tin 22.5 × 12.5 × 7 cm (9 × 5 × 2¾ in) or 1½ litre (2½ pint) capacity.

3 Sift the flour, baking powder and spice into a large mixing bowl. Stir in the eggs and the fruit mixture. Turn quickly into the prepared tin and scatter the almonds over the top.

4 ■ ■ Bake at the front of the grid shelf on the floor of the ROASTING OVEN with a cold roasting tin on the top runners. After 20 minutes, add 1 litre (1¾ pint) cold water to the roasting tin and continue to cook for a further 25-30 minutes, or until a skewer inserted in the centre of the loaf comes out clean.

■ ■ ■ Cook on the grid shelf on the floor of the BAKING OVEN for about 1 hour, or until a skewer inserted in the centre of the loaf comes out clean.

5 Turn the loaf out of the tin while it is still hand hot. Serve sliced and spread with butter.

BANANA TEA BREAD

PREPARATION TIME:
15 MINUTES +
COOLING

COOKING TIME:
45 MINUTES-
1¼ HOURS

140 CALS PER
FINGER

MAKES ABOUT
24 FINGERS

FREEZING: SUITABLE

This tea bread is an ideal recipe for using up bananas when they are over-ripe.

75 g (3 oz) butter, plus extra for greasing
225 g (8 oz) self-raising flour
1.5 ml (¼ level tsp) bicarbonate of soda
2.5 ml (½ level tsp) salt
150 g (5 oz) caster sugar
1 egg

450 g (1 lb) ripe bananas
125 g (4 oz) chopped mixed nuts, e.g. hazelnuts, walnuts and Brazil nuts
apricot jam, dried banana chips and toasted walnut halves

1 Grease and base-line a 450 g (1 lb) loaf tin. Sieve flour, bicarbonate of soda and salt into a bowl. Rub in butter; stir in sugar and egg.

2 Mash the bananas. Beat the banana and chopped nuts into the flour mixture. Turn the mixture into the prepared tin.

3 ■ ■ Bake at the front of the ROASTING OVEN with the grid shelf on the floor. After 20 minutes place the cold plain shelf on the second runners above and cook for a further 20-25 minutes or until a skewer inserted into the centre comes out clean. Transfer to the SIMMERING OVEN if brown on top but not cooked in the centre.

■ ■ ■ Bake on the grid shelf on the bottom runners of the BAKING OVEN for 1-1¼ hours or until a skewer inserted into the centre comes out clean. Transfer to the SIMMERING OVEN if brown on top but not cooked in the centre.

4 Cool in the tin for 10 minutes; cool completely on a wire rack (see Cook's Tip). To serve, brush with warmed apricot jam. Cut into thick slices, then cut each slice into three fingers. Decorate with banana chips and walnut halves.

COOK'S TIP
The cooled tea bread can be wrapped in greaseproof paper and stored in an airtight tin for up to one week.

HAZELNUT AND CHOCOLATE OAT COOKIES

PREPARATION TIME:
10 MINUTES

COOKING TIME:
12-25 MINUTES

MAKES 36

170 CALS PER
BISCUIT

FREEZING: OPEN
FREEZE AT THE END
OF STEP 2. THESE
COOKIES CAN BE
COOKED FROM
FROZEN,
ALLOWING 1-2
MINUTES EXTRA
COOKING TIME.

Freshly-baked biscuits are so special and delicious, so keep a bag of ready-to-bake cookies in the freezer and avoid the temptation to nibble.

200 g (7 oz) hazelnuts, chopped
150 g (5 oz) good plain chocolate
200 g (7 oz) butter
200 g (7 oz) pale muscovado sugar
2 eggs

5 ml (1 tsp) vanilla essence
200 g (7 oz) self-raising flour
5 ml (1 tsp) salt
200 g (7 oz) porridge oats
75 ml (5 tbsp) milk

1 Coarsely chop the hazelnuts and chocolate and set on one side. Cream together the butter, sugar and eggs.

2 Fold in remaining ingredients until just evenly mixed. Place large tablespoons of the mixture on a baking tray.

3 ▧ ▧ Bake on the grid shelf on the floor of the ROASTING OVEN with the cold plain shelf or roasting tin on the second runners above. Cook for 10-13 minutes, turning the tray round after the first 7-8 minutes to ensure even cooking. Then transfer to the SIMMERING OVEN for a further 15 minutes until well cooked, and cool on the baking tray.

▧ ▧ ▧ ▧ Bake on the third runners of the BAKING OVEN for 12-15 minutes, turning the tray round after 8-9 minutes.

ALMOND AND CREAM CHEESE BISCUITS

PREPARATION TIME:
15 MINUTES

COOKING TIME: 7-
12 MINUTES

150 CALS PER
BISCUIT

MAKES 36

FREEZING:
COMPLETE TO END
OF STEP 2. OPEN
FREEZE ON TRAY
UNTIL FIRM, THEN
BAG AND FREEZE
UP TO 2 MONTHS.
BAKE FROM
FROZEN, FOR 10-13
MINUTES.

Freshly-baked biscuits are always delicious and these can be prepared ahead, ready to bake straight from the freezer a few at a time.

200 g (7 oz) caster sugar
200 g (7 oz) butter
250 g (9 oz) cream cheese

225 g (8 oz) plain flour
2.5 ml (½ tsp) vanilla essence
200 g (7 oz) flaked almonds

1 Cream together the sugar, butter and cream cheese. This may be done in a food processor or in a bowl. Lightly work in the flour and vanilla essence.

2 Place almonds on a plate and then put half a dozen heaped teaspoons of biscuit mixture on the nuts. Roll each into a ball coated with nuts, set on a tray and flatten lightly with the fingertips. Continue making biscuits until all the mixture is used up.

3 Bake a few freshly made biscuits on a baking sheet on the grid shelf on the floor of the ROASTING OVEN for 7-9 minutes, until pale golden. Freeze the remainder. Serve dusted with icing sugar.

COOK'S TIP

If only baking a few biscuits, place them on the front of the baking sheet well spaced. If baking a trayful, turn the tray around after two-thirds of the cooking time to ensure even colouring.

INDEX

INDEX